MW01711607

A Century of Excellence

A Century of Excellence:

Prince of Wales College, 1860–1969

Marian Bruce

Island Studies Press/
PWC Alumni Association
Charlottetown
2005

A Century of Excellence: Prince of Wales College, 1860–1969
© 2005 by Marian Bruce
ISBN 0-919013-45-7

All rights reserved. No part of this publication may be reproduced, stored in a retrieval system, or transmitted, in any form or by any means, without the prior written permission of the publisher or, in case of photocopying or other reprographic copying, a licence from access ©, The Canadian Copyright Licensing Agency.

Cover image: In this rare 1919 panorama, students pose in front of the second Prince of Wales College building, opened in 1900 and destroyed by fire in 1932.
Editing: Edward MacDonald
Design: UPEI Graphics
Printing: Friesens

Library and Archives Canada Cataloguing in Publication

Bruce, Marian
A Century of Excellence: Prince of Wales College, 1860–1969 / Marian Bruce.

Includes bibliographical references and index.
ISBN 0-919013-45-7

1. Prince of Wales College (Charlottetown, P.E.I.)—History. I. Title.

LE3.P82B78 2005 378.717'5 C2005-903050-X

Island Studies Press
University of Prince Edward Island
Charlottetown, Prince Edward Island
Canada C1A 4P3
www.upei.ca

Prince of Wales College Alumni Association
c/o Advancement Services
University of Prince Edward Island
Charlottetown, Prince Edward Island
Canada C1A 4P3
www.upei.ca

Printed in Canada

Dedication

To the memory of Annabelle Bruce Brehaut (1936–2003),
and to the many other young men and women who entered adulthood through the portals of Prince of Wales College

Contents

Acknowledgements

Many people contributed to this book. Thanks are due, first and foremost, to the Prince of Wales College Alumni Society for initiating the project and financing the book, and for granting me the privilege of writing it. I also am grateful to the dozens of people — alumni, former faculty and others — who shared memories and memorabilia relating to Prince of Wales College. I am especially indebted to Dr. Ian Ross Robertson, history professor at the University of Toronto, Scarborough. He generously contributed a substantial amount of research material, including letters from the Macphail Papers, which otherwise would not have been accessible, and read a final draft of the manuscript.

Work on the book started in the summer of 2002, when two University of Prince Edward Island students, Carolyn Roberts and Ryan O'Connor, began conducting interviews and identifying, collecting, and documenting college-related material in local libraries and archives. Their research proved invaluable. My role began only in the late spring of 2003. Throughout the subsequent year-long research and writing process, I leaned on the sound judgement of the patient and good-humoured project editor, UPEI history professor Dr. Edward MacDonald. I am most grateful for his advice.

Thanks also to Simon Lloyd, in charge of Special Collections at the Robertson Library, who also chaired the University's Histories Table, overseer of this project; Leo Cheverie, also of the Robertson Library; the staff at the Provincial Archives and Records Office; historian Wayne MacKinnon, who read a draft of the manuscript; and the talented team who turned the manuscript into a book: editor Laurie Brinklow and book designer Matthew MacKay, both of the UPEI Graphics department. The UPEI Histories Table included members Simon Lloyd (chair), Laurie Brinklow, Lawson Drake, Harry Love, Douglas Boylan, Andy Robb, and Mel Gallant, with editorial advice from Edward MacDonald.

Finally, a special thank you to Dr. Ian Brown, former history professor at Prince of Wales College. Cheering from the sidelines, he contributed unflagging moral support and what was, from my point of view, the greatest gift of all: faith in a storyteller's ability to do justice to the history of a period in which feelings often ran high, and of a place that so many people still hold dear.

— **Marian Bruce**
High Bank, Prince Edward Island
July 2005

Foreword

The manner in which an institution is formed can play a significant role in its subsequent life. Some, such as Acadia, Mount Allison, and St. Dunstan's have their roots in religious denominations and a desire to educate religious and other leaders. Others, such as Nova Scotia Technical College (now Technical University of Nova Scotia), were nonsectarian in origin, founded to provide education in a specific field. Still others, such as Prince of Wales College, trace their roots to a political decision and a desire to provide, from public funds, higher education for all the youth of a political jurisdiction. A publicly funded institution arising out of a political decision is often prey to the vagaries of politics, financial resources, and other non-academic factors. Over the years, those who believed that education was too important to be left to the professionals often subjected these institutions to many demands and much scrutiny. Prince of Wales was no exception. Marian Bruce carefully and engagingly takes the reader through the Prince of Wales story from its beginning as the Central Academy to its conclusion with the formation of the University of Prince Edward Island.

By any standard, the cast of Head Masters and Principals who served Prince of Wales College was remarkable. Marian Bruce gives attention to all of them and provides the reader with new insights on each. The success of these leaders and their supporting faculty in starting many youth of this province on the path to regional, national (even in a few cases, international) success is a testament to their tenacity and hard work under sometimes difficult conditions. They were all highly educated men who demanded a correspondingly high academic standard from faculty and students.

A media headline version of the history of Prince of Wales College would focus on political decisions, disasters such as fires that destroyed buildings and their contents, and the many minutiae which distracted from the efforts to provide a good education to the students at the College. Marian Bruce, while citing some of those headlines and recording some of the trivia, is not distracted by them. In her telling of the highly regarded worth of Prince of Wales College she remains focussed on the human dimension of a College experience that has profoundly affected generations of Island youth.

Harry Love and Lawson Drake
Prince of Wales Alumni Association

Chapter One

Bibles, Bigotry, and Beardless Youths

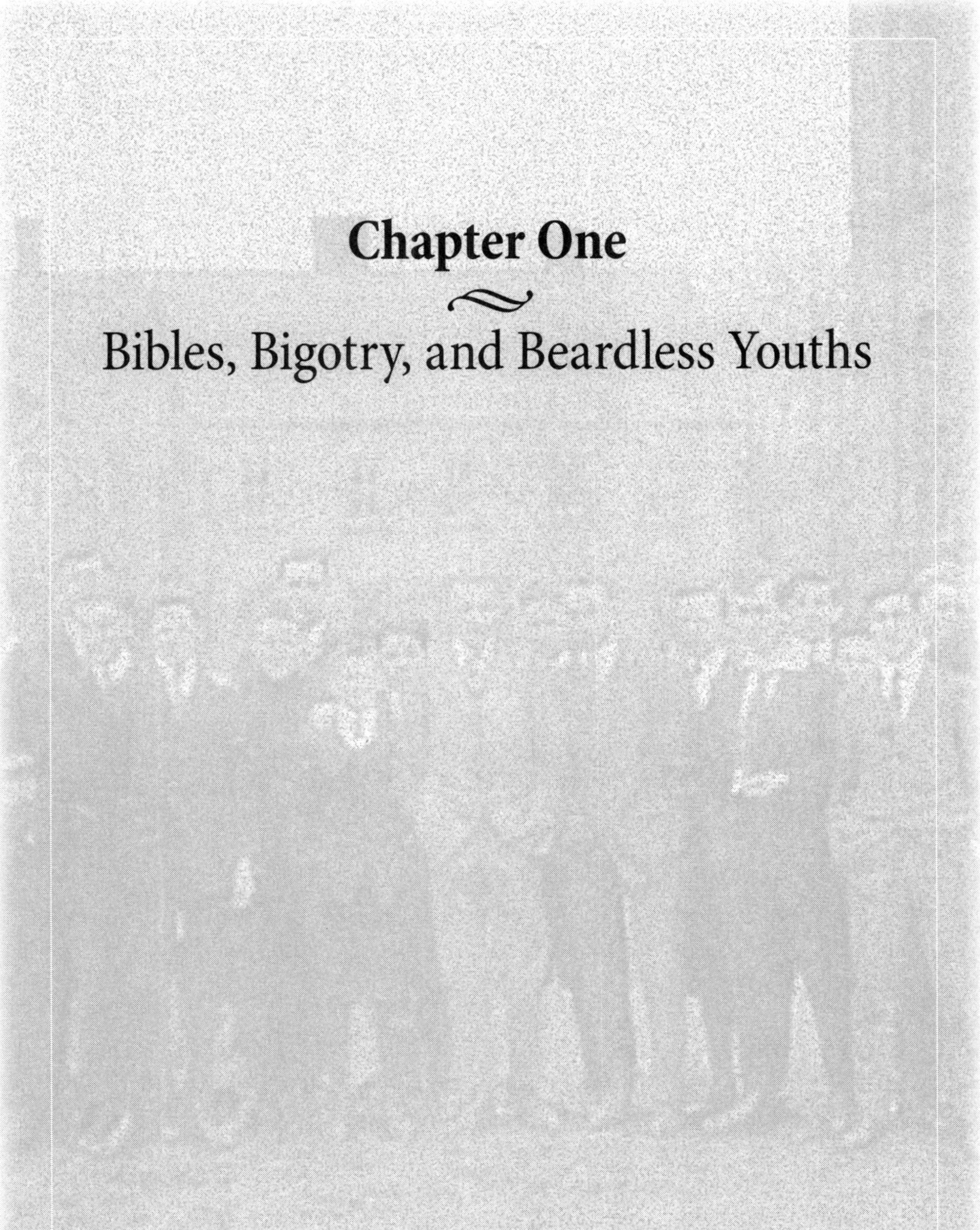

1

"What advantages would not a College afford for the cultivation of the highest orders of Youthful intellect and genius amongst us!"

—John Lawson, city recorder, 1856

In 1832, John Lewellin Lewellin, a Welsh-born agent for a large landowner in Prince Edward Island, wrote what amounted to an early visitors' guide. His advice for prospective settlers included this hint: "Don't forget to put up your Bible, with any other good books, and school books for your children, if you have a family. Education is now estimated at something like its value. The Legislature have shewn a laudable desire to promote it...."

Like most visitors' guides, Lewellin's looked on the bright side, finding a silver lining even in the long winter, which "much assists the farmer, fertilizing the earth ... and enabling it to produce tolerable crops under very indifferent management." He also exclaimed over the lovely soil, the climate, the topography, the economic opportunities, and the low cost of living in Charlottetown, and promised that an immigrant would find "no direct taxes ... no poor-rates, no tythes, no yellow fever, no ague, no hurricanes, and few cases of consumption."[1]

Lewellin was right about the school books and Bibles, but not about a few other items, including the education system. It was, in a word, dismal. For decades, the school system had been lurching down a rocky road, plodding ahead in fits and starts. For those who cared about such things, this must have been disappointing, considering early expectations. In 1804, Lieutenant-Governor Edmund Fanning had set aside 10 town lots in Charlottetown, bounded by Grafton, Weymouth, Kent, and Cumberland streets, in the sparsely settled east end of the town grid, "for the purpose of laying the foundation of a College for the Education of youth in the learned languages, the liberal arts and sciences and all the Branches of useful and polite literature...." It was almost two decades later, in 1821, that a school finally opened on that site, and it would be stretching things to call it a college. It was known variously as Kent College (in honour of Prince Edward, Duke of Kent), the National School, or, more commonly, Breading's School, after the first principal, James Breading. While theoretically an institution of higher education, the National School probably did not rise much above the common schools that were sprouting in various parts of the Island, often in private homes.[2]

Citizens of the little colony no doubt did their best under difficult circumstances. It was, after all, a pioneer society. Boatload after boatload of immigrants, mostly from Scotland, England, and Ireland, were docking at Island ports in the first four decades of the century. By 1827, there were 23,266 residents, most of whom occupied the land as small freeholders or tenants. They were preoccupied with clearing land and growing crops. The government — a lieutenant-governor, an elected assembly, and an appointed legislative council — was preoccupied with land ownership, the struggle for responsible government, and, especially by mid-century, religion. In government circles, there always seemed to be something other than education to create an uproar. Occasionally, disagreements led to intemperate behaviour, as in the dispute that two pistol-packing politicians tried to settle with a duel. As author and educator Frank MacKinnon has observed, the colony was "a small community which frequently made vital crusades out of ordinary issues."[3]

One of those issues was how the Island's meagre revenues should be spent. Money was in short supply, both in the public Treasury and in private homes. Most of the Island was owned by absentee proprietors, who were supposed to pay quitrent to the Crown but usually didn't. Revenues for the colony came from liquor sales, land taxes (after 1832), and an annual grant from the British government, which harboured the fond hope that the colony would soon pay its own way. The Mother Country also had final say over all legislation passed in the little colony, including financial bills.[4] There was not always enough money to pay the salaries of the many government officials, let alone construct roads, bridges, government buildings, and schools. The lieutenant-governor was without an official residence until 1835, and the Legislature met in a wooden courthouse until 1847.[5]

In 1825, when the Island government took charge of education — after a fashion — the public Treasury contributed small grants to help build schools and pay teachers. In 1832, for example, the legislative grant for the entire Island was 562 pounds and 10 shillings.[6] Student fees made up the bulk of a teacher's wages. Such school buildings that existed were often in poor condition, and the schools sometimes moved from district to district. Because books were in such short supply, the Bible often had to substitute as a textbook. Few students attended school regularly. Almost anybody could be a teacher. Some were farmers who, exhausted from their principal occupation, found the classroom a good place to take a rest. Some were, according to the *Prince Edward Island Magazine,* "persons of shipwrecked character and blasted prospects in life, after every other resource failed ... sometimes a man too proud to beg, too upright to steal."[7] The curriculum consisted of what the teacher decided it would be. Illiteracy was prevalent.

By the time John Lewellin Lewellin's hints for immigrants were published, however, two encouraging signs had appeared. In the 1830s, the first advances in the education of teachers, and higher education in general, came with the establishment of two classical schools, one government-sponsored and the other run by the Roman Catholic Church. These schools were the first institutions in a parallel system of higher education that would operate on the Island — not always in a happy co-existence — for almost a century and a half. From the beginning, the two systems were competing for a share of the government's meagre resources. That competition fed the embers of religious bigotry immigrants had carried across the ocean, along with their Bibles and fiddles, and retarded the progress of both systems for generations.

The Roman Catholic school was established first, in 1831. Angus MacEachern, the first Roman Catholic Bishop of Charlottetown, installed St. Andrew's College in his own home, a modest, two-storey wooden structure in the community of the same name, near the head of the Hillsborough River. While intended mainly as a school that would prepare young men for theological training, it was also open to non-Catholics, and was to include students preparing for secular careers. However, when MacEachern asked the House of Assembly in 1829 for a government grant in aid of the proposed Catholic college, he was turned down.[8] The legislative committee appointed to study education decided against recommending aid for an institution under the tutelage of Catholic priests. Besides, the government had plans of its own. Prompted by Lieutenant-Governor John Ready, the Legislature decided that spring to build a government-operated school of higher learning that would be "quite free and open to the youth of all persuasions."[9]

A committee of the House, appointed to prepare a specific plan for the government-run college, recommended that it should be built in Charlottetown and called the Central Academy. Its curriculum, like that of Pictou Academy and Dalhousie College in Nova Scotia, would follow the pattern of Scottish universities by including science and mathematics, as well as the classics.[10] Branches of education to be taught were "the Greek and Latin languages, Belles Lettres [literature], the French language, Geography connected with Astronomy and combined with General and Natural History, English reading, Grammar and Elocution, Elementary and Practical Mathematics and Theoretical and Practical Arithmetic." The school was to be under the control of nine trustees, all prominent government officials or members of the Legislature, who would report to the lieutenant-governor. No clergyman "having the Spiritual charge of any Parish or Congregation" was to be eligible to teach at the Academy. (Two clergymen in a row, one Anglican, the other Presbyterian, taught at the school in its first decade, but presumably not while in charge of a flock.) The school's two masters were to receive a salary of 150 pounds each a year, plus an equal share of the tuition money. They were also expected to take in boarders. The salaries were high in comparison with those of other teachers: district school teachers with the highest-class licence received about 40 pounds,[11] and teachers at grammar schools as much as 100 pounds,[12] but qualifications of teachers at the Academy probably were correspondingly superior.

The Academy, after all, was founded with great expectations. First of all, it would allow boys and young men to obtain an education on the Island and would also upgrade the academic qualifications of district teachers. And in future, some thought, it would grow into a university. In an attempt to set standards in education, the Legislature had passed an Education Act in 1830 establishing an appointed, five-member board of education that would certify teachers and supervise all schools in the colony. In addition, grammar schools were to be set up in each county. In this new, improved public education system, the Central Academy was to be the crown jewel.

Unfortunately, the Academy got off to a bad start. Like its sister institution, St. Andrew's College, the Academy suffered from the beginning from a shortage of funds. At the time, the government had two major construction projects on its plate: the proposed new Government House and the Academy. Trouble was, the colony's revenues for the year amounted to only 4,060 pounds, just about the contemplated cost of the two buildings.[13] The government tried to negotiate a loan, and failed. The Legislature then passed an act under which land was to be taxed at the rate of two shillings per 100 acres to pay for these and other buildings.[14]

Once the money was obtained, there were more delays. Construction of the Academy did not go smoothly and, in keeping with a long tradition in government projects, went over-budget. John Macdonald, a Charlottetown builder and contractor, and Robert Patten had contracted in April 1833 to build the Academy for 1,210 pounds. The building was to be completed by November of the next year. In February 1835, Macdonald reported to the House of Assembly that he had completed the project at a loss of 137 pounds, and complained that his partner had absconded after obtaining an advance of 50 pounds. Macdonald had a large family to support and claimed he was facing "utter ruin" unless the government covered his losses.[15] His claim was eventually settled by arbitrators, who awarded him about 315 pounds.[16]

The new Academy was located in the eastern end of Charlottetown and on the south side of the block that Fanning had set aside for a college. It was a square, two-storey, Georgian-style wooden building, somewhat similar in design to Government House, although much less grand. The trustees would soon discover, to their dismay, that the Academy building was cursed with shoddy workmanship. But in the spring of 1835, they proudly announced in the newspapers that a "commodious building" had been erected "in an eligible and airy part of the Town" and that they were looking for two masters for the new institution. In July, the trustees placed another advertisement, announcing that, because they had not been able to take possession of the building, they had decided not to start hiring.[17] Finally, in December, they appointed Rev. Charles Lloyd, a 34-year-old Anglican clergyman, as principal and Alexander Brown, master of the Charlottetown Grammar School, as his assistant.

Lloyd, a native of Ireland, had been educated at Westminster and Cambridge and had served as a curate in Devonshire before immigrating to the Island. He was appointed classics and mathematics teacher at the

Academy, but, for a time at least, continued to preach in Charlottetown and in a rural church on alternate Sundays.[18] Brown, according to the minutes of the school trustees, was to serve as master "of such other branches contemplated by the Act as to the Trustees may seem meet."[19] The school opened on January 19, 1836, with 58 male students enrolled.[20] Lloyd did not last long; he resigned in September of the first year, pleading ill health, and the next year took a post in Milton, an English settlement a few miles west of Charlottetown, as a missionary for the Society for the Propagation of the Gospel. He was replaced by another preacher, Rev. James Waddell, a Presbyterian minister from Nova Scotia, who happened to be a zealous champion of the cause of temperance. [21]

The Academy had created quite a stir in the Island newspapers before it even opened. There were, of course, complaints: the construction had bled the Treasury, one correspondent grumbled, and taxed "the comforts of the poor."[22] The school would benefit only Charlottetown residents, another writer predicted, and the money would have been better spent on instituting a uniform system of education in the district schools.[23] In defence of the Academy, an anonymous correspondent to the *Royal Gazette* replied that such complaints were nothing new: rural Islanders grumbled "at every advantage conferred on the capital, in which themselves do not immediately participate."[24]

It soon became obvious that some Island legislators sympathized with citizens who saw the Academy as a school for the Charlottetown elite. Waddell had asked the trustees to build a separate entrance and a second kitchen in the Academy at a cost of 100 pounds. One of the perks of the job was that teachers were entitled to live in the school building. Alexander Brown and his family lived in the western end, and were using the only kitchen in the place. The Waddells had to make do with a cottage at the corner of Weymouth and Fitzroy streets. The trustees forwarded Waddell's request to the Legislature, which turned it down. A committee of the House refused to recommend any spending on additions or alterations, "the present expenses of that institution being far beyond any corresponding benefit which the people of this Colony derive from it."[25]

The next year, a special legislative committee went even further, recommending a salary cut for the two masters. They should receive salaries equal to those of the highest class of district teachers, the committee said. As compensation, they should be allowed "the benefit of the ample accommodations which the building affords both for tuition and comfortable residence." The committee had undertaken a cost-benefit analysis of schools in the colony, including the Academy. The building, including desks, had cost the Treasury more than 1,355 pounds. The average cost per year of operating the Academy, in which an average of 54 students were enrolled, was 396 pounds. Since 1836, the average cost to the Treasury per year of supporting country schools, which had a total enrolment of 1,649, was 441 pounds. The committee considered this an unfair distribution of public funds.[26] To adjust the scales somewhat, the committee recommended that country students be exempt from paying tuition fees, which ranged from one to two pounds a term, depending on the subjects studied. For two years, the trustees had offered to educate four pupils from each county tuition-free, but only one from outside Charlottetown — a boy from Charlottetown Royalty — had enrolled, perhaps because room, board, and laundry cost the rural students 24 pounds a year. Charlottetown residents, the committee decided, could well afford to pay: "There has been laid before your Committee a catalogue of the pupils attending the Academy, from which your Committee should infer, that the parents of the pupils are, for the most part, of such a class in society as to be well able to provide, from their own resources, the means of educating their children."[27]

Most Islanders lived in the country, so it is no wonder that the cost of running the Academy irritated them. As the years went by, though, the rural enrolment gradually increased. By 1844, 5 of the 79 students enrolled came from outside Charlottetown: William Macdonald of Tracadie (the future tobacco king, son of prominent landowner Donald McDonald[28]) was studying mathematics, English, and Latin; William Jarvis (son of Chief Justice Edward Jarvis) of Mt. Edward, classics and English; Allan Frazer of Belfast, classics and English; Daniel McLaren of The Hermitage, English; and Alexander McNeill of Lot 49, mensuration (drawing).[29] Students ranged in age from six to twenty. Most were teenagers. All were boys or young men. At the time, girls and women were generally excluded from institutions of higher learning; in case there might be any doubt, the trustees had quickly established rules that prohibited female students, as well as boys under the age of six.[30]

As enrolment increased, so did the teaching staff. In 1843, the trustees had dismissed the two masters, for reasons that are unclear, and advertised for three replacements in newspapers in the Maritimes, the eastern United

States, and the British Isles. The headmaster was to receive a salary of 150 pounds, plus half the tuition fees and the use of "commodious apartments in the Academy, with the privilege of taking boarders, and a good kitchen garden." The second master would receive a salary of 100 pounds and a third of the fees, and the third master, 50 pounds and one-sixth of the fees.[31]

The new headmaster, Edward Rupert Humphreys, was imported from England. An erudite man, he had studied medicine at Cambridge University, wrote textbooks, made translations for the district schools, and was a popular lecturer at the Mechanics' Institutes.[32] Although he was only twenty-four years old when he arrived at the Academy, Humphreys ran a tight ship. He was a stickler for correct behaviour on the part of both students and teachers. The school doors were locked whenever classes began at 9 A.M. Tardy boys were shut out for the day and deemed to be absent. Too many absences led to suspension, as did insubordination. Corporal punishment was used infrequently; Humphreys preferred more refined methods of discipline. In a memo to the trustees in November 1845, he reported having chastised the third master for having "displayed much want of temper towards [a student] in my presence, addressing and reprimanding him, instead of making his complaint to me only." Any complaints to the headmaster about a student must be in writing, he insisted, "and not personally." Besides, he said, in dealing with youth, "*quiet* determination" worked better than anger, "or too many words."[33]

Humphreys banned snowball fights and hurley (the predecessor of hockey) on the school grounds, as well as conduct he considered improper anywhere else in the community. One day he expelled eighteen-year-old Alexander Desbrisay, a student from a leading Anglican family, on the grounds that he had "in my presence been guilty of misconduct in the Mechanics' Institute last evening," and had subsequently refused to do the required penance (a "task" not specified in the memo). Desbrisay had mistakenly thought students should not be subject to the headmaster's rules after school. The trustees later overruled the headmaster by reinstating Desbrisay — perhaps not surprising, given his family's status — but conceded that the duty of the masters was "to check any impropriety whenever they may observe it."[34]

While enrolment at the Academy was increasing, there remained a chronic shortage of funds to pay the masters a decent salary and to repair

Memories of the Central Academy

(In the winter of 1855, John Thomas Mellish was a small boy at the Central Academy. In this excerpt from his memoirs, he recalls an occasion in which he incurred the displeasure of the headmaster, William Cundall.)

"A boy used to note on a slate the names of any he saw whispering in class— the penalty for which was to remain in ten minutes after school. One day my name was in the last read out just before the dinner recess, and with several others I went forward to offer excuses. After explaining that I openly answered a boy who had first spoken to me, I coolly rubbed out my name from the list on the slate lying before the headmaster. This greatly annoyed him, and he said that for this gross offence committed right before his face I would have to stay in school for the whole recess — an hour and a half. I remained and one of the Perkins boys brought me some lunch. Composition day fell a little later. I took for my subject 'the Abuse of Power.' Starting with Nero I referred to the tyranny of sundry kings, military commanders and sea captains, winding up with a strong protest against the injustice and wrong done many boys by teachers of our own time and country and even very near home. Seated at his desk Mr. Cundall quietly examined the exercises. Watching him closely I saw that on reading mine he looked very serious and went over it several times. A faculty meeting was called and held then and there — the boys taking their ease back at their desks, I being the only one among them who knew what the fuss was about. My composition was now carefully read over by the other teachers. I saw a merry twinkle in LePage's eye, while Kenny kept rubbing his hands and working the muscles of his face. There was some earnest conversation between the three masters, in subdued tones, of course. Finally, to my great relief they all joined in a hearty laugh, and that was the end of the matter."

a building that was forever needing work. Year after year, the trustees went to the House of Assembly with requests for money to shore up the building. In fact, the school had not been operating a year when the trustees wrote to Lieutenant-Governor John Harvey, asking him to use his influence with the British government to obtain a grant to spruce up the school grounds, and to buy books and laboratory equipment, including "an Electric Machine, Voltaic Battery and apparatus, Chemical Apparatus and tests, telescope, microscope, barometer, hygrometer, thermometer, sextant and surveyors' measuring chain."[35]

In March 1842, the trustees asked for an annual grant from the Legislature, noting that they had personally inspected the Academy building and found the foundation in a dilapidated state, "and other parts of the building out of repair."[36] Three years later, complaining to the lieutenant-governor about the shortage of money for teachers' salaries, the trustees suggested that the Central Academy emulate two British schools, Eton and Winchester, where two classes of students enjoyed similar educational advantages, the wealthier students largely supporting the institution through substantial fees, and the poorer ones paying little. The trustees repeated that suggestion the next year. "By an arrangement similar to the one mentioned," the trustees wrote, "the Central Academy might be made all that the Island at present requires, and it would not then be said, as it has been said now, that we have the material for forming a permanently good School, but are too poor to support it, as it ought to be supported, and too proud to adopt a very simple plan for remedying this embarrassment."[37]

That year, the Legislature did provide for a second scale of tuition fees,[38] but the Academy's financial woes continued. In that respect, the Academy was not much different from other Canadian schools of higher education. For example, Acadia College (now Acadia University) in Wolfville, Nova Scotia, opened in 1839 in rooms provided by a secondary school, and still had no building of its own by the time the first graduates received degrees four years later.[39] The Acadia professors, who each had to teach half a dozen subjects, no doubt could sympathize with teachers at the Central Academy, who seemed to feel obliged to spend their own money on the school. In 1847, Humphreys asked the Assembly to reimburse him for the 70 pounds he had spent on books, fuel, and maintenance.[40] When he resigned that year, ostensibly because of ill health, his letter to the trustees included a plea to attend to "the very dilapidated state of the building, which gives rise to many injurious remarks."[41] Perhaps Humphreys was simply sick and tired of low pay and poor working conditions; in any event, he left Prince Edward Island for good and went on to a distinguished career as an educator, author, and journalist. Soon after leaving the Academy, he took a post as classical master at Merchiston Castle Academy, near Edinburgh; he later obtained his doctorate, was appointed headmaster at another British grammar school, and eventually immigrated to the United States, where he became assistant editor of the Boston *Post*.[42]

Humphreys' replacement was William Cundall, a well-bred shopkeeper and owner of a large Island estate, half of Lot 20. One of his students in the mid-1850s, John Thomas Mellish, remembered him in later years as "a real worker, forceful and enthusiastic, a man of kindly heart, but generally strict in his dealings with the boys." The other teachers on staff were John Kenny, a native of Ireland, and Island poet John LePage. Kenny was a striking young bachelor — slim, fair, and clean-shaven — and a popular teacher. "It was a real privilege to be in Mr. Kenny's class," Mellish recalled. "In the reading class, for instance, he treated expression, the meaning and derivation of words, and the historical references in the most interesting manner, and at the same time took pains to lead the boys to express themselves correctly. A man of twenty or over having come in from the country to the teachers' examination joined the advanced reading class for a few days. Mr. Kenny asked him the meaning of the word 'Agriculture.' 'To farm' was the reply. 'How the d---l,' said Kenny, turning red in the face, 'can you expect to teach others when you are ignorant yourself? The word is a noun, and you cannot define it by a word alone.' The poor young fellow's face flushed redder than the teacher's."[43]

Mellish's other classmates included Louis H. Davies, later a judge, premier, and Member of Parliament; his brother Robert Davies, who became a captain in the Royal Navy; and George Alley, who became a judge. The Academy was training future members of the Charlottetown elite, and it was run by gentlemen. Like other gentlemen of the day, they were elaborately polite, and would not be seen on the street without their beaver hats, knee breeches, and swallow-tailed black or blue coats. But they weren't prosperous enough to avoid working for a living, and their workplace was hardly fit for such men of distinction. Cundall left the Academy in 1856 to become manager of the newly founded Bank of Prince Edward Island,

and John Kenny took over as acting headmaster for the next three years. (Kenny later returned to his native Ireland and, according to Mellish, fell in love, got married, and fathered fourteen children.)

At one point during Cundall's tenure, the trustees complained to the Legislature that the Academy, built in an "insufficient and unworkmanlike manner," was in such bad shape, "it has now become in its external appearance a disgrace to the Colony; that because of the original insufficiency in its building, it has rapidly fallen into decay, and in Winter is, on many occasions, almost uninhabitable." In 1850, the House authorized a grant of 100 pounds for repairs, and permitted the trustees to raise tuition fees for the same purpose.[44]

In presenting their request for funds, the trustees assured the politicians that they were satisfied with the quality of education at the Academy, and that rural Islanders were then benefiting from its existence. Of the 117 students enrolled in 1851, 17 planned to become district teachers; of the 126 boys and young men registered in 1853, 19 were from rural districts.[45] Certainly, teachers who had attended the Academy were at an advantage. The Island's first school inspector, John McNeill, reported in 1845 that teachers who had spent time at the Academy were "more esteemed and sought after" than those who had not.[46]

And, by mid-century, education on the Island appeared finally to be estimated, in John Lewellin Lewellin's words, "at something like its real value." In 1852, after the Island had achieved responsible government, the new premier, George Coles, initiated his first reform — one which would, in theory at least, place the Island at the forefront of educational progress in the British North American colonies. A few years previously, Coles had visited Ohio and Massachusetts, and had been impressed by the system of state-sponsored education he had seen.[47] Under the Free Education Act introduced by his government, all children over the age of five could attend school free of charge. Teachers would be paid from the provincial Treasury, instead of relying on handouts from often-improvident rural residents. All the local districts had to do was to provide and maintain a school building.[48]

It was a watershed year for education, and an auspicious time for reforms that would cost money. After the hard times of the 1840s, prosperity came to the Island in the 1850s, thanks to the thriving shipbuilding industry and exports of farm products. Self-sufficient in its food supply, the

Island was sending oats, fish, cattle, and timber in ships to Great Britain, the United States, and Newfoundland. With the ratification of Free Trade came a steady growth in exports to the United States. In the early years of the decade, the public debt was reduced to 3,000 pounds from 28,000 pounds, and the annual revenue increased to 35,000 pounds from 22,000 pounds.[49] The immigration years were coming to an end, but large families were boosting the population rapidly — from 62,678 in 1848 to 71,496 in 1855. In Charlottetown, residents were building houses on almost every street, as well as shops as high as three storeys, with big glass fronts. Many of the homes and shops were gaslit.[50] In the country, the number of schools doubled in two years, and enrolment tripled. By 1856, the government was devoting a third of its budget, or 12,000 pounds,[51] to education.

The colony was making great strides in encouraging young people to go to school. What they learned there was another story. Besides expanding the school system, the Free Education Act was meant to improve teaching standards. It stipulated that all teachers' licences were to be cancelled at the end of the school year, and the Board of Education had to examine a teacher before issuing a new licence. Those who did not pass the examination could study at the Central Academy free of charge for up to six months. Shortly after the Act went into effect, it became clear that those measures were not sufficient. In his first year-end report, the new school inspector, John M. Stark, praised the government for promoting school attendance, but was less complimentary about the quality of instruction. "I could scarce believe," he reported to the superintendent of education in 1854, "that there could have been in any part of the world so numerous a staff of teachers where so few had even a shadow of a qualification for their important office."

Stark was a Scottish educator who had been lured to the Island in 1853 from Stow's Normal Training Seminary in Glasgow to serve as a school inspector, lecture on agricultural chemistry, and generally rescue the colony's school system. The Stow school founder, Glasgow merchant David Stow, described him as "well-educated, and of gentlemanly manners."[52] Perhaps. But he was not a tactful man. With some exceptions, he wrote in 1855, education was "in the hands of beardless youths, and of uneducated, untrained men of every age and calibre. A meagre knowledge of English grammar, geography, arithmetic and mensuration, with scarce the power, in many instances, to write a sentence grammatically and orthographically correct, is a preposterous title to the office of a schoolmaster."[53] Stark's vision of a reformed school system included, above all else, a Normal School where teachers could learn *how* to teach. In his native country, the teacher-training school for the Society for Propagating Christian Knowledge had been operating for more than a century. "The art of teaching," he once remarked, "is an art like all others, to be learned, to be studied, to be taught."[54]

Stark was no doubt mollified when the House of Assembly passed an act on April 17, 1855, providing for a Normal School in Charlottetown "for the training of male and female teachers."[55] The new teacher-training institution would be located in the old National School, which had closed, perhaps because of lack of support.[56] In the summer of 1856, William Monk, a teacher in Lancashire who had worked with Stark at Stow's teacher-training school in Glasgow, was hired as headmaster. Because work on enlarging and renovating the building was still not completed, he began teaching a class of twenty-two students in July in temporary quarters, the board room of the Central Academy.[57]

A little over two months later, on October 1, 1856, the new school was officially opened, with great fanfare. It was a glittering social event, bathed in the light of pride, hope, and a touch of self-importance. Everybody who was anybody was there — the lieutenant-governor, the premier, officials from the Board of Education, teachers from across the Island, and journalists — all, of course, with their ladies. At 3:30 in the afternoon, about 300 ladies and gentlemen gathered in one of the classrooms, admired the 14 well-laden tea tables and applauded lustily as the dignitaries congratulated each other and themselves on their foresight. Lieutenant-Governor Dominick Daly, who presided over the event, forecast that the school opening would mark the beginning of "a perpetual course of improvement and prosperity to the people of this Colony." Premier Coles pronounced the moment "the proudest of my life." Edward Whelan, a journalist and member of the House of Assembly, remarked that, although the Island was the smallest and poorest of the North American colonies, "we are entitled to boast that we have taken the lead and set an example to all the others in the important matters of education."[58]

In a way, it was John Stark's evening. He had been promoted to superintendent of education and was also superintendent of the new teacher-training school. His dream for the Island was finally being realized. "When on the other side of the Atlantic," he told the audience, "the attraction which shone the brightest in inducing me to leave my native country for a time was the establishment of a Normal training school in Charlottetown, Prince Edward Island."[59] The teaching method he imported from Stow's school was a revolutionary one in an era when learning was mainly by rote. "There will be no parrot work," Stark promised the crowd. "No child will be allowed to repeat by rote a lesson which he does not understand. Everything read or committed to memory will be thoroughly understood ere a new lesson is attempted; and thus, by picturing out in words, by ellipsis, by questions given individually and to the whole class, the children will be brought thoroughly to understand every subject which the lesson embraces, led to their own conclusions, and trained to think for themselves, and encouraged to express their own opinions in their own language."[60]

What many people in the audience may not have known was that the Stow method also included an inflammatory principle: teachers should impart a religious message to school children through the use of the Bible. In describing the work of the Normal School at the opening, Stark announced that the instruction would include a daily Bible lesson "in which the truths and facts of Scriptures will be brought before the children's minds by illustrations and picturing out in words, in language simple and easy to be understood, from which every thing sectarian or controversial shall be carefully excluded." For a man like Stark, an adherent of the Free Church of Scotland who refused even to travel on Sundays,[61] that was a proper course of instruction. Many Protestants in Prince Edward Island agreed with him. The mainly Protestant, seven-member Board of Education, which oversaw all of the Island's public schools, did not. Neither did many Roman Catholics. For a start, there was the issue of which translation of the Bible would be used — the Protestant version or the Roman Catholic one. And what interpretation of the Scriptures would a teacher give? Would Protestant teachers use the Bible to proselytize Catholic students? Although Roman Catholics comprised almost half the population of the Island (45 per cent to the Protestants' 55 per cent), they were not well-represented in the government of the day; they had won the right to vote and hold office only a quarter of a century earlier, and they tended to equate government authority — and government-run institutions — with British Protestant authority.

Nevertheless, during the orgy of self-congratulation that took place at the opening of the Normal School, nobody seemed to notice the storm clouds gathering on the horizon. At least, nobody had the audacity to mention it at the time. In fact, a journalist who covered the gala event mentioned that various passages of Stark's speech "drew forth most decided tokens of approbation from the meeting; and, on its conclusion, the learned gentleman was warmly applauded."[62] Perhaps the audience was overcome by the euphoria of the occasion. Only in retrospect would the Normal School Soirée be recognized as the forerunner of a series of squalls, involving education, religion, and politics, which would sweep across the Island over the next century, preoccupying legislators, toppling governments, and splitting the population in two.

The uproar created by Stark began soon after the Normal School opening. The Roman Catholic Bishop of Charlottetown, Bernard MacDonald, had missed the festive event, but discovered an account of the evening in a Halifax newspaper a few weeks later. From then on, it was all downhill for Stark, and for Protestant-Catholic relations.

Stark's statement on Bible-reading did not reflect the policy of the Board of Education, and, within two days of the Normal School opening, the Board explicitly excluded the Bible from the list of texts approved for use in the Normal School. Unfortunately, the Bishop was not aware of this.[63] In the first of a series of misunderstandings of comic-opera proportions, he wrote to the secretary of the board expressing concern about proposed changes in the teacher-training program. In the Normal School, he complained, "a certain formula of prayers" was being forced on the students, "many of whom are Catholics and are besides made to listen to lessons from a version of the Scriptures, in the correctness of which they do not believe. This introduction of religious matters into our public mixed schools is the Rock of Scandal.... If the friends of education wish our mixed schools to prosper, their wish can only be realized by allowing these schools to be godless, under the present circumstances of the country. The Catholics, I am bound to say, will be satisfied with nothing else...."[64]

The Liberal premier, George Coles, whose party relied heavily on the vote of poor Roman Catholic tenants, immediately assured Bishop MacDonald that Stark had made his remarks on his own hook. The Bishop replied that he was satisfied with this explanation, that he had acted as the result of a misunderstanding, and that Coles could show this letter to anyone concerned. Unfortunately, Coles neglected to do so.[65] And, unfortunately, the Bishop's *original* letter surfaced at a meeting of the Board of Education. The Board then ordered Stark to investigate the nature and extent of Bible-reading in the public schools. Stark found that Bible-reading was actually decreasing. Now it was the turn of the evangelical Protestants to express shock and dismay. They launched an aggressive campaign for the legal establishment of the Bible in the public schools, including the Central Academy.[66]

For years, the Island Legislature had resisted attempts by Protestant organizations, notably the Auxiliary Bible Society, to force Bible-reading into the Central Academy. In the district schools, local trustees and parents had the authority to decide whether to permit Bible-reading, which they did without creating any kind of a fuss. Then came John Stark's speech.[67] Like a lightning strike in a dry forest, it set off a conflagration that swept over the Island for more than a decade. In the 1850s and 1860s, the Island endured nine changes of government, partly because of denominational strife. In the 1859 election, with religion as the main issue, the Liberal government of Premier George Coles was defeated. Protestant voters had rallied to the support of the Conservatives, who advanced themselves as the champions of the Bible-reading camp. The Conservative-dominated Legislature then amended the Education Act to allow Bible-reading, without comment by the teacher, in the Central Academy and the public schools if parents so desired it. With that, the furor over the Bible Question fizzled out. By then, though, the damage had been done. Island society was split into two solitudes, one Catholic, the other Protestant.[68]

And what of John Stark, the man who — probably innocently — had fanned the flames of religious bigotry? Unfortunately for his career, he was seemingly incapable of discretion. A few months after the Normal School opening, he told the press that the government had directed him to introduce the Bible as a class book in the schools. Coles denied this. Relations between the school superintendent and the government grew more tense. There were questions in the Legislature regarding Stark's alleged failure to carry out his duties as school inspector. He wrote to the government, saying that he wanted to relinquish his duties by May. The government suggested he could leave right away. On that note, the Island's first qualified superintendent of education resigned. Predictably, newspapers on either side of the religious fence saw his downfall in totally different lights: the Protestant-allied *Protector* considered him a martyr to "Romish intrigue," while the *Examiner*, owned by Coles's political ally, Edward Whelan, diagnosed him as "a sort of loose screw on the State Coach."[69] What was indisputable was that his short-lived career on the Island was over. He went back to Scotland.[70]

Stark's much-longed-for Normal School would not have fulfilled his expectations, anyway — at least, not in the beginning. For one thing, he believed that student teachers needed three years of training. The Normal School program was only three months long. When the first class completed the course in October, only three of the twenty-two students passed.[71] Not surprisingly, some students complained bitterly about the institution. Some thought that the course should have guaranteed them a teacher's licence. Some argued that the Normal School should have instructed them in subjects in which they were deficient. At that time, any person over the age of 16 and possessing "good moral character" could enrol in the Normal School, regardless of qualifications. Poor William Monk, the headmaster, barely had time to teach the Model School children, who numbered about seventy, let alone help would-be teachers learn material they should have mastered in the district schools. He had no help at the Normal School, and, because he had to do so much remedial work, he neglected courses for which the Normal School had been set up in the first place — the art of teaching. The student-teachers watched the headmaster teach in the Model School, and then practised on the children, but didn't know enough about teaching to do themselves or the children any good. As the School Visitor reported to the Legislature in 1862, the quality of graduates from the Normal School didn't seem any better than teachers who had attended only the Central Academy.[72]

By the late 1850s, the Academy was offering an impressive course of studies. A notice in the *Royal Gazette* in 1859 listed reading, writing, English grammar, French language and literature, natural philosophy, Greek and Latin classics, algebra, geometry, analytical trigonometry, and differential and integral calculus, "with their application to Mechanics and Land Surveying, Navigation and Astronomy, including the use of all necessary instruments."[73]

By then, though, two new institutions of higher learning, more advanced than the Central Academy, were in the works. Roman Catholic officials were planning a diocesan college, intended primarily to produce candidates for the priesthood and, secondarily, secular professionals who would stand up for Catholics' rights and interests. The Legislature, probably recognizing that St. Andrew's College was fulfilling a need, had reversed an earlier decision not to fund a sectarian institution, and in 1834 had begun giving annual grants of 50 pounds to the college.[74] Ten years later, however, the school's finances were still in bad shape, and enrolment had dropped to ten. Bishop MacDonald closed the college and began collecting building materials for a new one on a tract of land he had bought on the eastern side of the Malpeque Road, just outside of Charlottetown.[75] The new college was formally opened in January 1855 under the name of St. Dunstan's College. Three years later, the rector, Rev. Angus MacDonald, requested a grant from the Legislature "for services rendered to education during the last three years," plus an annual grant to help the college keep operating. Despite MacDonald's description of the financially troubled college as the only institution of higher learning on the Island that poor country people, including Protestants, could attend, his request was turned down. He did, however, receive a consolation prize, a specific grant of 75 pounds — much to the displeasure of some Island Protestants, who tried to present counter-petitions to the House.[76]

The Bishop's timing could hardly have been worse. Premier Coles's Liberal government was in trouble over the volatile issue of Bible-reading in the schools. And the government had on the back burner its own plan for higher learning — in a sense, an institution parallel to and competing with St. Dunstan's College. There had been talk about such a college for years. Lieutenant-Governor Fanning, of course, had set aside land for a college half a century earlier. And, in 1843, the editor of the *Islander* observed that the Central Academy "ought ... to be regarded as the nucleus of a future university, and should receive that liberal support and consideration which are due to an Educational Establishment of the highest order...."[77] During the infamous Normal School Soirée, John Lawson, the city recorder, remarked that he had long hoped for this eventuality. "What advantages would not a College afford for the cultivation of the highest orders of Youthful intellect and genius amongst us!" he declared. "That it will not — now the march of intelligence is here commenced — I for one will not believe."[78]

Lawson's prayers were answered in the Speech from the Throne on February 16, 1860, when Lieutenant-Governor George Dundas spoke of the need for "perfecting the system of education throughout the Island."

The Legislature should consider "the propriety of re-constructing the arrangements on which the Central Academy is now based, in order that the increasing requirements for instruction in the higher branches of learning may be met, and the usefulness of that establishment augmented."[79]

On April 28, 1860, the Legislature gave first reading to a bill that would incorporate the Central Academy as a college "in which first class Mathematical, classical and philosophical education may be obtained as it is not desirable that the Natives of this colony should have to seek in other lands the attainment of a college education."[80] The bill went to some lengths to ensure that the proposed institution would be non-sectarian. The college was to be incorporated under a ten-member board of governors appointed by the lieutenant-governor. As in the Central Academy, no religious instruction was prescribed, and "no Clergyman, Pastor or Minister of any sect or denomination of Christians, having the spiritual charge of any Parish or Congregation" could teach at the college;[81] no student would be barred on the basis of religion.

The debate that followed indicated general agreement for updating the Academy. T. H. Haviland, a member of Premier Edward Palmer's cabinet, noted that the Academy was "but a day school for Charlottetown, and the sooner it is placed on a footing of a collegiate institution, the better...."[82] Liberal leader George Coles agreed. Young Islanders should have access to an education equal to that in other colonies, he said. The previous government had considered making changes to the constitution of the Academy, he said, but religious feeling was running so high at that time, it was not deemed advisable to introduce the change until the atmosphere cooled down.[83]

The atmosphere obviously hadn't cooled quite enough. Francis Kelly, a Catholic member of the Opposition, tried unsuccessfully to have third reading of the bill postponed. Then he called for the public endowment of St. Dunstan's College. Roman Catholic taxpayers, Kelly pointed out, would be contributing nearly half the funds for the government-operated college. That amendment was defeated by a vote of 10 to 5. On third reading of the bill, Kelly proposed adding a clause by which the government would pay St. Dunstan's professors the same amount it was planning to pay those at the other college. Again, Kelly's motion was defeated.[84] To Catholics, that indicated pure vindictiveness on the part of the Protestant legislators. To Protestants, Kelly's request was one more example of Roman Catholic aggressiveness. It was, *The Protestant* newspaper complained, "one of the coolest attempts on the part of the Romanists, to thrust their hands into the public chest of a Protestant country of which we have ever heard."[85]

Despite Kelly's opposition, the House of Assembly passed the act establishing the new college on May 1, 1860. Besides the Roman Catholic college, the colony now could boast a system of free education for all grade-school children, an imperfect but promising method of training people to teach them, and the groundwork for a new secular college that finally would occupy the land set aside by Governor Fanning a half-century earlier. The Legislature was truly showing, in John Lewellin Lewellin's words, "a laudable desire" to promote education in Prince Edward Island.

In the mix of religion, politics, and education, there would be rough roads ahead. But, after decades of false steps, the colony was making a veritable leap forward. "Looking at the velocity with which the great engine of education is now travelling on its magnificent way," the committee in charge of the Normal School opening wrote a few years earlier, "it is not to be expected that it will or can stop short."[86]

Like many colleges of that era, the Island's new institution would have to make do with a modest (if not downright uncomfortable) building, poor equipment, and very limited finances. It would offer a few more courses than the Central Academy, and an incentive for students from the country to enrol — six scholarships of 20 pounds each would be provided for students from the three counties[87] — but in the early years the staff would be smaller than that of the Academy, consisting only of two professors. Still, some of the colony's leading citizens pinned great hopes on the new institution. Some predicted that it not only would train young people from the Island for the learned professions, but would attract students from other lands. Some, like John Arbuckle, a teacher at the Central Academy who later became a school inspector, thought that the college would uplift the entire community. "No one, who has lived in a community where a college has existed for a long time," he declared, "can have failed to have observed its beneficial expression on the public mind, in elevating and refining the tone of society."[88]

An institution with the weight of such expectations on its shoulders surely deserved an appropriate name. What could be better than the title of a royal personage? By happy coincidence, Albert Edward, the eldest son of Queen Victoria, was coming to the North American colonies that summer. Island legislators hoped that he might be able to include the Island in his itinerary. In April, they wrote a letter to his mother, Queen Victoria, asking whether the Prince of Wales might stop off in Charlottetown. Two months later, they closed the Central Academy, and waited for it to turn into Prince of Wales College.

Chapter Two

The Prince and "The Princely College"

2

"Prince of Wales College is, we are pleased to find, altogether devoted to secular learning. This, in a country where every man is free to worship God in the manner he considers right, is as it should be."

—The Monitor, May 16, 1860

Let acclamations loud and long
Ring o'er our hills and dales!
God save the Queen, our loyal song,
And bless the Prince of Wales.
Where thousands press to see his face,
The foremost place we claim,
This beauteous Isle, our dwelling place,
Records his Grandsire's name...

— *From a poem by John LePage on the occasion of the visit to Charlottetown in 1860 of the Prince of Wales.*[1]

Albert Edward, Prince of Wales, was not highly regarded in the bosom of his own family. His mother, Queen Victoria, considered the future King of England dull, ugly, and lazy. "He is not at all in good looks," she once complained in a letter to her daughter Victoria. "His nose and mouth are too enormous and he pastes his hair down to his head, and wears his clothes frightfully ... His natural turn and taste is very trifling, and I think him a very dull companion ... Handsome I cannot think him, with that painfully small and narrow head, those immense features and total lack of chin."[2] The Prince, otherwise known as Bertie, also reminded Victoria of her lascivious uncles, and, perhaps, as monarch-in-waiting, of her own mortality. In an effort to stave off any inclination for frivolous activities such as cricket and billiards or, much worse, sexual dalliances, the Queen and her consort kept Bertie's wings clipped, denying him the companionship of people his own age and confining him to long hours in his school room. His visit to the North American colonies in the summer of 1860, when he was 18 years old, gave him a rare chance to escape the royal nest.

The official reason for the visit was the opening of the Victoria Bridge in Montreal, built by the Grand Trunk Railway, and the laying of the cornerstone of the Parliament buildings in Ottawa. The underlying reason was that the Queen owed the colonies a favour. During the Crimean War, Canada had raised and equipped at her own expense a regiment of infantry, which was incorporated into the British Army as the 100th Regiment, or the Royal Canadians. When the Canadian government was asked how such loyalty could be rewarded, the response was a request for a State visit from the Queen. Victoria had no desire to travel so far from home, but she promised to send Edward when he was old enough. The Victoria Bridge was just being completed, and the Canadian government asked that the Prince visit in time to declare the bridge open.[3] It was decided that he would also tour the United States and stop in Newfoundland, Nova Scotia, New Brunswick, and — to the indescribable delight of Islanders — the smallest colony of all, Prince Edward Island.

Like residents of other stops on the Prince's tour, and, unlike the Queen, the Islanders found Bertie to be handsome, charming, and full of vitality. "His Royal Highness," the *Islander* pronounced in a long and detailed account of the visit, "has a strikingly handsome and intelligent countenance, and a large and beautiful eye. It is impossible to look at him and not find that he is one of 'nature's gentlemen.' The ease, dignity and gracefulness of his manner are of a character few young men of his years can boast...."[4]

The newspaper was no less impressed with the way the little colony had risen to the occasion. "We feel sure," the *Islander* bragged, "that ... a reception given by Prince Edward Island to the eldest son of the Queen, has been but little inferior to any of those lately accorded him by Provinces vastly in advance of us, both as regards wealth and population."[5]

Certainly the colony spared no effort. When the Prince's ship docked at Charlottetown on the morning of August 9, huge crowds thronged the streets. Queen, Prince, Kent, and Water Streets were adorned with arches. Flags and banners were waving in all directions. The Colonial building was turned into a drawing room and banquet hall. The visit began with a parade to Government House, which included the Royal party, government officials, cavalry, judges, the clergy, members of the military, and various societies. At Rochford Square, a thousand school children brought tears to the Prince's eyes by singing the national anthem. Like most Royal visits, this one was packed with events. The Prince visited a farm, went riding, watched a fireworks display, held a levee, attended a ceremony at the Colonial building, and danced "with much spirit" at a ball in the Colonial building until three o'clock in the morning. When he returned to his ship the next day, he left behind him several mementoes. Sarah Harris, mother of soon-to-be-famous Robert and William Critchlow, observed in a letter to her mother-in-law that his spurs had torn several ladies' dresses at the ball, "and they intend keeping them as a memorial of his royal highness."[6] He also presented a diamond bracelet to the lieutenant-governor's wife, and a purse, variously described as 100 and 150 pounds, for charity. The other gift, less tangible but more durable, consisted of permission to use his name on the new college.[7] At some point, the Prince also decreed that Prince of Wales College could use his plumed crest and motto, *Ich Dien*.

The visit had cost the colonial government 3,000 pounds. At least one prominent Islander thought that was too much. Edward Whelan, a journalist and member of the Legislature, complained in the House: "Our resources were so diminished in regaling a few hundred individuals, chiefly from Queen's County, who happened to flock to this small city ... that not one pound more can be voted for the service of Roads and Bridges. If forty years hence he should be crowned King of Great Britain, it is not likely he will retain very vivid recollections of his hasty visit to this Colony; and if he should, to what avail would they be to the inhabitants of this Province, or how could they conduce to the interests of our children?"[8]

Whelan, of course, was a native of Ireland and possibly not disposed to working up much enthusiasm about an English prince. His newspaper, *The Examiner*, which served as a voice for Island Roman Catholics, displayed even less affection for the college that would bear the Prince's name. *The Examiner* took to referring to the new college as "the new sectarian institution"[9] — a term that must have sounded a bit spiteful to Protestants, in light of the government's expressed desire to free the college from any religious taint. Letters to the editor were even less complimentary. Some called Prince of Wales "the cow college" — a reference to the rumour that John Arbuckle, a teacher at the Central Academy, had kept a cow in the cellar. (The rumour would have been all the more delicious to Catholics given Arbuckle's reputation as an ardent Orangeman — and, coincidentally, a former drinking man.) More commonly, it was "the Protestant College." In the fall of 1860, "A Lover of Justice" wrote, "The establishment of this Protestant College is, without doubt, one of the most flagrant and outrageous acts of injustice towards Catholics ever perpetrated in this Colony. I for one loudly protest against the gross injustice of using public property for a Protestant College. The Academy was built by the money of Catholics as well as of Protestants, and the land which is attached to it is public property.... I protest also against the injustice of devoting a large portion of the public revenue to a Protestant or sectarian College, unless at the same time an equal amount, or an amount in proportion to their numbers, be given to Catholics...."[10] The Protestant press insisted, with some satisfaction, on the secular nature of Prince of Wales. "Prince of Wales College is, we are pleased to find," the *Monitor* commented, "altogether devoted to secular learning. This, in a country where every man is free to worship God in the manner he considers right, is as it should be."[11]

In those days, Catholics may have sincerely viewed Prince of Wales as a "Protestant" institution by virtue of being sponsored by the government of a British colony. Still, that description fit neatly with a strategy to obtain grants for St. Dunstan's College: if the government supported a "Protestant" institution, it should also fund a Catholic one.[12] In any case, the extreme language in the press of the day indicates the extent to which religion continued to get mixed up with politics and education. Delays in opening the college gave the two sides another chance to trade insults. In the summer of 1860, some citizens had hoped that the Prince of Wales would be opening the college bearing his name. In his travels across North America, the Prince did visit many colleges and universities. Prince of Wales College was not one of them. The old Academy building was empty, and badly in need of renovations by painters, carpenters, and masons. The government had closed the Academy in June, and had promised to hire two professors for the new institution, at a salary of 300 pounds each. The first one did not arrive until October.

Alexander Inglis was from Scotland, which was not surprising, given the number of Scots who had played prominent roles in the Island's education system thus far — among them, John McNeill, the first school inspector; John Stark, the first superintendent of education; William Monk, the first principal of the Normal School; and John Arbuckle, a teacher at the Academy and later a school inspector.

Born in Montrose, Scotland, Inglis had attended Aberdeen University, and had served as classical master in Aberdeen, schoolmaster at Fettercairn, and rector at Arbroath, Moffat, and Bathgate. Since 1851, he had been rector of Bathgate Academy in central Scotland. By the time he left for Prince Edward Island, he was 46 years old, bearded, balding, and bookish. By his own admission, he was something of a recluse, and had not cultivated many friendships during his nine years in Bathgate. Nevertheless, before his departure, the leading citizens of the area held a dinner in his honour at Robertson's Hotel. The chairman lauded him as "not only a profound and excellent scholar, deeply read in the classics, but a diligent and successful instructor of youth. His knowledge of general literature is also varied and extensive, and in addition to this, his kindly manner endears him to all his pupils."[13]

Inglis appeared chagrined by all the attention, and modestly chose to view the evening as a tribute to his profession rather than to himself. "I can only say that, since my appointment to the Prince of Wales College," he said, "I have studiously kept more than usually aloof from my friends, that I might not appear to evoke any demonstration.... I do not flatter myself that the distinction bestowed on me is on purely personal grounds. I have mixed but comparatively little in the general current of social life, and, consequently, have not cultivated acquaintance, nor ripened friendship into endearment so extensively as might have been done by one less tinctured with a love of books and a trace of professional ambition."[14]

Inglis arrived in Charlottetown in October 1860, but the new college was not yet open for business, a situation that annoyed some citizens greatly. "Will you have the goodness to inform me what has become of that Institution?" James Warburton, a prominent Liberal, wrote in a letter to *The Examiner* in November. "My son was a student in the Academy. He has been home since June, losing the time he ought to be occupied in attending to his studies, while the taxpayers are supporting an embryo Institution at a cost of 600 pounds per annum."[15] In fact, the taxpayers were paying the salary of only one professor by that point, although some money — 700 to 800 pounds, according to *The Examiner* — was being expended on repairs to the college building.

In early December, the trustees announced in *The Royal Gazette* that the repairs for that season were nearly finished, and the new college would open on December 10, "under the management of Professor Inglis, solely, *pro tem*."[16] *The Examiner* corrected that information a week later: the college would not open until after the Christmas holidays. *The Examiner* wondered why the board of trustees had not moved faster. "Whether it was their own stupidity that stood in the way — or the belief that 'the time had not arrived' for the opening of the College — or a difficulty in getting two professors, we cannot tell. We only know there is neither College nor Academy in existence. The old institution was closed at an early period of the summer; and the young gentlemen of 'the aristocracy' who attended there ... have been making wonderful progress in forgetting their unfinished tuition."[17]

The Examiner probably was right in thinking that the trustees were having trouble finding a suitable second master for Prince of Wales. Otherwise, why would they end up with William Monk, former head of the Normal School? Monk had arrived on the Island with good references from the Stow training school in Glasgow, where he had taught with John Stark, later the superintendent of education on the Island. But, only a few months after the Normal School opened, Stark's opinion changed. In a letter to *The Protector*, he wrote that Monk's "public and private conduct since coming here has given me the keenest and bitterest disappointment of my career in this Colony."[18] The government must have been disappointed in Monk, as well; in the spring of 1859, it fired him, along with R. B. Irving, then inspector of schools. Monk had an impossible task in trying to run the Normal School single-handed. Did it drive him to drink? Certainly Irving was a little too fond of the bottle; he occasionally appeared in court on charges of being drunk and disorderly. Perhaps Monk had repented of his sins, whatever they were. In any event, he took up his new post in the New Year. He was paid 200 pounds a year, plus 35 pounds for his house rent.[19]

In January, an announcement about the college appeared in *The Protestant and Evangelical Witness*, amidst advertisements for Ayer's Sarsaparilla and Watson's Cramp and Pain Killer and notices about stray cows: Prince of Wales College would open on January 7. The preparatory department "embracing the ordinary branches of a good Education" would be conducted by William Monk; Professor Inglis would teach Greek, Latin, French, German, mathematics, and natural science. The curriculum, probably influenced by the number of Scottish-trained educators on the Island, was consistent with the Scottish view that higher education should embrace science as well as the classics.[20] Students could enrol in one or both terms, extending from January to July and September to Christmas. Fees would be 10 pounds for each student, eight pounds for the second student from the same family and six pounds for the third. Like the Central Academy, the college would subsidize the education of rural students: those from outside Charlottetown would pay half the city rates. The notice, signed by John Longworth, secretary of the board of trustees and governors, invited the public to hear Professor Inglis's inaugural address in the hall of the college.[21]

The Protestant treated the opening ceremonies with reverence, noting that those attending included Lieutenant-Governor Dundas and other "highly respectable" ladies and gentlemen, and running the entire text of Inglis's address. It was a very long, very professorial address, embalmed in formal language, poetic imagery, and literary allusions, and, in a sense, it set the tone of the college for generations to come. Inglis proclaimed the value of studying not only the classics but also the more practical subjects, mathematics and chemistry. He exhorted prospective students to study from a love of learning, instead of from duty alone. And he assured them that the person who toils with the brain "belongs no less to the class of productive labourers than he who plies the anvil or ploughs the field." In his conclusion, perhaps mindful of the college motto, "I serve," Inglis urged students to use their education for the benefit of others. "The world is in a progressive condition," he said, "destined by an innumerable combination of co-operating agencies to culminate in universal knowledge and general felicity. This consummation is to be accomplished by human instrumentality. It can be realized not by passive content and listless inactivity, but by active exertion and strenuous perseverance. He who is content in ignorance, and aims only at personal goodness, is both selfish and short-sighted. We are here as units of one vast aggregate, and in a nobler sense than that of the poet may I address you and all men: *Et vos apes non mellificatis vobis*, which may not unaptly be translated, in the words of one no less distinguished for intellectual grasp than sublimity of moral purpose — 'None of us liveth to himself.'"[22]

Predictably, a letter in *The Examiner* that month mocked Inglis's flowery turns of phrase, criticized him for placing too much value on the classics, and berated the government for the money spent in turning the Central Academy into "the princely college." In appearance, the writer contended, the college was "the same dirty, dilapidated condition as it was when Professor Arbuckle is said to have made it the place of resort for his animals of the useful, if not ornamental, 'bovine species.'" The only repairs done to the Academy, the writer claimed, were a half-dozen steps to the front door. "The rest is the direct opposite of what a college should be. Not a library, not a map, not even a proper class book, have the Government provided, and for this winter, at least, the Prince of Wales College is but another name for a district school." This, the writer noted in an aside, was in contrast to St. Dunstan's College, which was properly equipped, despite a lack of financial aid from the government.[23]

Another correspondent complained about the tuition fees, contending that the government had planned the college only for children of the wealthy — "the young Havilands, Orlebars, Hancocks, Longworths, DeBloises, &c." — and described the building as "a perfect disgrace" to the colony. "It is better for a Cowhouse than for a College," the writer maintained. "Professor Inglis cannot maintain a very high opinion of those who sent for him, and praised this place up to the skies. When he was delivering his inaugural address the other day, the Government should have blushed with shame at the exceedingly shabby appearance of their College, the study room of which resembles a Smokehouse, for its ceiling is as black and dirty as smoke can make it. The whole building, with its smoky ceiling, broken plaster, &c., presents a most wretched and dilapidated appearance."[24]

Indeed, one can only speculate as to why Professor Inglis decided to leave Bathgate Academy, where, he observed during his farewell dinner, he had spent the happiest years of his life. Was it a fit of mid-life madness? The promise of a higher salary? The average salary for rectors in Scottish academies at the time was about 220 pounds a year;[25] at Prince of Wales, Inglis would receive 300 pounds. Compared with his new school, Bathgate was quite grand — an elegant stone building, crowned by a bell tower, with two wings connected by a colonnade, and a centre block containing the rector's house. There were five large classrooms, a library, and an acre of playground. At Bathgate, Inglis was in charge of a staff of four masters and more than 500 students.[26] In the early years at Prince of Wales, Inglis and one other master would preside over a college with an enrolment of only a few dozen students. If the newspapers were not exaggerating, the state of the college building must have given the new immigrant an unpleasant surprise. And was he prepared for the hornet's nest of religion-based backbiting that awaited him on this side of the Atlantic? Professor Inglis did not share his thoughts on these and related subjects for posterity. He was a man who kept his own counsel. With his wife and two children, he settled into a house at the corner of St. Peter's Road and Cumberland Street, and concentrated on making a success of the new college. The only evidence of any extracurricular activities is a mention in the newspapers of his becoming vice-president of the Young Men's Christian Association and Literary Institute, an organization that sponsored a wide range of educational talks. (One notice of a meeting advertised a lecture by Rev. David Fitzgerald on "Human Physiology, Digestion and Circulation, illustrated by Diagrams," and a discussion on "The Massacre of Glencoe — was William III implicated in it?"[27])

Aside from that mention, Inglis surfaced only once in eight years in the local newspapers, when he was reluctantly drawn into a dispute over religion and education. The *Vindicator*, a mouthpiece for the Roman Catholic bishop, had been bandying his name about, suggesting that he had been dabbling in local politics in an article in the *Protestant*. That accusation must have driven Inglis wild, because he actually responded. "I have no recollection of ever having spoken to the editor of the *Protestant* on any matter of politics," Inglis wrote to *The Examiner*. "I most solemnly declare that I have never heard of the article in question before its publication, and that I never made the slightest allusion to it, after its publication, to any individual beyond the circle of my own family. Moreover, I aver that I never wrote one word of a political nature or otherwise, except advertisements, to any editor of any newspaper in this Island — so studiously have I abstained from mixing myself up with any political section. I deem this positive declaimer due to myself, in order that my friends in this community may become aware that my motto is, and ever has been, to mind my own business, and nothing else."[28]

For a man with a keener appetite for local controversies, the 1860s would have furnished a veritable feast. Land ownership, Confederation, railways, and, as always, religion — they were all hot topics in the newspapers, in the Legislature, and, presumably, on the street. It was a topsy-turvy time on the Island. Confederation was one of the most acrimonious issues. Island politicians haggled with the Canadians over the terms of a marriage, advanced close to the altar, turned back, haggled some more. Delegates to the now-famous Charlottetown Conference came and went. Island governments — five in all — rose and fell. And, as usual, religion continued to rile the waters. In the name of religion, political alliances shifted back and forth. One election, in 1863, was fought almost solely on religious issues, with the Conservatives sweeping to power on an "anti-Popery" platform with an all-Protestant government. Roman Catholics and Protestants traded the most outrageous insults in the Legislature and in the newspapers.

In the middle of the fray was the rector of St. Dunstan's College, Father Angus MacDonald, who, in contrast to Professor Inglis, apparently relished a good public row. MacDonald was reputed to be editor of the Catholic *Vindicator*, and engaged in a number of inflammatory debates about religion in the press. In the early 1860s, facilities at his college were in even worse shape than those at Prince of Wales; in fact, the entire building had to be rebuilt. When, after an extraordinary community effort, a new brick shell was erected, MacDonald's paper threw this achievement in the face of the enemy. "The building is now a splendid brick edifice," the *Vindicator* boasted, "second to no educational establishment in the Lower Provinces; it is a credit to the Catholic community and an eye-sore to the whole fraternity of Orange bigots."[29]

While St. Dunstan's managed to pay for the repairs through various community fund-raising schemes, its operating costs remained too high, and its revenues too low. Throughout the decade, Bishop Peter McIntyre, a dynamic and determined supporter, tried in vain to obtain government support for St. Dunstan's. In the late 1860s, he coupled his request to the Legislature with a plea for aid for three convent schools, on the grounds that, like the college, his schools were doing some of the work of the public education system.[30] Again, he was unsuccessful.

While St. Dunstan's existed mainly to prepare students for religious seminaries, gave religious instruction, and hired priests and seminary students as faculty, its secular curriculum resembled that of Prince of Wales, on paper, at least. St. Dunstan's offered Greek, Latin, English, French, algebra, arithmetic, geometry, trigonometry, astronomy, geography, philosophy, natural philosophy (physics), chemistry, history, vocal music, and "problems on the terrestrial globe."[31] Prince of Wales, according to the act by which it was established, was to offer Greek and Latin classics, French,

German, mathematics, natural philosophy, metaphysics, logic, rhetoric (exercises in analysis and composition), political economy, and history. (On paper, the intended curriculum also resembled that of the first-year course at McGill in 1860 — classics, French or German, English literature, mathematics, history, elementary chemistry — although it is debatable how this translated in practice.) About the same number of students, and the same percentage of rural students, attended the two schools. St. Dunstan's even had a few Protestant students. Female students were admitted to the Normal School, but not to either St. Dunstan's or Prince of Wales. This was standard policy for the times in Canada: in 1860, only the Canadian Literary Institute (later, McMaster University) and Mount Allison College offered higher education to women.[32]

Predictably, the annual reports of the first Prince of Wales principal revealed little about the workings of the college. They do not record the religious affiliation of students, or hint at activities at the college. Accounts by former students provide some clues. According to one such student, at least one enduring tradition was forged in those early years. In a letter to his grandmother in 1862, Tom Harris of the soon-to-be-famous Harris family reported that the Prince of Wales boys had formed a debating club under the patronage of the principal. The principal's reports consisted mostly of enrolment numbers, with a breakdown between rural and town students. In 1863, for instance, Inglis reported an enrolment of 53 students, 30 of whom were from Charlottetown. In 1864, enrolment fell to 22 students, of whom 12 were from Charlottetown; in 1865, enrolment stood at 27, with 13 from Charlottetown.[33] Although the enrolment appears very small, especially in comparison with that of the Central Academy, the college building also housed a grammar school, established in 1863 under the direction of the Prince of Wales trustees, with Leander G. MacNeill as principal.[34] Some of the grammar school students received instruction daily at the college. Thus, Inglis's 1866 report showed an enrolment of 34 students at Prince of Wales, plus 16 from the grammar school who had received instruction at the college.[35] And, to put the numbers in perspective, in 1861-62, Acadia College in Wolfville, Nova Scotia, had an enrolment of only 37 students; The University of King's College in Windsor, Nova Scotia, 39; and Mount Allison Wesleyan College, 10.[36] By the time Inglis left the college in 1868, attendance at Prince of Wales had climbed to a total of 72, of whom 39 attended the college exclusively, and 33 were enrolled in the grammar school.[37]

In 1868, when Inglis was fifty-four years old, he left the Island and went back to Scotland. Little is known of his life there. When he died at the age of eighty, an obituary in the Bathgate *Gazette* furnished only the barest details of his life and career. After his return to Scotland, it said, he lived in Portobello; he devoted much of his time to working with the Young Men's Christian Association in Edinburgh; he died "due to failure of the heart's action" after an attack of pleurisy. At the time of his death, he was visiting his son-in-law, a clergyman, in Kilmarnock.[38] Perhaps back in Scotland he lived as quietly, and minded his own business as diligently, as he had in Prince Edward Island. William Monk went back to Scotland as well. The trustees discharged him in 1862; he became master of the Summerside Grammar School, tried to set up a rival college, and left the Island in 1864.[39]

Monk's replacement at Prince of Wales was another Scot, Alexander Anderson, a man whose personality was as vivid as Inglis's was low-key. Anderson arrived on the Island in November 1862, shortly after marrying Catherine Stewart Robertson of Alloa, Scotland. In December, *The Islander* reprinted this notice from a Halifax newspaper: "Among the passengers by the *Africa,* from Liverpool, was Professor A. Anderson, who has been appointed to a professorship in the Prince of Wales College. We have reasons to know that Professor Anderson stands very high as a Mathematician, Chemist, Geologist, and Zoologist, besides being an excellent classical and philosophical scholar. We congratulate the friends of the Prince of Wales College on this valuable addition to their staff." *The Islander* had no doubt that the appointment would give "great satisfaction, and prove of special service to the country."[40]

For once, such praise was well-merited. Alexander Anderson was barely twenty-six when he took over the post of second master at Prince of Wales, teaching mainly mathematics and science, but he had already made a name for himself in Scottish education circles. Born in Aberdeen in September 1836, Anderson had attended school in Aberdeen until 1854, when he led all of Scotland in the examinations for his year and won a scholarship to Moray House Training College in Edinburgh. He attended the college for two years, was appointed a master in the training department, and later entered the University of Edinburgh. At the end of four years there, he won gold medals in mathematics and natural philosophy, and a medal in chemistry.[41]

Anderson became principal of Prince of Wales in June 1868. He was only thirty-one years old at the time, but he was a brilliant, dynamic, and demanding teacher, and he was destined to leave his mark on the Island's entire public education system. Under his leadership, the "cow college" would develop the reputation for excellence that it maintained for the rest of its existence.

Chapter Three

The Lion of Prince of Wales

3

"A breach of discipline was looked upon by himself [Alexander Anderson] and his pupils as an offence against his own dignity and therefore against the eternal order of the universe."
— Sir Andrew Macphail

Alexander Anderson was a short, powerfully built man, with a beard, a thick shock of grizzled hair that stood straight up, and dark eyes that suggested he might have a sense of humour. Marching down the halls of Prince of Wales College "like a sergeant-major on parade," in the words of a former student, he presented a picture of dignity bordering on pomposity. Always impeccably dressed in his cutaway coat and tails, he carried himself ramrod straight — so straight, he almost leaned over backwards. He was capable of savage sarcasm, but, in the two years that Sir Andrew Macphail attended the college in the 1880s, Anderson never once so much as uttered a rebuke to any of his students. "A breach of discipline," Macphail wrote later, "was looked upon by himself and his pupils as an offence against his own dignity and therefore against the eternal order of the universe." The secret to his success in disciplinary matters, perhaps, was that he treated boys just off the farm with great respect, as if they were young gentlemen destined for greatness. And some of them were. The secret to his academic success was that Anderson loved to teach.[1] "He has a wonderful tact in finding out and developing talent in his pupils," a 19th-century biographer wrote, "and many a young man has been started by him in a career of usefulness and distinction, who might otherwise have remained unknown."[2]

In the first decade of Anderson's thirty-three-year reign as principal, Prince of Wales College began developing the reputation for academic excellence that it retained to the end of its days. Prince of Wales then offered high school and the first year of university, and graduates who transferred to universities on the mainland, the United States, or Great Britain did remarkably well, many of them winning scholarships and prizes. Many went on to become doctors, lawyers, university professors, legislators. Ironically, that didn't mean that the college was safe from either criticism or the threat of abolition. In fact, that sword hung over its head at least until the 1880s. As if that were not enough, Anderson had to deal with a dizzying turnover of staff and a building that became more and more inadequate as the years went by. Fortunately for the college, Anderson hung on, through thick and thin. He had his compensations: a salary, in the early 1870s, of $1,298 a year; the satisfaction of seeing the college grow; praise from mainland universities; and the everlasting gratitude of some of the super-achievers who had passed through the doors of his school.

One of them was Jacob Gould Schurman, who became president of Cornell University in Ithaca, New York, and later American envoy to China and ambassador to Germany. He once described Anderson as the greatest benefactor the Island ever had. "I have sat under many instructors," Schurman said, "speaking in different languages — German, English, French, Italian — but I have never yet met such a great teacher as Prof. Anderson; and calmly reflecting on the matter I believe there is none to whom all considered, I personally owe so much as to him."[3]

Schurman began his life as a poor farm boy in Freetown, near Summerside. In the 1860s, he left home at age thirteen to work in a country store, decided three years later to get a college education, and, after a year of intense study, took the examinations for the $60-a-year scholarships to Prince of Wales College. He led all the candidates across the Island. "I have been fortunate since then," he recalled years later, "and have had some rewards that most persons would consider very much greater than this modest prize of $60 a year. But I tell you that this was the greatest success I ever won. That $60 a year made all the difference in the world to me then. With it I could continue my education; without it I could not have gone on."[4] At the end of his first year at Prince of Wales in 1871, he captured prizes in Latin, Greek, geometry, algebra, trigonometry, chemistry, and physical geography. Then he went on to greater rewards: a $500-a-year Gilchrist Scholarship in a Dominion-wide competition to study at the University of London, a doctorate from the University of Edinburgh, two years of study in Germany, France, and Italy on another academic award, and, finally, a brilliant career as an academic and diplomat.

Some of the bright students at Prince of Wales had such good connections, they probably would have gone on to successful careers with or without Anderson's help. The thirty-three young men enrolled in the senior year in 1869 included a number of names of the Charlottetown elite — Pope, Palmer, Laird, Haszard, Haviland, Peters, Longworth, Brecken. Joseph Pope was the son of William Henry Pope, one of the Island's most powerful politicians, and the nephew of Conservative Premier James Pope. Joseph enrolled in the Prince of Wales grammar school in the 1860s, at age eleven, and studied under Anderson for five years. Although Joseph didn't go on to university, he managed to do very well for himself. After leaving Prince of Wales, he entered the public service, thanks to a job offer from his grandfather, the colonial treasurer. He eventually became private secretary to Sir John A. Macdonald and Under-Secretary of State for Canada, and in 1911 was knighted by the King. Sir Joseph Pope maintained a life-long admiration for his old teacher: "Of Dr. Anderson's faculty for imparting knowledge I cannot speak too highly," he wrote a half-century after his years at Prince of Wales.[5]

And Pope's was not the only success story. Many farm boys of that era — boys like Schurman, with no money or connections — also distinguished themselves. Martin Martin, the son of a farmer in Grandview, attended Prince of Wales in the mid-1870s, entered medical school at the University of Toronto, and graduated with first-class honours. A contemporary, George Carruthers of Bedeque, enrolled in Queen's University and later in McGill medical school, where he graduated second in a class of thirty-six. James Rodgerson of Pisquid completed his arts degree at Dalhousie University, and won the gold medal when he graduated from medical school.[6] John Alexander Nicholson of Eldon studied at McGill, and served as superintendent of education on the Island in the early 1890s and later as registrar at McGill, a position he held for twenty-eight years.[7]

Such triumphs did not go unnoticed. Even *The Examiner*, previously no great friend of Prince of Wales, mustered faint praise for the college in a report on the 1871 mid-summer examinations, where the students "acquitted themselves much more creditably to themselves and the Institution than we had been led to expect."[8] During the 1875 convocation of Dalhousie College, *The Examiner* reported that a "Professor McDonald"[9] had called attention to Jacob Schurman's Gilchrist Scholarship, and his tenth-place standing among about 500 candidates for entrance to London University: "The first praise is due, no doubt, to Mr. Schurman himself," the professor said. "It is but fair to Prince of Wales College and to Acadia College ... to believe that they did much to produce this gratifying result. We can say from long experience of them, that our students from 'the Island' are among the best we have, and those who have come to us from Prince of Wales College have been exceptionally grounded in the elements of a College course."[10]

What makes this solid grounding truly remarkable is that the district school system that fed Prince of Wales was still woefully inadequate. Year after year, the school visitors' reports told the same story: poor attendance, ill-equipped classrooms, a hit-and-miss curriculum, unqualified and poorly paid teachers (the lowest salaries in North America), vacant schools. In 1871, of a total school-age population of 25,952, only 9,337 pupils were attending regularly.[11] The Normal School, while gradually improving, was still the subject of considerable ridicule in the press and criticism in the Legislature. It was a good primary and secondary school, a Legislative committee reported in 1876, but had ceased to be a teacher-training school.[12] In fact, prospective teachers were not required to attend the Normal School, and were offered little incentive to do so. Students who wanted to enrol in either the Normal School or Prince of Wales College could do so pretty much by knocking on the door. Some had only an elementary-school-level education. Consequently, they were not always prepared for either institution.

In the case of Prince of Wales, this meant much remedial work, especially in Anderson's early years at the college. "I found that, if success was to be attained," he once confided to a friend, "a great deal of elementary drudgery had to be gone through, as no solid foundation had been laid. But the natural ability of the students was very encouraging, and consequently the results were gratifying."[13] In his annual report for the 1874-75 year, Anderson noted that, of the 70 students enrolled, 13 were in a preparatory class, receiving instruction in grammar, geography, history, arithmetic, writing, and reading, presumably to get ready for the regular curriculum. In his regular classes, Anderson taught Latin ("Latin Grammar, Bixce's Reader, Virgil and Latin Composition, Cicero and Horace and Latin Composition, Tacitus and Latin Composition"), Greek ("Greek New Testament, Homer, Greek Composition, Greek Tragedy, Medea"), geometry (junior and senior plane geometry, solid geometry, conic sections, analytical geometry, and differential calculus), algebra, and arithmetic. The second master, Alexander Lowe, taught preparatory English, grammar, "scientific lessons," English literature and composition, French grammar and composition, German, ancient history and English history, geography, and bookkeeping. To accommodate all these classes, Anderson observed, the two professors were working long hours, teaching from eight in the morning until four in the afternoon. "In fact," he said, "there is an abundance of work for another teacher."[14]

As it was, people were already complaining about how much Prince of Wales was costing the taxpayer — at that point, about 1,000 pounds a year. In 1871, when only 20 students were enrolled in the senior department and 28 in the grammar school, Lowe's appointment triggered an anonymous diatribe in *The Examiner* about the extravagance of paying 300 pounds a year to a second professor. An ordinary grammar school teacher could have done the job at a third of that cost, the correspondent wrote. "A large number of the people of this Island look upon the maintenance of Prince of Wales College, at an expense to the Country of nearly 1,000 pounds per year, as a great injustice to them. And so it is." The writer suggested that the college could be transformed into a teacher-training school and graded school, or replaced by an institution "with Professors representing all denominations."[15]

The latter suggestion apparently was a backhanded reference to the aroma of Protestantism that still hung over Prince of Wales. But opposition to the college was not confined to Roman Catholics. Some influential Protestants were just as hostile. Rev. Stephen Lawson, a Presbyterian minister who published *The Presbyterian,* complained in his paper that the college did not meet the needs of the Island. James Fletcher, editor of *The Island Argus,* agreed. Fletcher, a native of Orwell who had been trained as a teacher, was a champion of non-sectarian schools, but apparently not of the non-sectarian college. Week after week, Fletcher attacked the college for placing too much emphasis on the classics, for hiring teachers from abroad — "We have tried Scotland long enough" — and for failing to educate students for the professions. And, in an echo of criticisms levelled three decades earlier against the Central Academy, he dismissed the college as a school for the rich. "We condemn the Prince of Wales College," he wrote, "because it is not properly conducted — because it takes a large sum of money to run it, and yields very little in return. The leading men on both sides of politics condemn it.... Every man who wishes well to our Free system of Education condemns it as at present constructed, and the time to have it supplanted by something better has arrived."[16]

David Laird, the Liberal and Protestant editor of *The Patriot,* and a strong supporter of secular education, fired back a rebuttal, as did some of his readers. One blunt correspondent, dismissing Fletcher's editorials as being remarkable "only for the ignorance and stupidity which they display," pointed out that young men who had attended Prince of Wales were able to enter the second year of "the most celebrated Colleges and Universities of the Dominion and Great Britain." If anything, the writer contended, the government should spend more money on the college, not less.[17] The editor of *The Patriot* noted that the college was designed to offer a liberal education, not a professional one, and pointed to achievements of some of its graduates. "The honour lists of Dalhousie, Windsor and Edinburgh, can produce proof ... of the eminence of our College students, together forming a list, which we challenge any Institution, established for an equal time, and with equal resources, to excel."[18] As if to underline the point, the newspaper ran a news item the next week about Islanders at McGill College in Montreal: Duncan C. McLeod graduated with a Bachelor of Arts, with honours, won a gold medal, and gave the valedictory address at the convocation. Robert Weeks, the best student in his class at Prince of Wales, was studying engineering, and stood first in his class in drawing, construction, mathematical and experimental physics, zoology, and French.[19] James McLeod graduated in medicine. "Boys of Prince Edward Island," the paper exhorted, "see that year after year our little Colony may have the pride of hearing of some of you carrying off similar prizes in competition with students from the rest of the Dominion. There are some valuable prizes annually offered at McGill College; all you have to do is go up and win them."[20]

No doubt some of these bright young men would have succeeded at university regardless of their earlier training. And no doubt they were the cream of the academic crop. Despite Fletcher's allegations, Prince of Wales could not be accused of being the purview of wealthy Charlottetown boys: as early as 1864, almost half of the 22 boys enrolled in the college were from the country; by 1874–75, 30 of the 70 students were from the country, and 3 were from the mainland; by 1878, the farm boys outnumbered the city students, 33 to 27, with "all denominations represented," according to the Board of Education.[21] If the college represented any select group, it was the academic elite. As historian Ian Ross Robertson has pointed out,

Prince of Wales was run on the "old elitist principle of excellence." Education was meant to draw out the best in a young man, "and to draw the best men out of the common herd of humanity."[22] Robertson observes that, for many Scottish Islanders, with the collective memory of land clearances engraved in their psyches, a superior education was the route to social and economic security.[23] A good education also meant freedom from drudgery, of which there was plenty on a Prince Edward Island farm. At Prince of Wales, Macphail recalled, "it was well understood that the intention of coming to school was to escape from work by sitting in a professor's chair or on a judge's bench, by standing in the pulpit or before the altar, or moving at leisure in professional or political office."[24] A good education implied high standards — which left little room for indifferent students. By the time Andrew Macphail entered Prince of Wales, the policy was to shut them out — or drive them out. "If the boy had no aptitude or books," he wrote, "he should not waste his time, but had better betake himself to the land, the sea or the workshop, lest he might fall into that abyss of unemployment and poverty that lies between a profession and a trade."[25] Entrance examinations, initiated in 1880, were one way of selecting the best and brightest of Island students. The scholarship program was another. In Andrew Macphail's day, the scholarships had been increased to $80 a year, plus free tuition. "With due economy the amount was adequate and they were sought after like a secret piece of prey," Macphail recalled. "Failure meant that the boy might have to go to work for a living."[26]

In Macphail's case, that catastrophe fortunately did not occur. The son of school inspector William McPhail,[27] young Andrew was expected to carry on the tradition of his father's family: none of them, his grandmother once remarked — "part in sorrow, part in pride"[28] — had ever worked. At age fifteen Andrew took the two-day examinations for the coveted scholarship in the summer of 1880, competing against 149 other candidates. In the fall, scholarship in hand, he entered Prince of Wales College. His books for the year cost him a total of $10.25.[29]

By the time Macphail arrived, the college had undergone a decade of expansion: in five years, enrolment had almost doubled, to 91 from 51 in the mid-1870s. Anderson had also added new courses. In addition to Latin, Greek, English, geometry, algebra, trigonometry, history, geography, and music, there were new courses in French, natural philosophy (physics), chemistry, and agriculture. In classics, Anderson reported, "we read selections from Thucydides, Euripides, Horace and Livy"; in mathematics, students wrestled with "Higher algebra and Solid and spherical Geometry."[30] The addition of science and agriculture was a bow to demands from the community for more practical courses. The act establishing Prince of Wales College had specified that science, French, and German would be part of the curriculum. The first principal, Alexander Inglis, had made a point in his inauguration address of stressing the importance of science education, and apparently he taught both German and natural science. Under Anderson, though, the college was like most institutions of its day: science and modern languages were given short shrift. Even the University of Toronto, for example, had very little laboratory equipment before the mid-1870s; natural history and zoology were taught on the blackboard in a lecture room.[31] Prince of Wales had neither the facilities nor the staff to do justice to a science program. Anderson, despite his academic triumphs during his own student days in Scotland, probably wasn't very interested, anyway. His heart was in the classics. "But in time," Andrew Macphail recalled, "the rising cry for the practical in science was heard.... Principal Anderson was compelled to meet the charge that the old system was obsolete by adding new courses...."[32]

Adding agriculture to the curriculum certainly fit the tenor of the times. Farming was a serious business. Most Islanders lived on farms; more than 20,000 people made their living in agriculture. The buzzword of the era was "scientific agriculture," which meant using the latest techniques of cultivation and livestock breeding and maintenance. To encourage scientific farming, agricultural societies tried to educate farmers through lectures, lending libraries, newspaper articles and courses in the schools. Anderson was more at home with classics than with cows, but he made at least a token effort to bow to popular demand. The course leaned heavily on a small textbook, which, Macphail said, could be learned "like a catechism or the Ten Commandments." At the end of the year, a young woman from Charlottetown won the agriculture prize awarded by a Farmers' Institute, "although she entertained the private belief that the tubes which a cow displays were designed to yield milk and cream from separate reservoirs."[33]

Anderson had to take on the new courses without any increase in staff or pay, so perhaps he could be forgiven for making compromises and cutting corners. In one year-end report, he claimed that the college was devoting an hour a week each to chemistry and physics. In Macphail's memoir, possibly exaggerated for humorous effect, Anderson disposed of physics in one hour of the school year. "His appliances," Macphail recalled, "were a large magnet, a Leyden jar, an enormous stick of red sealing wax, a wet battery, and an air pump. He never deigned to manipulate this machinery, but would stand by with an air of sardonic amusement, whilst his son delivered a current of electricity into a semi-circle of the newer boys with joined hands, or exploded a square bottle by extracting the air."[34] And that, according to Macphail, was enough science for the year. "Principal Anderson had yielded to the modern scientific spirit and to the reformers of education. 'Tomorrow morning at eight o'clock,' he said, 'we shall resume Arnold's Greek Prose Composition.'"[35]

Anderson was never happy about the way French was taught at the college, which wasn't surprising, given that he was one of the instructors. His much-vaunted gifts as a teacher did not compensate for his inadequacy in the language. "He had learned his French in Edinburgh as if it were a dead language," Macphail recalled, "and now being compelled to teach French, he taught it as a purely intellectual exercise. He had declared to the disturbers of his academic peace and freedom that the only way to speak and understand French was to bring a French baby into the family and learn from him, but his college was no nursery. He eventually went so far as to affirm that the attempt to teach French from books would forever make it impossible for the pupil to speak of understanding it. The remembrance of the grammar would leave him dumb and speechless; when he opened his mouth the grammar would short-circuit his brain. There were two French boys in the class who were preparing for the priesthood. He proved his point; he addressed them in French, and they were compelled to admit that they understood not a word he said. To complete the proof, he had them speak to the class in French with the same result. But he continued the course, always pronouncing the words as if they were English words; he thought the attempt to imitate the French vowel sounds produced an unseemly distortion of the Scottish countenance."[36]

History was more to Anderson's taste. To teach ancient history, he would read whole Shakespearean plays and expound on their setting. His method of teaching modern history, Macphail recalled, was to read from the masters of English prose, describing the circumstances under which the texts were written.[37] Physical education was not part of the curriculum. All students had to take part in infantry foot-drill, but that was the extent of the program of physical exercise. "The Principal contended that boys came there to learn, not to engage in that voluntary labour known as exercise; enough of that on the farm in the summer time."[38]

If the teaching of modern languages and science at Prince of Wales was as perfunctory as Macphail suggests, it didn't hurt his career. After two years at Prince of Wales, he studied medicine at McGill, taught the history of medicine there for thirty years, edited two national medical journals, wrote many books, and became famous as a scientist, writer, and social critic. In *The Master's Wife,* published six decades after his Prince of Wales days, he remembered Anderson with enormous respect and affection. "Of the many teachers I have known," he said simply, "he was the best."[39] In fact, Anderson inspired a kind of hero-worship among many leading citizens of his day. "Members of the government, of the judiciary, and of the professions had all passed through his school," Macphail said, "and they retained for him a respect and fear not unmixed with affection. In addition, the best schools were taught by his pupils, and they helped to propagate the legend of his power."[40] Some of his former pupils also returned to teach at the college, and carried on Anderson's philosophy of education long after he was gone.

Unfortunately, neither Anderson's personal magnetism nor the undeniable success of his college could protect Prince of Wales from the fallout over interminable disputes in the community over religion, politics, and education. As Sir Joseph Pope observed many years later, politics ran high in that small place, "I suppose on the principle that the smaller the pit the fiercer the rats fight."[41] Some of the fiercest fights stemmed from the old School Question. The issue, as always, was whether the government should give grants to public schools and the secular college, Prince of Wales, and not to Roman Catholic schools and the Roman Catholic college, St. Dunstan's.

In the years when Prince of Wales was expanding and making a name for itself on the mainland, the Catholic college was floundering, and becoming more and more desperate for help. Chronically in debt and facing dwindling enrolment, St. Dunstan's depended for its survival on fees, grants from the Society for the Propagation of the Faith, and donations from the meagre resources of the faithful. Bishop Peter McIntyre continued to press for government aid, but it was a discouraging struggle. "From the fact of our never having received any assistance from the Legislature, as other public Institutions have done," he observed in his Lenten Pastoral for 1871, "and as the board and tuition fees of students were not sufficient to meet all current expenses, we were necessarily obliged either to go in debt or have the establishment closed. We had hoped all along that when gentlemen of education — not bigots — men of enlightened and Christian views and advocates of even-handed justice would find their way into Parliament, our case would be duly considered and our grievances attended to. Thus far, however, our hopes have not been realized."[42]

In spite of his lack of success with the college, the Bishop's vision of government aid expanded in the 1870s to include a complete system of separate schools for Roman Catholic children. The argument was the same as that for aid to St. Dunstan's College: the schools and the college represented the religion of half the Island's population, performed a valuable service to the community, and relieved taxpayers of the burden of educating a large portion of the student population. Catholics were paying taxes for a school system they didn't use.

The education issue muddied the waters of the important 1873 election, which ostensibly was about whether the Island should join Confederation. In a desperate attempt to attract Catholic voters during that campaign, Conservative leader J. C. Pope led Catholic voters to believe that his government would provide aid for separate schools. When the Island's Protestant clergy reacted with outrage, Protestant voters exacted from some of the Tory candidates — even J. C. Pope — a pledge that they would not change the existing educational system. At the end of this confusing campaign, the Conservatives won the election, but the promised support for Catholic schools did not materialize. However, the School Question did not go away.

The other big issues of the mid-1800s — land ownership, Confederation, and the railway— had been laid to rest.[43] Islanders, having resisted for a decade attempts to lure them into a marriage with Canada, finally gave up the fight. Faced with increasing pressure from the mother country, as well as yearly deficits, a sagging economy, and a massive debt from building the railway, the Island reluctantly entered Confederation in 1873. Under the terms of Confederation, the Island was in a position to buy back lands owned by the proprietors. The Dominion government had also taken a burden off the provincial treasury by assuming ownership, maintenance, and operation of the Island's 200-mile railway system. In addition, the Dominion had promised an efficient steam service with the mainland, which seemed to solve the problem of economic weaknesses caused by isolation.[44]

The only burning issue in the mid-1870s was the interminable School Question. The Education Act needed revision, and that debate gave Island politicians another golden opportunity to dust off old religious biases. Inevitably, Prince of Wales College became entangled in the ensuing web of half-truths, hyperbole, and outright mendacity. In a debate in the Legislative Assembly in 1874, Conservative W. W. Sullivan attacked both the college and the Normal School for costing taxpayers too much for too little gain. The college, he said, cost about $2,600 a year to run, employed professors from Scotland, was in reality only a high school, and benefited mostly boys from the city. The Normal School, at a cost of about $1,500 a year, was of no benefit "for the purpose for which it had been intended."[45] Opposition leader Liberal Louis H. Davies, a staunch promoter of secular education, was an alumnus of the Central Academy and Prince of Wales College — and a loyal one. In a speech in the Assembly, as reported in the *Parliamentary Reporter,* Davies took issue with those who wanted to abolish Prince of Wales. "If the College had, during the last ten or twelve years, turned out young men who had made their mark, and at no very distant day would take charge of the destinies of this Island, it was an institution which should not be abolished. He had received but a small part of his education in the Prince of Wales College, but he looked upon it as his *Alma Mater* and defended it."[46]

In the mid-1870s, Davies headed a special committee of the House that investigated the state of the school system. The committee reported that education was badly in need of repair, and that religion was being taught in some public schools in spite of the prohibition against it. Religion in the schools became the sole issue in the 1876 election campaign. Davies, a champion of non-sectarian schools, led an all-Protestant coalition of Liberals and Conservatives to victory. The voters had finally decided that religion and education do not mix. The next year the government passed the Public Schools Act, which proclaimed that all public schools were to be strictly non-sectarian. That didn't end religious divisions on the Island, although it did drive them underground. Theoretically, religion was dead as an election issue — but not in the kitchens and political backrooms. Resentment toward Prince of Wales didn't end, either. If anything, the election, in re-affirming Protestant power, reinforced Catholic perceptions that the government college was a Protestant college. And it was clear that the government had scuttled any hopes the Bishop might have harboured for a bailout of the Catholic college and the Catholic school system.

The economic depression that took hold in the province after Confederation must have made St. Dunstan's money troubles seem even more hopeless. As it turned out, Confederation didn't bring prosperity to the Island at all. A crucial promise — continuous communication with the mainland — was not fulfilled. Shipbuilding was in decline. Trade was disappearing. The province was going further into debt every year. It was not a good time to look for help for higher education.

To make matters worse, St. Dunstan's had lost the one top-flight professor that had burnished its academic credibility while toning down its priest-dominated image. John Caven, a Scot who had been educated in Edinburgh and Rome, joined the staff of St. Dunstan's in 1869 at a salary of 100 pounds a year, more than double that of the clerics on the faculty, but only a third of what professors at Prince of Wales were making. After four years at St. Dunstan's, Caven left to become editor of the Catholic *Herald,* and, in 1880, joined the faculty of Prince of Wales College.

Caven was neither a priest nor an ecclesiastic, but he was a staunch Catholic. His presence on the staff of Prince of Wales not only added lustre to its academic image but also gave it a slightly more interdenominational aura. It is impossible to know for sure how many, if any, Catholics attended Prince of Wales in the first two decades of its existence. According to Sir Andrew Macphail, two francophone boys studying for the priesthood were in his class in 1880–81. By then, the names of Catholic students studying to be teachers had also begun appearing on the register. That breakthrough came about through the much-maligned Normal School. So did another threat to the existence of the college.

By the mid-1870s, conditions at the Normal School were gradually improving. Five different principals had run the school between 1856 and 1877: William Monk, Joseph Webster, John Arbuckle Jr. (son of the former teacher and school inspector), Donald Montgomery, and John Harper. Not all of them had an unblemished reputation. Monk was fired twice, once from the Normal School and once from Prince of Wales College. Webster, born and educated in Nova Scotia, was castigated in the Catholic press for everything from his "foreign" background to his alleged incompetence to sexual impropriety. In the early 1860s, when he was a thirtyish bachelor, the *Vindicator* suggested that he had improper relations with female students. The matter ended with a libel suit and a retraction by the newspaper publisher, but not before entertaining Islanders with the most sensational news event of the year.[47]

Under Webster, the Normal School term was increased to five months from three, and two teachers were hired for the Model School. Montgomery, who took over in 1874, was a graduate of the school, and had spent time in the United States investigating systems of teacher training. Under his direction, the program was increased to two five-month sessions, and candidates for the school had to have at least a basic academic background. According to the year-end report of the board of education in 1875, students had to be able "to read with ease and fluency, parse a common prose sentence, ...write readily, legibly and correctly, give the definitions of geography, have a general knowledge of the relative positions of the principal countries, with their capitals, the oceans, seas, rivers and islands of the world — be acquainted with the fundamental rules of arithmetic, common or vulgar fractions, and simple interest."[48]

In the late 1870s, the Normal School acquired a new principal and new quarters. John Harper, who took over in 1877, at the age of thirty-three, was a native of Scotland who had taken teacher training in Glasgow, and had served as headmaster of schools in Nova Scotia and New Brunswick. Harper came armed with a good reputation as a teacher, although some Islanders never forgave him for his foreign origins.[49] Under Harper, the school had a staff of four; unfortunately, the building had only three rooms. To acquire more space, the school moved to the upper storey of the Wesleyan Academy on Upper Prince Street.

In Harper's day, standards for teachers were becoming stricter. Candidates for the Normal School had to pass a two-day, written examination — in 1879, only half of the 120 applicants were admitted — and prospective teachers had to pass an exam given by a licensing board composed of members of the executive council, the chief superintendent of education, and the principal of Prince of Wales. Anderson also helped draw up the Normal School curriculum. By the late 1870s, that curriculum was starting to look like the one at Prince of Wales — uncomfortably so, in the view of those who saw the duplication of courses as evidence that one of those institutions was redundant. The Normal School offered Greek, Latin, geography, the chemistry of common things, and school management; Prince of Wales students studied the Greek and Latin classics, French and German languages, metaphysics, logic rhetoric, and political economy. The curriculum of both schools included mathematics, history, and natural philosophy. Prince of Wales graduates were even obtaining teachers' licences. Of 97 candidates appearing before the licensing board in June 1878, 10 were teachers trying to upgrade their licences, 2 were inspectors of schools, and 9 were graduates of Prince of Wales. Despite their lack of professional training, the Prince of Wales students had to pass an exam in school management. That wasn't much of a challenge, though, and they had a better academic background than the Normal School students. Consequently, they were obtaining the highest class of teachers' licences, and the best schools. To some people the question was, why bother with a separate Normal School? Alternatively, why pay for a separate college?

Those questions became more pressing in the months that followed. In the 1879 provincial election, Louis H. Davies, who was a good friend of Prince of Wales College, was defeated by Conservative W. W. Sullivan, who wasn't. Sullivan, the Island's first Roman Catholic premier, was a lawyer who had been educated at the Central Academy and St. Dunstan's College, and had supported efforts to obtain funding for separate schools. By the time he took office, the government was having trouble funding public education. Davies had attempted, unsuccessfully, to balance the provincial budget by imposing direct taxation, much to the indignation of voters. Sullivan was determined to address the deficits. As an alternative to taxation, Sullivan promised retrenchment and pressure on the Dominion government for more money. To save money, he eliminated the secret ballot, cut salaries of public officials, and reverted to statute labour on the roads. He also set his sights on the two publicly funded institutions of higher learning. For at least five years, he had been complaining about the expense of running Prince of Wales. Together, the college and the Normal School cost $6,000 a year to run.[50]

The new provincial superintendent of education, Edward Manning, was unequivocally opposed to shutting down the college, "the one public institution of the Island which has gained and deserved a reputation abroad." Without it, he wrote in his January 1879 report, the education system "would be but a truncated one, wanting its crowning glory."[51] Instead, Manning suggested, the college and Normal School should be amalgamated. The combined institution could be managed by four professors instead of six. The college principal would oversee the regular work of the college, as well as the academic courses of students aspiring for first-class teachers' licences, and the Normal School principal would attend to the professional training of student teachers.

The amalgamation idea opened the door to an even more revolutionary one — offering higher education to women. As early as 1842, school inspector John McNeill, a man clearly ahead of his time, bemoaned the fact that few girls were attending the district schools. A woman needed to be educated for "the right discharge of all the duties of social life," just as a man needed an education for "the proper discharge of his duties of operative or commercial life." In fact, McNeill hoped that every district on the Island would encourage female students to qualify for the teaching profession.[52] In the 1850s, two factors contributed to a rise in the number of female teachers: the Free Education Act provided for a salary from the government of 30 pounds a year for female teachers, so long as they taught only girls and boys under the age of twelve, and the Normal School opened its doors to both men and women.

In the school's first year, 15 of the 58 teachers-in-training were women, which made the school something of a pioneer. Both Prince of Wales and St. Dunstan's colleges were male preserves, and colleges in other parts of Canada started opening their doors to women only in the late 1870s (Mount Allison was the first, granting a bachelor of science degree to a woman in 1875). Even in the cities, there was much concern about the consequences of admitting women to the same classes as men — so much so that McGill College initiated a parallel set of arts lectures, one for men, another for women. In the 1880s two medical colleges for women opened in Ontario to overcome the embarrassment of having mixed classes attend lectures on such subjects as anatomy.[53]

On the Island, teaching was gradually becoming less male-dominated. By 1876, 157 of the Island's 335 teachers were women.[54] Their salaries were, of course, much lower than the men's, but at least they could study academic as well as professional courses in the Normal School. And the proposed amalgamation of Prince of Wales and the Normal School would open more doors for women. Some of the female candidates for teachers' licences would have to be admitted to regular college classes. "But why stop here?" Manning asked in his report to the Board of Education. "If these classes were thus open to young women who were preparing to be teachers, others who wish to prosecute their studies further than is possible in the public schools might as well be admitted also, taking care to allow country students to come in free, while the city students should pay a fee, as is now the case with the young men." Manning noted that private schools for young ladies in Charlottetown had been abolished, leaving female students with no option but to leave the Island if they wanted a higher education.[55] "Now under this plan," he said, "young ladies past the age of 16 would find in the College the best of finishing schools."[56]

Any opposition in the Legislature to the amalgamation idea was only a half-hearted one. The main objections came from Liberal Donald Farquharson, who fretted that the two principals would not see eye to eye, wondered whether the government intended to fire Harper, worried that there wouldn't be enough space in the new institution. The Normal School was working well, he said. Under the new system, "things would be turned upside down."[57] On this issue, Opposition members didn't have much of a case, since they, too, had broached the idea of amalgamation when in power. And the government was promising savings of $3,000 a year. In the current economic climate, it was too much to resist.

On May 29, 1879, the House of Assembly passed a bill creating the Prince of Wales College and Provincial Normal School. A principal and three other professors would be employed. The principal would be paid $1,500 a year; the first assistant professor, $1,200; the second, $1,000; and the third, $800. In addition to the six scholarships in each county, two awards of free tuition would be offered to students from Charlottetown and Royalty.

After amalgamation, the teacher-training department went back to its old quarters on Kent Street, allowing its students to take some classes next door at the college. Because both Catholic and Protestant women took the teacher-training program, Prince of Wales became the only place on the Island where Catholic women could obtain a higher education — and remained so until the 1940s. Little by little, the college was fulfilling its mandate as a secular institution. In fact, a decade after the amalgamation, Anderson reported that 38 of the 117 students enrolled were Roman Catholic. (In a curious departure from custom, he also broke down the Protestant contingent by denomination that year: 47 Presbyterians, 19 Methodists, 10 Baptists, and 3 Episcopalians.)[58]

Prince of Wales was also exercising more and more influence on the Island's entire education system. If the reputation of St. Dunstan's College, at least in the early years, lay in its production of would-be priests, the name of Prince of Wales became almost synonymous with teacher training. In the first term after amalgamation, 71 students enrolled in the college, only 20 of whom indicated they did not plan to teach. A couple of factors, both related to economics, contributed to the popularity of the teacher-training program. One was that candidates for teachers' licences did not have to pay tuition fees. Another was that the country school often served as a way station to other occupations. In those days, and for generations to come, many young people — including Andrew Macphail and J. G. Schurman — taught school for a year or two to make enough money for university and another career. And qualified teachers from Prince of Wales were a valuable commodity. There were still deficiencies in the public school system, the worst being poor attendance and the large number of farmer-teachers who still ran one-room schools. As late as 1879, school superintendent Edward Manning was complaining about teachers who were trying, unsuccessfully, to do two jobs at once. One such teacher, "dragging his weary limbs into the school room half an hour late, is so uninterested in the studies of ten or twelve youngsters that he soon drops off in a doze!... trustees have more than once described these farmer-teachers as 'just going into school to rest themselves.'"[59]

For Alexander Anderson, the most persuasive argument for amalgamation was that it could help raise the standard of the teaching profession. It meant that all newly licensed teachers on the Island had to pass through his hands, and obtain the benefit of a Prince of Wales education. With characteristic zeal, Anderson immediately embarked on a reform of the Normal School. First, he set aside seven hours a week for instruction in education. This class included lectures on the art of teaching, given twice a week by the master of school management. The textbook, the *Swett's Methods of Teaching,* covered almost anything connected with the classroom — the arrangement of furniture, the training and development of students' minds and bodies, discipline, and methods of teaching various subjects. Three days a week, groups of students would put these methods into practice in the model school, under supervision. Once a week, selected students would teach in front of fellow students, the principal, and the school-management master.[60]

Next, Anderson set the lofty goal of turning every professor in the institution into a model for the student teachers to emulate. They would learn from "the manners of the teacher in the presence of his class, the methodical distribution and arrangement of his work, his careful preparation for his class, and accurate acquaintance with the subject he is to teach, his clearness in exposition, expressiveness and power in arousing interest, his faithfulness in the discharge of his duty, his accuracy and regularity in examining Exercises and Examination papers...."[61]

In the first year, the role models were Anderson, John Harper, John Caven, John McSwain, and Annie Montgomery, the Model School teacher, and the first woman on staff. The next year, Harper, McSwain, and Montgomery were replaced by Thomas LePage and D. J. McLeod.[62] Of these, LePage and Caven were the most memorable. LePage, a son of poet John LePage, had been a brilliant student at Prince of Wales in the early 1870s, capturing top prizes in ten of his classes. He had studied at Dalhousie, intending to become a clergyman, but left before obtaining a degree. Only a teenager when he first joined the Prince of Wales faculty in 1876, he was, like his father, a talented poet and an equally talented and popular teacher, who took charge, at one time or other, of almost every class in the college. Macphail described him as "a man of the spirit," from whom a boy could learn "by way of Wordsworth that there was an inner and intimate world of poetry."[63]

Caven, who was fifty-one when he joined the staff, taught school management and the classics. During his days as editor of *The Herald,* he had a reputation for deadly sarcasm, but, according to the editor of a rival paper, the grey-bearded Caven was also "as full of fun as a kitten," and possessed "a tender heart and a kind disposition."[64] In addition to skills as an editor and historian, Caven was a good singer, one of several prominent vocalists with the Charlottetown Orchestral Club and a member of the St. Dunstan's Cathedral Choir. He loved the Greek language, reading it aloud, Macphail recalled, "with a continuous chuckle over its ease and beauty." He entertained his students this way for the entire class, "in the belief that if they learned the sound, the sense would take care of itself."[65]

Caven would remain on the faculty for two decades. That was untypical for the times. In a dozen years, thirteen teachers came and went through the revolving door of the college. Most stayed for only a year or two. One example was one of the brightest academic lights, William John Alexander. Born in Hamilton, Ontario, he had graduated from the University of Toronto, and had won a Gilchrist Scholarship to study at the University of London, where he obtained first-class honours in English. He was hired to teach at Prince of Wales in 1878, at the age of twenty-three. After only a year, he went on to further studies and eventually became a leading English scholar at the University of Toronto.[66] After Leander MacNeill, the second professor, left in 1870, Thomas May became second professor for four months. Benjamin Darby was hired for one year. Alexander Lowe, one of the longest-serving professors in that decade, stayed for four years, until the end of the 1875 year. J. C. Dunlop replaced him for the next year, after which Wellington Dixon and Thomas LePage, both Prince of Wales alumni, joined the staff for one year. LePage returned for a year in 1878, and again in 1880.[67] In the 1870s, Anderson was the only professor the public could identify with the college for any length of time. It was he who provided continuity and stability to the college and set its tone.

Fortunately, Anderson was much admired. In 1887, the year of his 25th anniversary at Prince of Wales, some of his old students held a banquet in his honour at the Hotel Davies in Charlottetown, and presented him with a monetary gift.[68] Naturally, they also offered many testimonials about his contributions to the college and to their lives. The praise was well-deserved. In his annual report in 1882, Anderson noted that Prince of Wales graduates had won five scholarships during the previous year at Dalhousie, in addition to one at McGill and one at Queen's. The scholarships, plus many prizes, "bear witness to the character of our work," he noted.[69] Three years later, he reported that professors at McGill, Dalhousie, and other universities "have not been sparing in their satisfaction" at the quality of students from Prince of Wales. In addition, the Presbyterian Theological College in Halifax had decided to accept as university-level equivalents Prince of Wales certificates in classics, mathematics, and English literature.[70] His 1888 report bore the news that five students from Prince of Wales had graduated from Dalhousie with honours. Three had obtained gold medals. Four others had "acquitted themselves with great credit" at McGill.[71]

Anderson's achievements did not go unnoticed in the outside world. In 1888, McGill awarded him a prize of his own — an honorary doctorate in recognition of his contributions to education. In the citation, McGill noted not only the academic success of his former students but also his influence over education throughout the Island. He was "a man of thorough and sound scholarship" who had raised Prince of Wales "to a very high degree of efficiency," and through it had greatly improved the Island's educational system. He had trained a large number of students for McGill, and "the Dean of the Faculty of Arts[72] bears testimony to the excellent training of these students and the high position they have taken in the examinations." Finally, the citation noted, "it is desirable to mark the appreciation of the University of the work of educators who have attained the highest places in their profession, and have, as in the case of Mr. Anderson, exercised an influence pervading a whole province."[73] From that day on, he was no longer "Mr. Anderson." His students and former students referred to him — behind his back, presumably — as "the Doc."

There were still dark clouds in Dr. Anderson's universe. He suffered a great loss in 1889, when Thomas LePage, probably the best-loved teacher next to the principal, died at age thirty-two after a long illness. His place at the college was not filled that winter. As a consequence, student Janetta Macphail wrote to her brother Andrew, "the teaching was unsatisfactory," and some students left at Christmas.[74] Some of the complaints apparently centred on weak discipline, notably in the classrooms of D. J. McLeod[75] and John Caven. In a letter to Andrew Macphail in 1883, student A. D. Fraser reported that Anderson had been absent for a few days, and Caven had taught in his place. "His discipline is rather lax but I was much pleased with the easy familiarity he displayed in teaching Latin and History. He also did Hamlet very well."[76] Two years later, Dan MacLeod wrote from Trinity College in Toronto: Trinity, he said, had "one or two weak men. Of course there is a Professor Caven in every College."[77] Janetta Macphail, referring to D. J. MacLeod's inability to keep order, wrote to her brother, "We like Mr. Anderson very well ... but we don't learn much from Mr. Caven and as for D. J. we give up all together."[78]

Weaknesses such as these must have grieved Anderson, a man who set great store by proper decorum, treated his students with great respect, and was, in turn, highly respected by them. But he still had much to be thankful for. With amalgamation, threats to the existence of the college had disappeared, or at least had gone underground. The new Entrance Exams had motivated teachers in the district schools to do a better job of preparing senior pupils. Enrolment at the college was climbing, mostly as a function of the teacher-training department: in 1885, 89 students were enrolled in teacher training, and only 20 were classed as "non-professional" students. Of the total enrolment, 70 were men, and 39 were women. Enrolment rose to its highest point of the decade in the winter and spring of 1887, when 137 students attended the amalgamated institution.[79] This was still a tiny fraction of the Island's population of 109,000, but it was about as much as the college could handle at the time.

In contrast, St. Dunstan's College, especially in the early years of the decade, appeared to be a dead man walking. In the words of historian Edward MacDonald, "the pulse of the college grew steadily weaker."[80] The rector's salary was only $250 a year; other faculty subsisted on pay as low as $25 a term. Enrolment shrank to 27 in 1882–83, and again to about a dozen the next year. Critics advised Bishop McIntyre to close the college. Only his fierce determination to save it, plus the sacrifice of the staff and parishioners who, after some arm-twisting by the Bishop, contributed money from their meagre funds, kept that from happening. In a pastoral letter in October 1883, McIntyre announced that a collection would be taken up for the college in each parish. Although he did not mention the rival Prince of Wales College by name, he did remind parishioners that it was not the only college with bragging rights. In spite of the government's failure to support St. Dunstan's financially, the Catholic college could point to "great numbers of its former students who hold a foremost place in the honourable walks of life. It can be safely said that, had it not been for St. Dunstan's College, our Island would have been deprived of one-half its talent."[81]

By the middle of the 1880s, with a new rector, Rev. Charles MacDonald, the anaemic patient began to rally. Enrolment at St. Dunstan's rose, hovering around 80 for the next decade; new courses were added; and public confidence in the college was restored. "There is no place of which we have any knowledge where young men and boys are better cared for than at this institution," the Catholic *Herald* declared in 1888. "Besides receiving an excellent intellectual training, they are surrounded by everything that tends to make them healthy, happy and comfortable."[82]

Well, not quite. Revenues at the college barely met expenses, and there was nothing left over for badly needed repairs or renovations. In that respect, Alexander Anderson knew just how Father MacDonald felt. While the rising enrolment at Prince of Wales could squelch criticisms that the college was failing to serve the community, the size of the student body was a mixed blessing. The college had been shoddily built to begin with, and now it was half a century old. In its earlier incarnation as the Central Academy, the trustees had pronounced the building almost uninhabitable, especially in winter. Now, with dozens of Normal School students crossing the lawn every day to take classes at Prince of Wales, the small, poorly built and badly ventilated classrooms, the narrow hallways, and the lack of an assembly room made life almost unbearable. When enrolment dipped to 100 in the fall of 1887, Anderson reported, with evident relief: "The air of the rooms has been sweeter, the classes of reasonable dimensions, and the distribution of students such as to secure a fair division of work." Still, he added, "we are constantly reminded of the inadequacy of our space and the unsuitableness of our building for our purposes."[83] In turn, Anderson constantly reminded the government of the situation. Repairs had been made every year, but there still was no real improvement as a result. What Prince of Wales needed was a new building.

Of course, the Island's two colleges were not alone in their struggles. Universities and colleges throughout the Maritimes were suffering from inadequate financial support. The Nova Scotia Legislature withdrew support from all institutions of higher education in 1881, leading to the shutdown of St. Mary's College for twenty-two years and the abolition of the University of Halifax. New Brunswick supported only its provincial university, and the annual grant of $8,844 remained the same for eighty years. Only Dalhousie made substantial gains in the late 19th century, attracting such first-rate scholars to its faculty as Jacob Gould Schurman, and developing into the strongest university in Canada outside of McGill, Queen's, and Toronto. Dalhousie had escaped its Presbyterian Church domination and its dependence on provincial largesse through a series of endowments. In doing so, it also escaped the sectarian rancour that poisoned the atmosphere when denominational colleges competed for government aid.[84]

Alexander Anderson and Prince of Wales had no such luck. Since amalgamation, the college had become a totally dependent ward of the government. The Sullivan government had abolished the college board of trustees and placed Prince of Wales under the control of the Board of Education. Donald Farquharson, the Liberal leader, was not happy about this. In the debate on amalgamation in the Legislature, he had sounded the alarm. Without a board of trustees, he warned, the public would have no way of knowing how the college was being run. Now the college was an agency of government that could be manipulated for political purposes. Farquharson was right. The Board had the power to make rules for the college, change them if necessary, prescribe what examinations should be held, specify what qualifications the teachers should possess. With that act, the government had removed the last thin layer of protection the college had against government interference or neglect, and had left it vulnerable to the whims of whatever politicians and bureaucrats happened to be in office. As the 20th century approached, it would take all of Alexander Anderson's legendary power to keep his little ship on a straight course.

Chapter Four

The Lion in Winter

4

"Of all the teachers I have ever sat under, none was to be compared to Dr. Anderson. I can see him now, standing before us, making the dry bones of Roman History live, and clothing even Greek verbs with charm and 'pep'...."

—Lucy Maud Montgomery, c. 1927

For almost two weeks in July 1893, eighteen-year-old Lucy Maud Montgomery waited in suspense for the newspapers to publish results of the Entrance Examinations to Prince of Wales College. She had just spent three days on the dreaded exams, and, like many another candidate for entrance to the college, she worried that she hadn't been sufficiently prepared. The young woman who ran the Cavendish school that year was a friend to her students, but not much of a teacher. English and history, the exams on the first day, were territory in which Maud felt at home. Latin, algebra, geography, agriculture, and even geometry — one of her weak points — were not as bad as she had feared. But the paper on her worst subject, arithmetic, was so terrible, she wrote in her diary, "it fairly made my hair stand on end." Maud was hoping to take teacher's training at Prince of Wales, and a passing grade in arithmetic in the Entrance Exams was a prerequisite for a teacher's licence. The more she thought about that arithmetic test, the more convinced she became that she had failed.

It wasn't an unreasonable fear. The failure rate of students taking Entrance Exams to Prince of Wales was notoriously high. That year, for instance, 264 students from across the Island wrote the exams in Charlottetown, Montague, Alberton, and Summerside; fewer than half passed. To Maud Montgomery's enormous relief, however, the exam results in *The Daily Patriot* finally arrived on July 18, with her name high on the list, making her "the happiest girl in Cavendish."[1] Annie Moore of Crapaud came first, with 491 marks of a possible 650; Maud came fifth, with 470 marks. After getting permission to skip a year, she began teacher's training and second-year work at Prince of Wales.

Classes began on Wednesday, September 5. By the following Monday, Maud had decided she loved Prince of Wales College. "It is simply delightful," she wrote in her diary.[2] She was not referring to the physical environment. As she recalled years later, the college was a shabby old place, then sixty years old, with a still shabbier Normal School across the lawn. Inside were overcrowded, stuffy classrooms, dark, narrow halls, sagging stairs, floor boards so thin you couldn't fasten a chair to them.

The two buildings were the bane of Principal Anderson's life. Year after year, he complained to the government about the classrooms, hallways, and stairs, the poor ventilation system, the lack of an assembly hall. In 1891, Anderson reported that the daily attendance of 123 students was "unwontedly large" — that is, too large for the facilities. By the time Maud Montgomery arrived, the daily attendance had climbed to 164, the highest thus far. Anderson, a stickler for decorum, complained that the overcrowding made it difficult to keep order: "When young men are crowded together, and stairs only admit of being mounted in single file, when it is necessary to have a classroom in a building apart from the College, the opportunities for, and the temptations to boisterous conduct are undoubtedly too great."[3] The presence of young ladies, he said, only made matters worse. The chief superintendent of education, J. A. Nicholson, criticized the lack of efficiency in the teacher-training department, but, as Anderson pointed out, the Normal School didn't have the facilities it needed. Normal School students practised teaching in the Model School, but there was no room large enough for them to watch fellow students teach or assemble for lectures and practical illustrations by the school-management professor. Students couldn't even gather comfortably for prayers and roll call. "This need has been brought home to me every morning for the last 10 or 12 years," Anderson wrote, "when all the students have met in my room for prayers and roll call, and when half of them have been standing around my desk owing to want of space...."[4] As the superintendent of education pointed out, the facilities were not in keeping with either the steadily climbing enrolment at the college or "the superior quality of the work performed and its wide reputation."[5]

Despite these difficulties, the college was still maintaining its good reputation and still inspiring the affection of students and alumni. At the

The Entrance

"Oh, I wish the entrance exams were over!" Lucy Maud Montgomery wrote in her diary on June 30, 1893, expressing the anguish of Island students for generations to come. "The Entrance," the gateway to Prince of Wales College, was regarded with almost as much hope, longing, and anxiety as were the Pearly Gates. "We heard about the Entrance exams from Grade One, almost, until Grade 10," Fleur Stewart recalled. "It was sort of a black cloud over you."

In Montgomery's day, half of those who wrote the exams failed. By the 1950s, the success rate was somewhat better, in the range of 60 per cent. But parents still complained that the exams were too hard, and teachers were still judged on their ability to get their Grade 10 pupils through The Entrance.

Some pupils switched schools for Grade 10, often at great inconvenience, in hopes of gaining an advantage at exam time. In the 1940s, for example, Grade 10 pupils from several communities in King's County travelled to St. Peter's Bay every day on the train to study under Dan MacDonald, who was famous for his Entrance successes. Many country teachers, overwhelmed by the task of dealing with many grades, patterned their entire Grade 10 curriculum on questions from treasured old Entrance Exams tucked in desk drawers. This practice did not endear the district teachers to Prince of Wales principals, who did not regard this as adequate preparation for work at the college. "Teachers shouldn't be teaching from old Entrance papers or terrifying pupils by magnifying the trials of Entrance," principal Frank MacKinnon wrote in 1949. "Most parents are sensible about it, but some make an almost incredible fuss, which only serves to alarm their children at Entrance time. If the students do their work well the examination authorities can be counted on to give them a fair deal."

Nevertheless, the entire experience was alarming, especially for rural youths who rarely, if ever, had spent much time among strangers. Some, like Lawson Drake, were still in short pants. In his day, you could write off three subjects —geography, Canadian history, and hygiene —in Grade 9. Consequently, he was only 12 years old when he first entered the doors of the Prince of Wales gymnasium — "the biggest hall I had ever seen." Clive Stewart recalled that one of his classmates, whether through nervousness or ignorance, made the mistake of entering the building with his cap on. "Dr. Steel met him at the door and said, 'Take off that cap!' And the poor guy— no wonder he failed. It was intimidating for some. They just froze when they got in there." Clive Stewart's memories of the exams will always be associated with a bad smell: "It was hot weather, and the wind was from the east, and down on the foot of Grafton Street was the Davis and Fraser pork factory where animals were slaughtered and canned. And the odour from that plant came wafting up into the hall as you were sitting there writing the exams."

The exams were written in the gymnasium on long wooden boards placed on trestles. Some of the boards were warped, so that if someone leaned too hard on one end, the board would lift at the other end. Each student had been given a registration number, which he or she wrote on the exam paper in lieu of a name. Looking over his or her shoulder were members of the college staff.

After the exams were over came weeks of suspense. At some point during the summer, names of successful candidates appeared in the Charlottetown newspapers, in order of their total marks. "The relief from the past ten days is enormous," Montgomery wrote in July 1893, when she found that she had done quite well. "I had worried so much over that arithmetic paper that I had begun to believe that I had surely failed." Those who failed a subject were branded with a star beside their names. That system lasted for generations. Until the exams were phased out in the 1960s, after the advent of a network of high schools, everyone on the Island had the opportunity of discovering who had passed, who had failed, and who the successful teachers were.

annual commencement exercises, the valedictorians usually threw in a complaint or two about conditions at the college — possibly for the benefit of politicians on the platform — but devoted most of their time to the standard, wistful recap of the college year, and their pride in their alma mater. The imposing figures who made speeches at those year-end closings were usually alumni, and usually nostalgic for their own college days. In 1894, Lieutenant-Governor George Howlan gave what *The Patriot* called "a tenderly retrospective" sketch of his Prince of Wales days, noting that "the trysts made at the old college gate remained unbroken through life."[6] Two years later, Andrew Macphail, then practising medicine in Montreal, donated a gold medal to the college "to acknowledge, in some degree, my indebtedness to the Prince of Wales College."[7]

The story behind that medal illustrates something of the character of both Anderson and Macphail. In the fall of 1895, after Macphail proposed donating the medal, Anderson insisted that it be called either the "Macphail Medal" or the "Uigg Medal," in honour of Macphail's home district.[8] A letter to Macphail from a "D. Ferguson" in Charlottetown (possibly Senator Donald Ferguson) warned that Anderson "does not seem in a mood to take suggestions. You know he likes to have things his own way pretty much. It would seem that he would like to have the Medal known as the McPhail Medal."[9] Macphail eventually agreed to present the medal — to Edwin Crockett of York, the top student at the college — at the May 1896 convocation. The next year Macphail insisted that Anderson's name be substituted for his on the medal. William Peterson, principal of McGill, designed the Latin inscription and said that, in his opinion, there was nothing inappropriate in giving such a medal in Anderson's lifetime. "My reason for giving this medal," Macphail told Anderson, "is expressed in the Legend upon the Reverse Side, 'In honorem Alexandri Anderson.' Permit me also to say that my appreciation of the work which you have done and are doing in the Prince of Wales College has increased every year during the seventeen since I was a student under you."[10] Anderson acceded to Macphail's wishes, but asked him to write a letter, which could be read at the convocation, "stating the conclusion you have reached respecting the naming of the Medal."[11] Anderson was a man who either did not seek glory or was canny enough to avoid appearing as if he did. Perhaps a little of both.

When it came to his college, though, he was not so modest. After almost forty successful years, he called attention to the success of former students at every opportunity, including commencement exercises and annual reports to the government: Ernest Brehaut of Guernsey Cove had won the "First Exhibition" at Dalhousie, Anderson noted in 1891; Richard Lea and Robert McKechnie had won gold medals at McGill; Frederick McLeod and Arthur Mellish had won scholarships to Harvard; Gordon Laird had had a fellowship at Cornell extended for a second year.[12] By then, the college's pride in its academic reputation had become the stuff of legend. Prince of Wales was now "Old Prince of Wales," with well-established traditions and fondly remembered foibles. The student body was still small enough to be a close-knit community — and, considering the admission criteria, a select one at that. Perhaps even the slight physical discomforts students and staff had to endure contributed to their sense of unity.

The year Maud Montgomery went to Prince of Wales, she complained bitterly and often in her journal about her living accommodations in Charlottetown: her landlady on Hillsborough Street skimped on meals, heat, and sanitation, and was definitely not a kindred spirit. But years later, Montgomery remembered her time at Prince of Wales as "the happiest year of my life."[13] Soon after her year began, she developed a busy social life, found her niche in student projects, and relished the novel intellectual rush of learning from bright, knowledgeable teachers. There were five professors on staff then, including two Prince of Wales alumni — Herbert Shaw, who had left the science department at McGill College to teach science and drawing, a new course that year, and Samuel Napier Robertson, a Dalhousie graduate who had just put in a year as principal of Alberton High School.

Not surprisingly, Maud Montgomery's favourite professor was the formidable Alexander Anderson. "Of all the teachers I have ever 'sat under,'" she recalled many years later, "none was to be compared to Dr. Anderson. I can see him now, standing before us, making the dry bones of Roman History live, and clothing even Greek verbs with charm and 'pep'...."[14] Anderson was, in fact, something of a showman. One of Montgomery's classmates, Ernest Herbert Ramsay, who later became a Presbyterian minister, once recalled this picture of Anderson in the classroom, drawing a circle on the blackboard: "With back to his class, his cutaway coattails hanging meekly down, his short legs apart, and head thrown back, he would, with one sweep of his arm pivoted at the shoulder, complete a circle as perfect as Giotto's, and then pause for the class to applaud."[15]

Anderson may have been an entertaining teacher, but he was also a demanding one. He taught Latin, Greek, history, and advanced mathematics, and he was known as a "hard marker," as Maud Montgomery discovered when he returned her Latin composition paper in December. Her mark was 44 per cent. "Isn't that awful?" she wrote. "I never made such a low mark in my life, even in geometry. I can't understand it, although Dr. A. is a merciless 'marker-down.'"[16]

Professor Caven, or "Old Caven," as students called him behind his back — he was then sixty-four — was not quite so formidable. One of the Island's first historians, he probably was as erudite as Anderson. But according to Ramsay, "he was humane where the Chief was masterful. Full of quiet humour and the power of epigrammatic speech, he often caused waves of laughter to flow and ebb in the classroom."[17] In Anderson's class, a student had no choice but to learn something; with Caven, you could read a novel, carve your name on the lid of the desk, or flirt with a young man in the next row. Still, Maud Montgomery absorbed a good deal from his classes, partly because he taught her favourite subjects, English, French, and literature, in addition to school management. He often wandered off course during his lectures, a habit that no doubt enhanced his popularity. "Such stories as he could tell," Maud recalled. "He would stand on the platform, tugging away at his long, gray, tobacco-stained beard... In a few minutes some literary allusion would suggest a story to him and he was off on the trail of it."[18]

Caven did have a mean side. His savage tongue reduced some girls to tears. In one of his rages, he informed one that "a decent pickpocket" would be ashamed to associate with her. But every year, he also singled out a girl in the class as his favourite. The year Maud attended, the lot fell on her — possibly, she concluded, because she appreciated his literary jokes. "He always looked at me across the sea of faces when he perpetrated one and we exchanged a fraternal grin." One day, he crossed the boundaries of their relationship by tugging on her long braid as she passed his desk. "I was brought up in my head-long career by a jerk that nearly wrenched my head off my shoulders," she recalled. "I turned in fury from the delighted class to see that diabolical old professor, still holding my hair with one hand, tugging at his beard with the other, and grinning like a benevolent monkey. 'One can't help doing that when a girl has hair a yard long, Lucy

Maud,' he said. It was weeks before I forgave him — and weeks before my neck ceased to be stiff and sore."[19]

Maud's least-favourite teacher was George Harcourt, who had been hired in 1891 from the agricultural college in Guelph, Ontario, to teach science and agriculture — presumably in an attempt to present these subjects in a more in-depth fashion than previously. Anderson had been urging the Board of Education for some time to appoint professors who could teach agriculture, drawing, and — for female students — sewing and domestic economy. Unfortunately, the agriculture teacher was not at all popular, and neither was the course. Anderson dropped it at the end of the next year, and Harcourt with it. Maud Montgomery would have been pleased. In later years — passionate as ever in her likes and dislikes — she described him as "a weak sneak" and "a nonentity," not respected by the students and not liked by the principal. One day, the teacher-training students brought four pounds of peanuts in the shell to his chemistry class. Soon, peanut shells, beans, and even the odd carrot were flying through the air. "Harcourt was furious but powerless," she reported in her diary. "He took down — or pretended to— a lot of names and I expect we'll hear something more of it yet; but they can't kill us and Dr. A., who dislikes Harcourt, never pays any attention to the latter's complaints."[20]

Anderson didn't usually tolerate such rowdiness in his kingdom, and he merely had to show his face to subdue the unruly. One day, students in the music class, then held in the Philharmonic Hall, got out of hand. The music teacher, Rev. F. E. J. Lloyd,[21] was a poor disciplinarian. His father, also a clergyman, happened to be present, and tried to restore order. "Never mind, Father," the teacher said, "they are just from the country, and do not know any better." With that, Ernest Ramsay recalled, "pandemonium prevailed, and the class broke up. Next day, The Doctor was on the platform, and we were as still as mice. He came several times in succession but soon grew tired of playing the policeman, and the class was discontinued."[22]

One day, a student in one of Montgomery's classes incurred Anderson's disfavour. "I remember the horror that pervaded us one day when a wretched student tried to 'answer back,'" she recalled. "I don't think he ever tried it again. One didn't — with Dr. Anderson. The good doctor could be bitterly and epigrammatically sarcastic when he chose. He delivered himself of some ironic remarks concerning the ancestry of the miserable youth ... winding up with a statement to the effect that said youth was an unanswerable argument for evolution. There could be no doubt at all that he had descended — very recently — from a monkey."[23]

Anderson could also bestow praise — sparingly. "Words of commendation from the doctor are like angel's visits," Montgomery wrote in her diary, "and hence much appreciated."[24] When someone handed him a copy of the college's first student newspaper, *The College Record*, he read it carefully, and pronounced his approval "with that air of finality that no one who knew him can ever forget," Ernest Ramsay recalled. One of Maud Montgomery's contributions — "How Girls Study" — evoked his greatest praise: "It is a work of genius."[25]

The appearance of *The Record* coincided with the beginnings of campus life outside of the classroom. In the mid-1890s, students could write for the newspaper, or join the literary society, a debating club, a hockey team, or a football team. There was not yet a student council but there was a college yell, with the appropriate name inserted to fit the occasion: "What's the matter with Dr. Anderson? He's all right! Oh, yes, you bet!"

The newspaper, an eight-page monthly sheet, was edited by Norman Hunter and Hedley MacKinnon,[26] with Talmage MacMillan as business manager. Maud Montgomery wrote five pieces for the paper, including poetry and the sketch that Anderson praised so highly. She later described it as "a spoof on schoolgirl studying — interrupted by gossip, candy and talk of new hats and boys."[27] The paper was not published the next year, but in 1896 reappeared under a new name, *The College Observer*. It failed to appear in 1898, but emerged the next fall with Arthur Cameron of Montague as editor and James D. MacLeod as assistant editor. The content of *The Observer* ranged from serious analyses of world affairs to sports news to humour columns that relied heavily on puns on students' names. The Boer War obviously was on everybody's mind. Britain had just sent troops to South Africa to defend British commercial interests in two republics, the Transvaal and the Orange Free State. Public opinion in Canada and elsewhere was divided on the justification for the war, but Anglophone Islanders were, in general, staunchly loyal to the British Empire and excited about the South African adventure. Prince of Wales students apparently were no exception. The lead article in the October 1899 issue of *The Observer* was devoted to an exposition on the Transvaal: "The attention of the world is now centred on this small republic which with its ally, the Orange Free State, has declared war against Great Britain."[28] Other articles in those early issues contained the usual, timeless preoccupations of student newspapers: sports, in-jokes about college life, and despair over the lack of student support for school activities.

The debating club tackled everything from war to love, art and politics. On November 18, in the first debate of the year, James D. MacLeod and Roy Conners tangled on this question: "Is the policy which Britain is pursuing towards the Transvaal justifiable?" MacLeod, who took the affirmative, won a majority of votes. Occasionally, Prince of Wales debaters tangled with St. Dunstan's College boys. In the winter of 1900, Prince of Wales took the affirmative in a debate over whether women should be granted the vote, an issue that would not be settled on the Island for another twenty-two years. According to a report in *The Observer*, A. C. McMillan from St. Dunstan's maintained that, in spite of his great admiration for the ladies, they should not be allowed to vote, "for political campaigns of the day were conducted with such bitterness and animosity, that perhaps those feelings would be introduced into the home, so that discord would reign supreme where once peace and happiness held sway." McMillan's team won by a close vote. The chairman cast the deciding vote — after "a lengthy and heated discussion."[29]

College debating in those days was as much a male prerogative as voting was. In fact, male students seem to have dominated most of the student organizations, a situation that, of course, reflected life in the outside world. It did not reflect the population of the college. Throughout the 1890s, more than a third of the students were women (70 women to 101 men the year Maud Montgomery attended), and, by the end of the decade, female students slightly outnumbered the men. "The lady students so completely filled the stage," *The Daily Patriot* reported after the 1897 convocation, "that the sterner sex were amassed in the front seats of the pit, the remainder of the Opera house being filled with one of Charlottetown's brilliant audiences."[30] Women often did well academically — in 1899, Maude Bremner won the college gold medal and gave the valedictory address — but tended to stick to such ladylike activities as reading essays or singing solos at the commencement exercises. At her graduation, Maud Montgomery read an essay on Shakespeare's Portia, an analysis, *The Daily Patriot* reported, "of a very high order." Annie Moore, one of the brightest students in the college, sang "Shall Our Parting Be Forever" and, as an encore, the popular air, "Two Little Girls in Blue." One female student, Cora White of North River, was listed on *The Observer* masthead in 1899 as "college editor." Presumably other girls and women wrote for the paper, as Lucy Maud Montgomery did for *The Record*, and belonged to the literary society. Away from the college, young women could amuse themselves — and, with luck, run into interesting members of the opposite sex — by promenading around town or through Victoria Park, or by attending church services, church socials, or a play at the new Opera House. *The Observer*'s "Etiquette Department," which purported to answer "all questions from correspondents on matters relating to history, science, law, etiquette, medicine and love," had some advice for its readers on this delicate matter:

"MD — Is it right for a timid young lady to allow a gentleman to escort her home from prayer meeting after night?

"Ans. — No, they should wait until daylight; furthermore, we would advise all timid (?) young ladies, when in future they go to prayer-meeting or any other meeting which may detain them until after night, to provide themselves with a bulldog and a lantern for their protection and guidance on their way home. These will serve them much more efficiently for purposes of defence than any gold-headed cane with a perfumed dandy attached to one end of it."[31]

In early fall, the young ladies of Prince of Wales could stand outside and watch their heroes practise football on the college grounds. Unfortunately, Prince of Wales boys were not known for their athletic exploits. They had a brief, shining moment in hockey in the winters of 1896 and 1898, when, according to *The Observer*, they pulled off a "brilliant performance," winning a trophy in 1898 for successive victories over rival teams. That was about it for the decade. In the fall of 1899, the football team took on two local men's teams, the Abegweits and the Anchors, and lost all three games (16-0 to the Anchors), even though some St. Dunstan's boys helped out. Some years, Prince of Wales couldn't even muster up a football team. "It is a regrettable fact," *The Observer* lamented, "that, season after season has seen the laurel wreath of victory crown other brows than those of Prince of Wales kickers, and season after season has seen athletics sink lower and lower at Prince of Wales College...." The college, unlike St. Dunstan's, had no indoor rink in which to practise, and the college grounds were often unfit for football. St. Dunstan's also had the advantage in retaining many of its student athletes for a six-year program; many Prince of Wales students enrolled for a short stint of teacher-training. Possibly the prevailing attitude at the downtown college didn't help, either. "It is a well-known fact," *The Observer* declared, "that many students, with more prejudice — possibly effeminacy — than good sense, shudder at the thought of what they term the brutal sports of the athletic arena. They lift their cultured eyebrows with ill-concealed disgust at the mere mention of football, a game which, in their opinion, reminds one of the gladiatorial shows in the time of Nero. It is also urged that college athletics not only undermine the intellectual interests, for the promotion of which a college exists, but that they also tend to cast down the laurels of learning and wisdom for the trophies of the athletic field." [32]

The college might boast of its laurels of learning (and often did), but in sports, it was outclassed by St. Dunstan's College. At various times of the year, St. Dunstan's students played cricket, baseball, hockey, handball, English rugby, and football. Football became especially popular on the Catholic campus when St. Dunstan's teams began defeating rivals on the Island and in Nova Scotia. Hockey was a new sport on the Island — the first men's game was played in 1890 — but it didn't take long for St. Dunstan's to embrace that game as well. In 1898, an indoor rink was built on the campus, and hockey took over from football in winter as a student preoccupation.[33]

Academically, St. Dunstan's was also making gains. In 1892, the college affiliated with Laval University in Quebec, one of the most highly regarded Catholic universities in North America. Under the affiliation agreement, students who completed the college course at St. Dunstan's and passed examinations set and corrected by Laval would be entitled to receive bachelor's degrees in arts, letters, and science.[34]

Alexander Anderson might be forgiven for feeling envious. As early as 1894, he was publicly hinting at his hopes for degree-granting status at Prince of Wales. During the closing exercises that year, he referred to "Prince of Wales University." Turning to Premier Frederick Peters, who acted as chairman of the event, he explained that he had used the word "university" prophetically.[35]

Anderson was being a bit overly optimistic. He was having enough trouble persuading his political bosses to give the college the support it needed just to stay alive. If rumours circulating in the press were correct, the politicians were eager enough to meddle in the academic affairs of the college: in 1895, *The Daily Examiner* alleged that the Peters government was using the school system, including the college, to further the interests of the Liberal party. As an illustration, the paper charged that the Liberal government had refused to hire a Conservative (identified only as a Mr. Duchemin) to replace Professor Samuel Robertson, who had resigned because of ill health. Instead, the government had hired E. E. Jordan, a Dalhousie graduate, and presumably a man with more suitable political credentials. *The Daily Patriot*, defending the hiring decision, described Duchemin as "an extreme partisan," an assessment *The Examiner* believed was an excuse for "an unjustifiable and contemptible act."[36] There were also controversies over alleged patronage in awarding scholarships. At the end of the decade, the opposition alleged that a young woman from Souris had won a scholarship to Prince of Wales because her father was a strong Liberal. Attorney-General H. C. McDonald refuted this charge. His explanation was that, although some had considered her ineligible for a scholarship because of previous attendance at the college, she in fact had been enrolled in the college for only ten days before taking ill. [37]

The politicians weren't quite so interested in the college when it came to spending money. In the early 1880s, when enrolment stood at fewer than 130, Anderson had asked members of the Legislature to tour the college. At the time, his major complaint was the lack of an assembly hall and cloakrooms. The politicians agreed that the buildings were inadequate, but did little or nothing about it. More than a decade later, when 246 students were crammed into the building, none of the classrooms was large enough. In his annual reports to the government, Anderson was starting to sound cranky. He had been tinkering with the curriculum, adding courses on an apparently trial-and-error basis. In 1891, he added botany and hygienic physiology, as well as "advanced instruction in English and French" for students who did not wish to take trigonometry and Greek. Both agriculture and drawing had been added and dropped because of lack of interest. But, in the mid-nineties, he put everything on hold. He wanted to improve teaching methods, courses, and organization, he said, but this was impossible until he had a new building, and could install all classes under one roof and under his supervision. Not only was it inconvenient to have to send students to the Normal School building for some classes; in wet or cold weather, it was also potentially unsafe. Floor space was so limited, "the students are not properly seated, but packed; and everyone who knows anything of class-work is well aware what difficulties arise in consequence.

Discipline is endangered, and is only maintained by vigilance, prudence and ability to interest, on the part of the teacher, and self-restraint on the part of the students." At exam time, students were packed closely together, which made "the opportunities for impropriety too favourable."[38] The only way to get rid of the stale air in the classrooms was to open the windows, which Anderson frequently did.

"We always nearly froze in Dr. Anderson's room," Maud Montgomery recalled, "especially we girls who sat in the row of seats next the window. The good doctor had a praiseworthy passion for fresh air and the lower sash of the windows must be opened to the limit. We sat there, often with wind, snow, or rain blowing in on us. Nor was it the least use to protest. The doctor smiled, patted the protestant on the shoulder and assured her that dampness was excellent for the complexion and fresh air for everything.... We were always glad to escape into Professor Caven's room, which was always warm and unhygienic. No open windows for Professor Caven."[39]

The winter of 1897 was so severe, even Anderson couldn't bear to open his classroom windows. That winter, and the next, saw unprecedented outbreaks of headaches, colds, grippe, measles, and other ailments. The college had in the past escaped outbreaks of serious illnesses, such as the smallpox epidemic that killed more than a hundred people in the fall of 1885. Anderson blamed the illnesses of the Nineties on overcrowding and the "re-breathing of the same air, fetid and poisonous, and laden with the germs of disease."[40]

Unless immediate improvements were made in the facilities, Anderson warned finally, the college would have to raise its entrance requirements. "I think I can safely affirm that there is no other educational institution, doing the same work, or engaged in educational work at all, in Canada or in the United States, in which the professors and students are so hampered by untoward conditions," he declared.[41] Anderson seems to have carried out his threat to raise entrance requirements. For the next two years, the enrolment was pared down to 233. The failure rate in the Entrance Examinations was extremely high. Of 337 students who took the exams in 1899, only 116 were successful.[42]

Throughout the 1890s, the province didn't pay more than $1,869 a year for fuel and repairs for both the college and the Normal School. Salaries for faculty cost another $4,000 to $5,300 a year.[43] Anderson's salary had dropped to $1,200 in 1890 from $1,500, probably because he was living in an apartment in the college. (Anderson and his wife, Catherine, and children, Alexander, William, Frederick, and Helen, had lived in at least two different locations, King's Square and Water Street, before moving to the college, apparently around the time of the amalgamation.) In 1897, superintendent Donald J. McLeod noted that the record attendance of 246 at Prince of Wales indicated the regard in which the college was held, "but in other respects the country has shown the Prince of Wales College and Normal School but scant generosity. The building has been allowed to remain as our forefathers left it forty years ago, and it is now far behind the requirements of modern Educational Institutions."[44]

Meanwhile, the politicians complained that education was costing too much — an average of about $122,000 a year, or almost half of provincial revenue in 1899, according to Premier Donald Farquharson, compared with 7 per cent in Ontario.[45] One reason for the rise in education spending was the increase in the number of teachers who had second-class licences, and therefore had to be paid more than third-class teachers. "Here we have 580 teachers to pay every year," Farquharson complained at the college closing that year, "and very little money with which to meet this demand."[46]

The province certainly was in dire financial straits. The shipbuilding industry was at an end. Farm incomes had declined. In the final three decades of the 19th century, 30,000 Islanders, many of them young and educated, left for greener pastures, often in the New England states.[47] In addition to the interminable expenses of building and repairing roads and constructing new bridges, including one across the Hillsborough River, the government was committed to a large public works project, an addition to the Hospital for the Insane. Every year, the province racked up huge deficits, and every year the politicians made pilgrimages to Ottawa, begging for more federal subsidies.

Anderson was determined to get a new home for Prince of Wales, however, and he had a scheme for doing so which, he said, would not add a penny to the province's debt. It involved collecting tuition fees from all students at the college. By law, students taking teacher training were not required to pay tuition fees, which amounted in the early 1890s to $14 for town students and $7 for those from the country. The teacher-training students far outnumbered the rest of the student body, which meant that the bulk of students were educated free of charge. However, some Normal School graduates didn't teach at all, but went on to university or some other career. In 1894, Anderson received permission from the government to collect fees from all students. The fees, then reduced to $10 and $5, would eventually be refunded to those who actually taught school for two years. His plan was to use the accumulated fees to pay the interest on the cost of erecting a new building. By 1896, the college had collected a total of $3,300, enough, Anderson said, to start construction on a new building.[48]

The new college, he assured students at their closing exercises in May, would come in good time. The valedictorian sounded less optimistic. "The same old building with its cramped accommodation and ... badly ventilated rooms, still gathers within its walls the hope of higher education of our province," Addison Anderson said. "Our students tried, year by year, to sing 'There's a Good Time Coming,' but it seemed to require strong faith to realize its approach."[49]

Hopes were revived the next spring, when the Legislature passed an act authorizing the government to build a new college and Normal School. Debentures of $18,000 were to be issued for a term of thirty years, with an interest rate of not more than four per cent. The government would set aside all fees collected from college students to pay the interest on the loan. The debentures were issued the next year, and tenders were called for a building with a separate assembly hall, but the estimated costs were so high, the government decided to revise the building plans. By then, the two major Charlottetown newspapers, *The Daily Patriot* and *The Daily Examiner*, joined Anderson's campaign. Besides its lack of space and poor ventilation, *The Patriot* said, the present building "is otherwise ill adapted to preserve the health, promote the comfort and facilitate the studies of the numbers of young men and women who attend the institution each year."[50] That week, *The Examiner* published a letter from a reader with quite a different point of view. "The tax-paying community has been startled of late by the revived rumor ... that in these hard times and times of threatened provincial bankruptcy, a grand new building is going to be erected in fulfilment of [former Premier] Peters's wild promises for a new Prince of Wales College," the writer said. Instead of government spending money it didn't have on "a palace for Dr. Anderson," the old building should simply be fixed up, and his apartment converted to classrooms.[51] In its editorial that day, *The Examiner* supposed that the letter-writer represented "a large proportion of not the most enlightened public opinion" on the Island. But the paper stood by its contention that erecting a new building would pay in the long run. Student fees had been collected to pay the interest charges; the money had been borrowed; the Legislature had approved the project; it was time to act.[52]

The government finally did. The building contract was awarded that year to Schurman and McDonald. Charlottetown architect C. B. Chappell designed the new college, a grand, three-storey structure of Island brick, trimmed with Nova Scotia granite, and topped with a slate roof. Located just east of the old college, the building measured 133 feet long from north to south, and, with 14-foot projections on either side, 100 feet wide on the section facing Grafton Street. It had 6,240 square feet of floor space on the ground floor and 7,058 square feet on the second.[53] There were six classrooms, four on the ground floor and two on the second. Each measured 40 feet by 27 feet, with 13-foot ceilings. There were two laboratories, each 26 feet by 34 feet — a chemistry laboratory with porcelain sinks, and a physics laboratory. Also on the ground floor were a principal's office, a teachers' room, washrooms with marble basins, and cloakrooms. On the second floor were two classrooms and an assembly hall, 69 feet by 42 feet, with a ceiling that rose to 24 feet in the centre. The hall had a raised floor and seated up to 500 people. In the basement there was space for two gymnasiums, one each for the gentlemen and the ladies. The third floor had room for a library. There were three entrances, on the east, west, and south sides, each opening into 14-foot-wide corridors. All of the work was done by local contractors, except for plumbing and heating, which was handled by a company from Galt, Ontario. The final cost was $36,000.[54]

A reporter from *The Patriot* toured the building just before students and staff moved in on February 5, and pronounced it "a lasting monument to the Liberal government, an edifice of which the workmen needeth not to be ashamed, a tribute to the untiring energy of Dr. Anderson, and, best of all, a source of pride to the intelligent inhabitants of this little Isle of the Sea." It was too bad, the reporter mused, that every man and woman on the Island could not visit Charlottetown to view the contrast between the old and the new at Prince of Wales. And not only did Charlottetown have a magnificent new college, it also had a brand-new hospital on Kensington Road.[55]

In fact, Charlottetown was quite the exciting place that winter. In the fall, four thousand people had given the Island's thirty Boer War volunteers a send-off when they sailed from the Charlottetown harbour. All that winter, the Charlottetown newspapers were filled with dispatches from the front. "There is something stirring and exciting and tingling about it all," Maud Montgomery wrote in her diary, "even here in this quiet little Island thousands of miles from the seat of war."[56] As the war progressed, the British-led troops had some terrible setbacks — two Islanders were among those killed in February — but, on March 1, they advanced on the town of Ladysmith, ending a long siege by the Boers. It was the beginning of the end of the war, and all of Charlottetown turned out to celebrate. Shops and schools were closed. Prince of Wales students, in a fever of patriotism that might seem excessive to more cynical generations, marched down the flag-bedecked streets, waving Union Jacks and cheering all the way. At each stop, they listened to speeches by politicians, sang "God Save the Queen," and gave three cheers for Her Majesty. At City Hall, they hanged Paul Kruger, the Transvaal president, in effigy, and, at Government House, they cheered the Queen, the British Army, and the Lieutenant-Governor. In the evening, despite falling snow and a biting east wind, the Prince of Wales students marched in a torchlight parade with students from St. Dunstan's, led by the Catholic college band.[57]

A little more than a week later, on March 9, students had another excuse to cheer, which they did, early and often. It was another big night in Charlottetown — the formal opening of the new Prince of Wales College. Long before the proceedings started, *The Examiner* reported, the hall was filled with students and others, "the former from time to time giving their college yell,"[58] and hundreds more were unable to get in. One of them was Henry Cundall, a prominent land agent and businessman who lived at Beaconsfield, Charlottetown's grandest house. With a companion, Eleanor Compton, he drove to the college well before the 8 o'clock start of proceedings. "We found the large assembly room completely filled," he wrote in his diary. "Many present unable to get in roamed around the building and others returned home. We remained and by standing on chairs outside got glimpses of the interior."[59] Inside, the hall was draped with the Union Jack and the Stars and Stripes, the latter presumably in honour of the American consul, who had been scheduled to speak at the opening but had to attend to other duties. Interspersing addresses by Premier Farquharson, Attorney-General D. A. MacKinnon, Principal Anderson, and D. J. McLeod, superintendent of education, were musical selections: two solos by Florrie Earle,[60] "The Absent-minded Beggar" and "Rule Britannia"; songs by a mixed chorus and a male quartet; a solo, "A Hundred Pipers," by Professor Caven; and a violin selection by Henry Vinnicombe, a Charlottetown orchestra leader and music teacher.

One of the guest speakers was the rector of St. Dunstan's College, Rev. A. P. MacLellan. As he rose to speak, the students gave three rousing cheers for St. Dunstan's, a welcome that surely must have warmed the heart of the Catholic rector and proved one of the salient points of his speech: he outlined the history of his college, showed its close connection with Prince of Wales, and "referred to the great friendship between the two colleges recently evidenced."[61] This was MacLellan's second appearance as an honoured guest of Prince of Wales. The previous summer, he had addressed Prince of Wales students at their closing exercises, urging them to direct their energies toward the development of their God-given talents. He probably felt quite at home in the downtown college. He was a trained teacher, a graduate of the Normal School, and he had taught in the district schools for a number of years.[62] While taking teacher training, he no doubt had formed at least a nodding acquaintance with students across the yard at Prince of Wales, if not with its principal. And times definitely had changed from the days when Father Angus MacDonald, the St. Dunstan's rector in the 1860s, railed in the press against "Orange bigots."

As the 20th century approached, the blatant religious bigotry that had poisoned the Island's political and educational systems in earlier times had subsided. Catholic and Protestant students were mingling in classrooms at Prince of Wales, at football, hockey, and debating matches, and at public events such as the Boer War victory celebration. The rector of the Catholic college remarked on that convivial spirit. "The most cordial relations have always existed between the two colleges," he told the audience at the Prince of Wales College opening. "Of this fact, abundant evidence was shown a few days ago when the students of both institutions were walking side by side under their respective banners, to celebrate a great national victory." The Catholic college, he assured Anderson, was "not jealous of your prosperity" in acquiring a new school.[63]

Indeed, MacLellan's own college was enjoying better times. In a reflection of the parallel course the Island's secular and sectarian colleges had taken for more than half a century, St. Dunstan's College had just moved into a renovated and expanded brick building, also designed by Chappell, although not built with public money. Enrolment at the Catholic college had hovered between 65 and 85 in the early years of the decade; by 1898, it reached a new high of 120. To cope with the expanded school population and modernize facilities, the college added a new wing, which included a dormitory for live-in students, a refectory, a science room, a laboratory, private rooms for senior boarders, and a chapel that could be converted to a convocation hall. Extensive renovations, including steam heating and new plumbing, were carried out in the old section of the building. The new wing was ready for use by the fall of 1899 — just a few months earlier than the new Prince of Wales College building.[64]

Anderson was grateful for his own new facilities. He found the building "spacious, convenient, substantial, admirably lighted and well furnished. It is heated and ventilated in the most approved manner, and every arrangement is made to secure the best results from professors and students." With all the classrooms finally under one roof, discipline was easier to maintain, and he could keep an eye on the school-management classes.[65] Now he could expand the time devoted to school management, add new courses, such as German, improve the teaching of French, and start acquiring books for the library.

First, though, he had a troubling personnel problem to handle. John Caven, the erratic, erudite professor of English, French, and teacher training, was turning into a liability. By the time the new building opened, Caven was seventy-one years old, past the age of retirement by today's standards. He had been a fixture at Prince of Wales for two decades, but, in Alexander Anderson's opinion, he no longer could handle his job. This had been troubling Anderson for a number of years, so much so that he had discussed Caven several times with Premier Donald Farquharson.

Anderson finally wrote to Farquharson "with great regret," asking him to take "such action as you deem necessary" to solve the Caven problem.[66] The grey-bearded Caven had always been volatile — "as full of fun as a kitten" one minute, savagely sarcastic the next. Students either loved or hated him. At the end of her college year, Lucy Maud Montgomery had made a point of going to his house to say goodbye, "for he has been a good friend to me..."[67] But his bitter tongue reduced some students to tears or fury. One of them was Adele Bremner, an exceptionally bright student who graduated in 1901. "The following are a few examples of the insulting language used by Professor Caven towards the undersigned and other students of PWC," she wrote in the spring of 1899. Her note, which was not addressed to anyone in particular, but apparently landed in the hands of the provincial cabinet, included these examples: "Did you see that fat

Bremner girl on the bicycle yesterday? It would have paid you to see her. There's money in it if she only knew it." And "Yes, you stick around here like fleas to a dirty beggar."[68]

Caven, in sharp contrast to Anderson, clearly did not respect his students, and in turn received little respect. Anderson had evidently tried to advise Caven about the art of establishing one's authority, but it did no good. Caven was incapable of keeping order. Sometimes, when the din in his classroom became too great, Anderson would poke his head in the door. The class would fall silent. "There, Mr. Caven," Anderson would say. "It isn't so difficult, is it?"[69] Anderson was as worried about Caven's teaching ability as he was about his discipline problems. Always conscious of the college's duty to the public school system, he felt that Caven was not doing a good job of preparing future teachers. "It is a well known fact that the work done by the student teachers in School Management is of very little service to them," he told the premier. "It is also a fact as well known that the professor in that department has lost the respect and control of his students." At the same time, though, he worried about Caven's financial situation. "I would beg of you that, should you appoint a professor in place of Mr. Caven, you would take into consideration the fact that he has been connected with the college since 1880, and that at his time of life it would be difficult for him to find other employment."[70]

At the time, Caven was making $1,000 a year. His wife, Catherine, had died a decade earlier, and his four children were all grown. The second-eldest, William, was working for the Dominion government in Montreal, but Caven may have been supporting the two youngest ones, Lucy and John. In any case, the aging professor had no pension and, presumably, little savings. William wrote to Farquharson that fall, asking him to either keep his father on at the college or find alternative employment. "I need not tell you what you must know, that he is without any means, and taking away from him what he has is about the same as placing him on the street. I know, Mr. Farquharson, your own good heart would not allow you to do this..."[71] Two months later, the Roman Catholic Bishop of Charlottetown, J. C. McDonald, wrote to the cabinet, reiterating William's plea. "Could he not be retained in the College as a lecturer on Literature or some other kindred subject, for which some moderate salary might be given? Or cannot some other employment be found for him to afford him a means of making a living? It would seem too bad to put the man on the street at his present advanced years..."[72]

The Bishop's prayers apparently went unanswered. When cabinet met on December 12, it decided simply to give Caven $300 "as a gratuity" when he left Prince of Wales at the end of that month.[73] The principal's annual report for the school year noted diplomatically that Caven, "wearied from the toil of active teaching, retired from the staff with which he had been connected for over twenty-one years.... His students in token of their regard presented an address and a tangible expression of their feelings to the kindly gentleman who had been so prominent in their lives."[74]

For the students and staff at Prince of Wales, a more earth-shaking event had already occurred that year. On March 1, 1901, they gathered in the convocation hall to say farewell to the revered professor who had been principal for four decades. Anderson was leaving to replace D. J. McLeod, the chief superintendent of education, who was moving to Sydney, Nova Scotia. In Anderson's remarks to the students, as reported by *The Daily Patriot*, he touched on his early days at the college, its continual growth, the construction of the new building and — as always — "the reputation PWC students had won for themselves abroad...." As for the future, "he had firm belief in the great possibilities of the institution."[75]

What Anderson did not reveal was his reason for leaving the college to which he had devoted most of his sixty-four years. It couldn't have been for money, because the superintendent's salary was the same as the principal's, with the addition of a $250-a-year travelling allowance.[76] Perhaps, like Caven, he couldn't afford to retire. Despite his undeniable devotion to his students, and the long hours he put in at the college, he had not received a raise in pay in twenty-two years. His children were grown and presumably out of the nest, but he had no pension and no home of his own. At the turn of the century, he was still living in an apartment in the old college. When the new one was built, the government offered him a housing allowance of $200 a year, which Anderson considered inadequate. He couldn't rent a suitable house near the college for that amount, he told the cabinet. "If the Government could increase the compensation to $300 a year, and give me permission to build such a house as the Principal of the College should have within the College grounds, I would erect it at once at my own expense."[77] Like so many of his requests to the government, this one was either rejected or ignored.

But Anderson finally had fulfilled his mission of acquiring a new building, and he evidently felt assured that he was leaving the college in good hands. Samuel Napier Robertson, a highly regarded colleague and former student, was the heir apparent. Cyrus Macmillan, an outstanding Prince of Wales alumnus who had just graduated from McGill with an honours degree in English and history, would be joining the faculty for the rest of the term.[78] Caven was on his way out. "Circumstances were very different from those under which I might have accepted the position on former occasions," Anderson told Andrew Macphail shortly after his departure. "Then I had no guarantee for the maintenance of the College as a training School for our teachers — in fact I was certain that the arrangement which would be made would soon bring it to the level of a common school. Now, however, the College has a good repute, the people look upon it with some pride, it is well equipped with teachers each well accomplished in his own department, and admirably housed. I can therefore, with some confidence, withdraw from its more immediate management.... I shall still exercise a general control over the College & see that the standard of work will not fall." He added that he intended to maintain a lively interest in the college, especially with regard to establishing strong instruction in modern languages.[79]

In a way, the school superintendent's job wasn't much of a stretch for Anderson. He had long regarded the college as the lighthouse for the Island educational system. It not only trained teachers for the public schools, but also set standards for the schools to aspire to. Many people then, and for years to come, rated teachers on their ability to get their senior students into Prince of Wales. In some of his annual reports for the college, Anderson had devoted as much space to the district school system as to the college. He had alternately cajoled, praised, and scolded district teachers, commenting on the quality of students entering Prince of Wales, making specific suggestions for improving the teaching of English composition, history, arithmetic, and geography. In his 1896 report, for example, he noted that geography and history seemed to be taught as exercises in memory. To foster a spirit of inquiry and encourage "the faculty of attention," he said, teachers should make history come alive by reading to their class adventure and travel stories, and ask students to summarize them in their own words. More exercises in dictation would improve spelling; greater attention should be paid to penmanship.

Now, travelling around the province, he could give his advice in person, watch teachers in action, and inspect the condition of the schools. In many districts, the facilities shocked him; he found conditions that must have brought back memories of the old college building: smoke-blackened walls and ceilings and cold, poorly lit and ventilated classrooms. The number of teachers leaving the profession, and the low salaries they were paid, also dismayed him. In report after report, he lambasted rural residents who failed to pay an adequate supplement — or paid none at all — to the teacher's government-issued salary.[80] One district, Kelly's Cross, had never paid a supplement to a good teacher who had run the school for many years. "Such treatment is not only selfish and unjust, but ungrateful and cruel," Anderson declared.[81] He was particularly incensed about the inequality in salaries for male and female teachers. Women received annual salaries of $130 to $230, depending on their class of licence, compared with $180 to $300 paid to male teachers. "Why ... should such discrimination exist?" he asked. "Surely the time has arrived when men and women, who do the same work, under the same exacting circumstances, shall be put on an equality by the school law."[82] It was an uphill battle, but after his years of hammering on the government's door on behalf of Prince of Wales, Anderson was used to seemingly hopeless causes.

As he neared retirement, Anderson was able to point to some improvements: school buildings had been spruced up; teachers' supplements had risen; students were doing better in matriculation exams. In his 1908 report, he expressed great pleasure over the number of candidates who had performed well in the previous summer's Entrance Exams — confirmation of his belief that the schools were improving. Teachers were showing "readiness and intelligence" in adopting his suggestions. There had been improvements in penmanship, arithmetic, history, and geography. In 1910, he reported that school facilities had improved considerably; in 1911, he observed that local ratepayers had increased their contributions to teachers' salaries (supplements) every year since 1901. The number of students proceeding to Prince of Wales was increasing: enrolment had climbed to 288 by 1911.

One of Anderson's great defeats was the death of school consolidation. Encouraged initially by the remarkable, if short-lived, success of an experiment in consolidation near Charlottetown, he had lobbied hard, in public and in private, for merging schools across the Island. In the 1908–09 school year, there were 479 district schools, 60 of which had an average attendance of fewer than 12 pupils. They were, he observed, "weak, not only in numbers, but in the quality of the instruction, and hopelessly weak from the indifference of the people." Ratepayers in the one-room school districts recognized that consolidation would improve the level of education, he said, but were afraid of higher taxes and jealous of their community rights and powers. By 1909, he concluded that the only solution would be to give the superintendent the power to consolidate certain districts, whether the ratepayers agreed or not.[83]

After a decade on the job, Anderson was still lamenting the fast turnover of teachers, the low salaries, the irregular attendance. Women teachers were still making much less money than men. Even for a man as dynamic as Anderson, the cumbersome, fragmented school system proved to be a difficult beast to turn around. In 1911, he submitted his resignation. Although he agreed to stay on another year while the government found a successor, he sounded discouraged in his final report. "The effects of a long and arduous service in the cause of Education extending over fifty years, and, latterly the hopelessness of my task rendered it impossible for me to persist in my struggle," he wrote.[84] Perhaps he was just tired. By the time he retired in 1912, he was seventy-six years old.

Thanks to William Peterson, principal of McGill, and his old friend Andrew Macphail, Anderson was able to obtain a pension. Peterson was director of the Carnegie Foundation for the Advancement of Teaching, which offered pensions to certain colleges for retiring professors and dealt with retirement provisions for professors. Technically, only McGill and Dalhousie qualified — professors in government and church institutions were normally exempted from the fund[85] — but Peterson applied on Anderson's behalf, at Macphail's request. Peterson successfully pressed Anderson's claim on his position as superintendent "and the fact he has been a pioneer who has rendered distinguished service."[86]

After Anderson retired, he and his wife, Catherine, moved in with their daughter and son-in-law in Halifax. Catherine died a few years later. In January 1925, Anderson's son-in-law, F. C. Kingdon, informed *The Patriot* of sad news: a couple of days previously, Anderson had dislocated his shoulder and was now unconscious. The shock of the accident, at his advanced age, had been great; pneumonia had set in. "He is worn out and tired out," Kingdon said. Two days later, on January 13, 1925, the old lion of Prince of Wales died. The funeral was held at his daughter's home, and he was buried in Fairview cemetery in Halifax. He was eighty-nine years old. "Dr. Anderson," Judge W. S. Stewart wrote in *The Guardian*, "has passed beyond the veil wearing the bright colours of a rich harvest of long, useful and valuable service, of which thousands, now and always, will reap the benefit."[87]

Valuable service, indeed. Alexander Anderson had devoted fifty years to the cause of education in his adopted home, apparently to the exclusion of all else, aside from his church (Presbyterian) and his family. In four decades at Prince of Wales, he had missed one day at work because of illness. While teaching and administering his staff, it was not unusual for him to spend one or two extra hours a day, throughout the term, with students who wanted extra help. "Although receiving but a small salary," Judge Stewart observed, "time and a half overtime was never a slogan of his."[88] Education was his passion. Aside from his work at the college, he occasionally travelled throughout the Maritimes, giving lectures on the writings of Burns, Shakespeare, and Savonarola. He also served as a director of the Dominion Educational Association and a member of its history committee, and as president of the PEI Teachers' Convention. In the eyes of many admirers, he had contributed hugely to the Island's educational system. Jacob Gould Schurman, scholar and diplomat, once described him as "incomparably the greatest benefactor the Island has had" in education: "If there be today in Prince Edward Island a good school system, good machinery, good teaching, scholars, it is all due, directly or indirectly, to his genius for education."[89]

Among Anderson's many accomplishments was one that was never publicly mentioned: in all his years amid the religious strife on the Island, he remained above the fray. In fact, he sent his daughter, Helen, to Notre Dame Convent school, perhaps because he had an exceptionally high opinion of it. The convent schools in Charlottetown, Summerside, Tignish, and Souris, taught by the sisters of the Congregation of Notre Dame, were technically not under his jurisdiction as school superintendent, but the Bishop and local priests opened them for his inspection. In one report, he noted that he had spent a day at St. Joseph's convent and two days, in company with the Bishop, at Notre Dame. "The children in both were exceedingly well taught," he reported. "The Senior Class in the convent de Notre Dame was a pleasure to examine. The girls were intelligent and well instructed in the subjects of study. The book-keeping work was beautifully executed, and the books spotless."[90] For a man of such exacting standards, this was high praise, indeed.

For himself, perhaps Anderson demanded too high a standard. In forty years at Prince of Wales, he had overseen the development of a tiny, obscure, underfunded college in a dilapidated building into an institution that was respected across the nation. Yet, one of his letters, in response to a request from Sir Andrew Macphail for information on his career, is a classic of understatement. "During those years [1862 to 1901] there is nothing to record of a sensational nature," he wrote. "Hard work and a great amount of pleasure derived from the answering enthusiasm of my students, and the attestation to the soundness of our work by McGill & other Universities, was the atmosphere in which I lived & toiled. Of the fruitage I say nothing."[91]

Of course, Anderson never saw the realization of his fondest hopes for the college. For many years, he had entertained visions in which bright young students like Lucy Maud Montgomery could stay at Prince of Wales instead of studying, at great expense, at universities on the mainland. Montgomery had followed a well-trod road: after leaving Prince of Wales, she taught school for a year before enrolling in the arts program at Dalhousie University for one year — all she could afford. Although she later regretted her decision to go to Dalhousie, she thought at the time that attending "a real college" would help her achieve her ambition to become a writer.[92] Anderson also had a personal interest in the lack of opportunities on the Island. At least two of his four children had left to further their studies elsewhere — Frederick spent four years at Royal Military College in Kingston, and Helen studied in Paris and Hanover. (Two other sons, Alexander and William, moved to New York. Alexander became general manager of the Electric Light and Power Company in Albany, and William worked as an electrician with the Edison Company in New York City.)[93]

When he retired from Prince of Wales, Anderson felt the time was ripe for degree-granting status: "Hitherto this had been impossible from want of accommodation and a disinclination on my part to encourage students to remain longer under such disadvantageous conditions," he wrote in his 1900 annual report. "These untoward circumstances no longer exist. Our new Building encourages us to hope for a great advance in the future, and a completion of the undergraduate course is one of the most important features of that advancement."[94]

All that was required, Anderson told the government, was one more professor on staff and a redistribution of work at the college. He was wrong. What really was required was the co-operation of his political bosses. That would prove surprisingly difficult to achieve.

Chapter Five

Working for the Government

5

"We are very desirous... to get our college—Prince of Wales—affiliated with McGill.... This matter, to my mind, is of great importance, and if a satisfactory arrangement can be arrived at our Province will derive a great deal of benefit."

—Premier Arthur Peters, September 13, 1906

The man with the formidable job of filling Alexander Anderson's shoes at Prince of Wales was a thirty-one-year-old protégé, Samuel Napier Robertson. Variously described by former students as "austere," "straight-laced" and "puritanical," Robertson was a tall, dignified bachelor with a sensitive, poetic face, who customarily wore a dark suit, white tie, and high white collar. Robertson and Anderson had much in common. Both were intellectuals who loved the classics, maintained high academic standards, and believed in shaping character as well as minds. But their temperaments were different. Their handwriting provides an interesting study in contrasts: Anderson's is extravagantly large, forceful and dramatic, the kind you might expect from a man who often told his students, "Speak loudly enough so that everybody can hear you, whether they want to or not."[1] Robertson's writing is small, neat and precise, as befitted a lower-key personality. Anderson had charisma, fire, and a wicked sense of humour. Robertson was careful. After several reminders to the government over four years about a salary increase that had been promised when he was first hired, Robertson wrote to Premier Farquharson. The tone of his letter bordered on the apologetic. "Your government very generously gave me my increase for last year," he concluded, "and I would humbly ask that you may see it proper to give further increase this year, and bring my salary up to the promised standard."[2]

Robertson would need all the force of personality he could muster to deal with the turbulent days ahead of him. After decades of relative stability, the new century delivered a road of twists and turns at Prince of Wales

— some of them minor, some momentous. Besides a new college and the departure of Anderson and Caven, the first decade alone would see additions to the building, the curriculum, the student population, and the staff. There was also increased tension about the college's role: should Prince of Wales serve primarily as a vocational school, churning out future teachers and farmers, or should it build on its fine reputation as a preparatory school and ultimately aspire to university status? The struggle to find that delicate balance led to an episode that came tantalizingly close to changing the history of the college and perhaps that of the province.

If the ground was shifting at Prince of Wales, there were tremors in the outside world as well. The Victorian Age ended with the death of the Queen, and the other Prince of Wales, Albert Edward, finally made it to the throne. The horse-scaring automobile arrived on the Island. A brand-new industry, fox-farming, was creating a get-rich-quick frenzy. Farmers were flexing their collective muscles, joining buying, shipping, and marketing co-operatives, and demanding an education system that better reflected the realities of rural life. Rumours foreshadowing a war in Europe were wafting across the ocean.

Even the provincial government seemed to shift shape every time you blinked. Although the Liberals had hung onto power since the early 1890s, the premiership had become a way station to more lucrative jobs. In 1901, the year Robertson took over the reins at Prince of Wales, Arthur Peters, younger brother of former premier Frederick Peters, became the third premier of the Island in as many years. The question of who became premier mattered quite a bit to Prince of Wales. The premier was effectively the boss. The principal carried out the orders. When students at the college organized a petition complaining of poor ventilation in the classrooms and asking for a recess of twenty minutes a day instead of two, they addressed their complaint to Premier Donald Farquharson.[3] Apparently it was the premier who oversaw even those minute details. The principal's opinion of the matter is not mentioned.

The new principal, unlike his predecessors, was a country boy, born and bred in Prince Edward Island. His father, a sea captain from Cape Traverse, had perished in a shipwreck off the coast of Newfoundland when Sammie was a small boy, and the family moved to the home of a relative in North Bedeque. Sammie attended a rural school during the week and almost certainly spent much of Sunday in the local Free Church of Scotland, where his uncle was an elder.[4] He enrolled at Prince of Wales in 1884, graduated three years later, and spent the next four years at Dalhousie University, majoring in the classics. After a year as principal of Alberton High School, he joined the Prince of Wales faculty in 1893, teaching English, Latin, and Greek. He left for a year, enrolling at Union Theological Seminary in New York, possibly with the intention of entering the ministry, and then studied briefly at Johns Hopkins University in Baltimore, Maryland, before returning to Prince of Wales.[5] In his absence, he won high praise from Anderson: "In the performance of his duties," he wrote, "he was uniformly able, earnest and conscientious, and as a colleague he was genial, helpful and gentlemanly."[6]

All of this was probably true. Certainly Robertson was an earnest gentleman. He was not keen on frivolity. He permitted sports, but only insofar as they contributed to the physical health of students. He insisted that male and female students use separate stairways. "Woe betide anyone caught using the wrong staircase!" recalled Joseph Devereux of New Haven, who enrolled at Prince of Wales in 1913.[7] "In his announcement of the regulations, [Robertson] had given special emphasis to this point: 'There must be absolutely no inter-mingling of the sexes.'" In the classroom, every moment had to count. Students who failed to pay attention in class, or displayed a lack of interest, were promptly reprimanded, or sent to the principal's office. Actual insubordination was practically unknown. Joseph Devereux could recall only one expulsion during his Prince of Wales days. A brash young man from Summerside announced near the end of the school year that he was going to "get a rise out of the Doc" by daring to smoke in the college. "When the bell signalled the recess, he lit a cigarette, strolled casually down the hallway, and stood before the open door of Dr. Robertson's office. Right at that point, his career at Prince of Wales came to an end. The fact of his having exceptionally high scholastic standing mattered not at all. He had violated the rules of proper conduct and there was no way in which he could escape the penalty."[8]

To his credit, Robertson practised what he preached: he was an exemplary role model, always working hard and doing good deeds. In addition to administering staff and students, he taught most periods of the college day. On Sundays, he put his theological learning to use by teaching a Bible class at the Free Church of Scotland, where he also served as an elder.[9] He took a great interest in all his students. "He was a man of vast sympathy for all in need of advice or counselling," Devereux wrote. "His patience was remarkable and his office door was literally always open. His duty, as he saw it, lay with the student who was encountering problems; many a confused boy and girl left his presence with renewed feelings of confidence."[10]

Robertson's main preoccupation, of course, was his students' academic welfare. By the end of his first year as principal, he remarked with satisfaction on the large, airy classrooms in the new building, the new chemistry laboratory, the examination hall. But two areas needed urgent attention: equipment for the physics lab and books for the library. The previous year, students had raised $200 for books, but the government would have to provide the foundation. "Additional and parallel reading in every subject of the curriculum must be done, if the student is to get a full and clear conception of the truth," Robertson wrote in his annual report. "But whither can he turn? Apart from books of reference, almost wholly dictionaries, there is nothing."[11] The next year, and for many years after that, he was still despairing over the lack of library books.

Robertson's heart, like Anderson's, lay in the classics, but he was making a valiant stab at answering an ever-growing clamour for more practical subjects. Possibly, given the way the college was run, he didn't have much choice. Manual training — carpentry courses based on the principle that the best way to learn is by doing — had been added to the curriculum in 1900, and the next year, Ewen McMillan, a graduate of the Ontario Agricultural College, was hired to teach agriculture, a course that had been neglected since the departure of George Harcourt in 1894.

At a time when 85 per cent of Islanders lived on farms, it was not surprising that many people were demanding that more attention be paid to agricultural education. The buzzword of the day was "scientific agriculture," the use of modern techniques of breeding, animal husbandry, and growing crops. When the province established a Department of Agriculture in 1901, its main function was to promote agricultural education. It encouraged the growth of Farmers' Institutes — self-help groups through which farmers exchanged ideas, bought supplies, and sold farm products — and published lengthy, detailed reports on topics such as dairying, fruit-growing, and noxious weeds. The district schools started teaching gardening in 1905, and, to prepare teachers for this subject, Dalhousie graduate Theodore Ross began teaching botany and "physical geography" to teachers-in-training at Prince of Wales. By 1906, the agriculture department at the college was extensive enough to require a full-time teacher to conduct classes in botany, physical geography, nature study, and agriculture.[12]

That was still not enough for S. E. Reid, commissioner of agriculture for the Island, who complained that Prince of Wales College paid more attention to Latin than to agriculture, botany, and physical geography combined. "We spend yearly on this school that devotes more than one third of its energies to the teaching of languages alone a large sum," he said. "We spend annually half of our revenue on our public schools, which are so conducted that the tendency is always from the farm, rather than towards it.... The time will come when it will be quoted as a stock example of our stupidity, that although more than 90 per cent of all those who enter the public schools shall live on farms and get their livelihood from agriculture, the whole atmosphere of those public schools, supported by farmers, should be cityward and tend to create within the pupil a dislike for rural surroundings, and a disgust for farm life in general."[13]

Islanders were indeed leaving the farm at a fast clip. Despite a high birth rate, the 1901 census showed the Island had lost 6,000 people in the previous decade. Young people who had gone to college were especially likely to head for the city. As historian Edward MacDonald has observed, "There were few opportunities for Latin and Greek scholars in a province of farmers."[14] It's doubtful that many young Islanders enrolled at Prince of Wales with the intention of becoming farmers. Most of them, like Sir Andrew Macphail in the previous century, went to college to escape the farm. The best and the brightest generally didn't even stay at teaching jobs on the Island for long. Alexander Anderson thought that higher teachers' salaries would staunch that exodus. "Salaries are so small," he said, "that the best students who leave Prince of Wales College either do not take situations as teachers, or if they do, they only remain for one or it may be two years, and then leave."[15] Critics like Reid argued that Prince of Wales was providing the wrong kind of education: young Islanders should be taught what they really needed to know — how to build barns, milk cows, and plant potatoes. If they were women, they needed to learn either how to teach school or how to put a good meal on the farm table.

One expatriate Islander with some sympathy for this point of view was Sir William Macdonald, an eccentric, cantankerous, fantastically rich bachelor who had left his home community of Glenaladale, east of Charlottetown, at age sixteen. He never completed his education, but that didn't prevent him from making a fortune in Montreal as the founder of Macdonald Tobacco, and perhaps inspired him to devote huge sums of money to educational causes. A man of firm opinions, Macdonald disliked religion, innovations like the telephone and the gramophone, and the product that had made him rich. "I am not proud of my business," he once said, "and that feeling, perhaps, has been the reason for my donations."[16] McGill University in Montreal was the main beneficiary of his philanthropy — over the years, he gave the university between $11 million and $14 million — but he also donated money for practical training in rural areas.

In 1899, Sir William established the Macdonald Rural Schools Fund, designed to encourage the teaching of subjects such as manual training, domestic science, and agriculture in selected schools across Canada. In Prince Edward Island, schools in Charlottetown and Summerside were chosen as sites for a three-year pilot project in manual training. Sir William also financed the establishment of the manual-training class at Prince of Wales, and agreed to maintain the course for three years. All students at the college were required to take the course, and, after three years, the government decided to continue it. Robertson applauded that decision — significantly, not because students were learning practical skills but because, in his opinion, they were building character. "The care and exactitude demanded in the work, the opportunity it affords the instructor to direct and govern the physical movements of the student, and in this way to pass on to the development in him of a respect for authority and government, makes Manual Training one of the important subjects in the curriculum," he wrote at the end of the three-year trial period. "Not too many influences can be brought to bear upon the wilfulness and irresponsibility of youth."[17]

Once the manual-training programs were established, Sir William financed another scheme designed to promote both practical and academic courses. James Robertson, the former federal agriculture and dairy commissioner who became principal of Macdonald College, encouraged Sir William to fund, as pilot projects, a series of consolidated schools in Eastern Canada. In addition to the usual academic subjects, the schools featured courses in manual training, agriculture, gardening, and other practical subjects. One school was to be built on the Island, a plan much to Alexander Anderson's liking. From the time Anderson had started his job as superintendent of education, he had conducted a crusade for consolidating some of the province's 470-plus school districts, believing consolidation to be the salvation of the Island's education system. In his reports to the government, in public lectures, and in private interviews, he urged Islanders to give up some of their one-room schools. Bigger schools, he argued, would enable taxpayers to employ better teachers, provide a more pleasant, more stimulating environment, and introduce rural children to subjects they'd otherwise never encounter. Samuel Robertson also favoured consolidation then, although he was to change his mind in later years; in 1908 he was appointed to a three-member commission on education that developed a detailed scheme for cutting the number of Island school districts in half.[18]

But Islanders tended to be suspicious of consolidation, fearing higher taxes, the risks to the health and safety of young children being transported long distances, and the loss of educational autonomy within their small communities. However, six districts agreed to participate in a pilot project financed by Sir William. In August 1905, the Macdonald Consolidated School officially opened in Mount Herbert, east of Charlottetown. Sir William had agreed to pay the $20,000 construction costs, plus salaries of the principal, teachers and support staff, and some operating costs for the first three years. The Macdonald Consolidated School experiment was a remarkable success. Besides the usual academic subjects, male students learned carpentry and agriculture; girls studied household science and floriculture. Five years before the school opened, the six districts supporting the school had sent only one student to Prince of Wales; in its first five years, the consolidated school matriculated twenty students from the six districts and another twenty from students who attended from other parts of the province. Since the idea was to keep young people on the farm, perhaps the school was a little too successful. In any case, it cost too much. After the three years paid for by Sir William, he extended his commitment to the school for another three years, but when that time was up, neither the provincial government nor the local districts were prepared to pay to keep the school open. Its benefactor sent his last cheque in 1911 with this terse message: "This is my *final* remittance."[19]

While the consolidation project was starting up, and Sir William was still in the mood to spend money on the Island, he agreed to pay for an addition to the north end of the college. The new wing, designed by Island architect C. B. Chappell, measured 70 feet by 100 feet, and included three additional classrooms for the Model School on the first floor and an assembly hall for examinations and physical education on the second. Much to Robertson's relief, the additional space gave the teacher-training program needed breathing space. With only two classrooms in the Model School in which about a hundred Normal School students could practise teaching, the practical work of the program had been almost nonexistent.

Five classrooms would allow an entire teacher-training class to spend a week at a time in the Model School. Household science was also added to the curriculum, and there were improved facilities for manual training, agriculture, and nature study.

It was not surprising that Sir William chose to send money to Prince of Wales instead of St. Dunstan's College. He had been brought up in the Catholic Church — his father was Catholic and his mother Protestant — but he renounced his faith at a young age and retained a dislike for organized religion for the rest of his life. When Lord Strathcona, a contemporary philanthropist, presented the Young Men's Christian Association in Montreal with a new hall, Sir William remarked, "Lord Strathcona has given a building for the Christians. *I* will give a building for *all* the students of the University."[20] Although Sir William had not attended the Island's nonsectarian college, he had gone to the old Central Academy, and perhaps harboured some affection for its successor.

From his safe distance in downtown Montreal, Sir William also clung — like many expatriates — to a nostalgic longing for life in the country. He viewed with reverence the workings of the natural world. He was a frequent visitor to the agricultural college he built at Ste.-Anne-de-Bellevue, outside Montreal, and once sat in silence for hours watching chicks hatch from an incubator.[21] With his largely rural native province, though, he had a more complex, love-hate relationship. Possibly this stemmed from his unhappy childhood and certainly from a transaction in the 1870s, when the government compelled him to sell his 10,435 acres of land at a price he considered too low. Charlottetown businessman Henry Cundall, an old friend from the Central Academy days, thought that a grudge from that episode had prevented Sir William for many years from spending "a very large sum of money" on the Island.[22] Fortunately for Prince of Wales, Sir William's heart had melted by the turn of the century.

The college expansion was completed in 1907. Henry Cundall, appointed overseer of the project, told Macdonald College principal James Robertson how happy he was to have enabled Sir William "to carry out his munificent and very costly work of enlarging and improving the College, and thus make it a very complete and efficient Educational institution for this Province."[23] Like many public-works projects, this one turned out to be even more costly than expected. First estimated at $20,000, the cost escalated to $55,000, much more than the entire building had cost at the turn of the century. Along the way, there had been changes to the design of the new wing, and the fund also had financed improvements to the heating and ventilation systems in the original building. Sir William sent the full amount, James Robertson reported, "with all good will."[24]

After lacking decent quarters for forty years, Prince of Wales now had a new building and an even newer wing. This was progress with a vengeance. But there was more to come.

In the late summer of 1906, Premier Arthur Peters floated another proposal for expansion at Prince of Wales. A certain Dr. Bagnall (probably Charlottetown dentist John Stanley Bagnall) had just visited McGill University while on a trip to Montreal. According to a report he wrote later for Premier Peters, Bagnall asked J. A. Nicholson, the registrar, and H. M. Tory, a McGill professor, about the possibility of affiliating Prince of Wales with McGill. It was an exciting idea. Certainly the timing was right. McGill was in the midst of a huge expansion program, thanks mainly to Sir William, who had financed the construction of engineering, physics, and chemistry buildings in the 1890s, and was building Macdonald College at Ste.-Anne-de-Bellevue, devoted to agriculture, teacher training, and household science. At the same time, McGill was extending its influence to colleges in other parts of Canada, partly in an attempt to raise educational standards, partly to expand its influence and recruit top-flight students. By 1906, Vancouver, Victoria, and Alberta colleges had affiliated with McGill, later to emerge as, respectively, the University of British Columbia, the University of Victoria, and the University of Alberta.[25] (Coincidentally, the principal at Vancouver College during its transition was James Curtis Shaw, formerly of Stanhope and a Prince of Wales alumnus.[26])

For Prince of Wales, affiliation with McGill would be a natural extension of links that had existed since the 1860s. In the 19th century, Prince of Wales became an "affiliated school," in that it prepared students for examinations set by McGill.[27] Over the years, Prince of Wales had sent many graduates to McGill, and many had done exceptionally well. One of them, Sir Andrew Macphail, was soon to become professor of medical history at McGill. The university was well aware of the academic standards at Prince of Wales: in recognition of Anderson's successes, McGill had given him an honorary degree in the 1880s. And, of course, the McGill registrar was a Prince of Wales alumnus. With a little fine-tuning, the curriculum for university-bound students could be made to jibe with McGill's. Bagnall said he was told that, by adding one or two more professors and expanding the curriculum, Prince of Wales could send students to the third year at McGill in arts, science, and scientific agriculture. He was also told that the "Macdonald Funds" would pay for the extra professors. "He [Dr. Tory] said, 'There are funds here that I am satisfied we can give them financial assistance from.'"[28] Bagnall didn't know how much money was available, but he thought the proposal was worth pursuing.

So did Premier Arthur Peters. A Charlottetown lawyer, Peters was an alumnus of Prince of Wales, but as premier was mainly preoccupied with prying more subsidies out of Ottawa, obtaining winter transportation to the mainland, and keeping his Second King's political fences in good repair.[29] In the fall of 1906, however, he latched onto the affiliation idea like a pitbull, launching an exchange of letters with McGill that continued until the next spring.

"We are very desirous," he wrote to registrar J. A. Nicholson in September, " ... to get our college — Prince of Wales — affiliated with McGill. We have a very fine college, and since the improvements made by Sir William Macdonald, which will be completed this fall, it cannot be equalled in the Maritime Provinces.... As the matter now stands with us, in order to carry out the Prince of Wales College system under Sir William Macdonald's grants, it will be necessary for us to supply two or three more professors. If we could have an understanding with your university that we could get affiliated, this I think could be done without a great deal of extra expense.... This matter to my mind, is of great importance, and if a satisfactory arrangement can be arrived at our Province will derive a great deal of benefit."[30]

Nicholson, a former superintendent of education on the Island, was understandably sympathetic. "I am delighted to learn of your interest in the proposed scheme of affiliation," he wrote, "... and am quite satisfied that with your influence and assistance the matter can be consummated."[31]

Peters wrote back immediately. "I assure you that myself and the Government here will do all we can to secure the affiliation of our College with McGill. I am very pleased that you look so favourably on the matter and feel so confident that it can be carried out."[32]

Charles E. Moyse, vice-principal and dean of arts at McGill, assured Peters that the faculty was in favour of the move, "not only on account of the thorough preparation of the many excellent students who have come to McGill from that College, but also because the expansion and consolidation of our academic interests seems more than ever forced upon us by our national outlook...."[33]

The McGill principal, William Peterson, who happened to be a close friend and next-door neighbour of Sir William's, sent his blessing. The benefits for his university included another source of students with qualifications he could depend on. "It would be good," he told Peters, "if you could turn students from Prince of Wales College towards Montreal, instead of letting them drift to the United States, as I am told they now do. Two years with you would be an admirable preparation, either for further work in Arts or as a preparation for professional training in Applied Science or Medicine or Law."[34]

Peters apparently had asked McGill about obtaining funds from Sir William. Peterson's reply was guarded, but positive: "I note your suggestion about further draft on Sir William Macdonald's munificence, and shall bear your needs in mind...."[35]

That fall, Premier Peters asked Nicholson to come to the Island at the government's expense to discuss the matter. Then, not wishing to bear too much of the expense, he wrote to the Intercolonial Railway, asking for a pass for the return trip from Montreal. (His request, unfortunately, was turned down.)

Until that visit, at least, the premier was directing the orchestra on the Island end. There is no evidence in the surviving official correspondence that Samuel Robertson had any role to play, aside from an unsigned, undated memo — presumably from Robertson — that outlines what changes would be needed at the college. Peters brought Robertson up to date by letter in November, on the eve of Nicholson's visit. "Of course you are aware that we are trying to get affiliation between our college and McGill," he wrote. "I wrote Dr. Peterson some time ago asking him to let me know what changes would be required to be made in our curriculum, and also asking him to use his good offices with Sir William Macdonald, to assist us in providing a larger staff than we have at present in Prince of Wales College. His answer is very encouraging and I have no doubt we will get this affiliation and possibly some assistance from Sir William along this line."[36]

After his visit to Charlottetown, Nicholson confirmed in a letter to Peters that, to start with, the college could affiliate up to the end of the first year in applied science, up to the end of the second year in arts, and for "a year or two" in connection with agriculture courses at Macdonald College, scheduled to open that year. Peters replied that he would present this information to his cabinet. "I almost feel confident that there will be no trouble at all."[37] Nicholson also noted that teachers at Prince of Wales would become professors of a college of McGill, have their names listed in the McGill calendar, and enjoy "a status they had not before."[38]

When the spring session of the Island Legislature opened on February 19, 1907, the government announced that the affiliation plan would "result in great benefit to our Island students."[39] A month later, Peters sent to McGill a draft of a bill that would designate the college as "The Prince of Wales College of McGill University," providing courses leading to degrees at McGill. The instruction of students at Prince of Wales preparing for degrees would be of standards similar to McGill's. The new act, to come into effect on July 1, would not affect the teacher-training program, which would remain under the Board of Education, as would decisions on tuition fees.[40]

On March 26, the bill was given first reading in the Legislature. It was scheduled to be read a second time the next day. Instead, it sank without a trace.[41]

On April 6, Nicholson advised Peters that the plan had gone through its final stage "in so far as the University is concerned, Corporation having approved of the proposal at a meeting held on the 3rd inst."[42]

Five days after that letter was written, and without the benefit of public debate, the government did a sudden about-face. Premier Peters announced in the Legislature that the government had dropped the McGill affiliation bill. *The Examiner* reported, "The Premier said that after consultation he found it would be better to hold the conclusion of the matter over for another year."[43] J. A. Mathieson, the Conservative leader, agreed. He thought Prince of Wales should first of all be a training school for teachers, the newspaper reported. "It will, of course, always happen that some of the pupils will go to universities. That is very well. But it should be incidental. A marked distinction would in his opinion be made between those who attend Prince of Wales College for the purpose of becoming teachers in our public schools and those who attend for the purpose of going to the university to prepare for a professional career. ... He approved of this delay." Another Liberal member, Francis L. Haszard, who later became premier, also supported the motion. "He thought it advisable to go slow."[44]

At this point, the administration at McGill had not one, but two, disasters at home to worry about. In early April, the Macdonald Engineering Building, a handsome greystone structure built with Sir William's money in the heart of Montreal, burned to the ground. Two weeks later, on April

16, the university's medical building was destroyed by fire in the middle of the night. Arson was suspected in both cases.[45] There was a sad irony in these fires, in that Sir William was inordinately anxious about fireproofing his buildings, perhaps in reaction to a fire at one of his factories in which four workers had died. While Macdonald College was under construction, he tested the fireproofing by soaking shavings on an office floor with kerosene, and setting them ablaze with a match. That building passed the test, although two of the college's farm buildings burned in the summer of 1907 after being struck by lightning. Macdonald rebuilt the engineering building immediately, and Lord Strathcona, another McGill benefactor, financed the construction of the medical college.

The day after the medical building burned down, Premier Peters sent his condolences to the McGill registrar, and broke the news about the government's abrupt change of heart. "I am sorry to have to tell you that for the present year we do not propose to carry out this proposition.... The House has received a number of petitions from Farmers' Institutes complaining that more money should not be expended on University Education before we have expended some additional on Agricultural Education.... Of course there is a strong sentiment among many of our people that this affiliation would be a good thing for our Province, but this is a matter that will have to stand for the present."[46]

In a second letter, Peters told McGill that the Farmers' Institutes and agricultural community "seem to think that the affiliation will cost the Province a large sum of money. This may or may not be correct." He did promise to "take measures this season to in some way obtain an agreement of opinion from the different centres of education on the Island on this matter."[47] Nicholson replied politely that it was perhaps better to get a consensus before proceeding. "I am sure from the point of view of the university we would prefer to have the scheme thoroughly well matured before being accepted. I trust, however, that in the end it will be found to be advantageous."[48]

The significance of the government's decision seems to have been lost on the local newspapers. At the end of that session of the Legislature, *The Examiner* expressed disappointment that the government had failed to pass a dog-control act, but did not mention the McGill matter. The student newspaper, *The Observer,* did raise an objection. "Notwithstanding the fact that many members of the legislature, many educational authorities, and many electors were in favour of the bill," the paper noted in its April 1907 issue, "still sufficient objection was raised to have it laid aside for this year and probably for good. To some of the students, at least, of this college, this result has been one of extreme disappointment, and we hope that, when the bill is presented again, those who are so opposed to it will lay aside all prejudice, reconsider the stand they have taken, and help to bring about this affiliation, which has done so much to promote educational interests in other provinces, and will do the same for ours."[49]

That, of course, did not happen. Peters had promised the McGill registrar that he would try to "obtain an expression of opinion from the different centres of education on the Island." Possibly he intended to do so, but he became ill from Bright's Disease that fall and died in office the next January. The affiliation plan died as well. Ironically, his obituary described him as a man who was "never a seeker after cheap popularity, and at times somewhat indifferent to the favour of the masses."[50]

Apparently, this was not one of those times. Prince of Wales had always been vulnerable to political pressure; without a board of trustees to defend its interests, it was at the mercy of politicians with one eye on the ballot box. This time, its fate appears to have been decided in the back rooms. Because the bill was discharged before second reading, there was no debate in the Legislature, and almost no publicity in the newspapers. Islanders weren't writing letters to the editor about Prince of Wales; they were too busy worrying about sheep-killing dogs, the hoped-for tunnel to the mainland, and changes to the game laws. It's hard to imagine who knew enough about the bill to persuade the premier to change his mind so abruptly.

In his bitter account of the life and death of Prince of Wales, former principal Frank MacKinnon alleges that the 1907 fiasco was just one more example of the damage caused by mixing religion, politics and education. In other words, the old religious wars were not over; they just raged behind closed doors. To MacKinnon, the villains of this piece were officials of the Roman Catholic Church. As evidence, he cites conversations he had with former McGill professors — H. M. Tory,[51] who had shepherded the Vancouver College affiliation; Frank Adams, vice-principal at McGill; Lemuel Robertson, who "went from McGill to the University of British Columbia and knew the whole story re PWC"; and George Robinson, a former Prince of Wales professor also at the University of British Columbia.[52] In addition, Walter Jones, a former principal of the Macdonald Consolidated School who later became premier, had told him about "a well-organized Catholic lobby that went among farmers and local groups and frightened the Cabinet and its weak premier."[53] MacKinnon saw the incident — and others to follow — as an illustration of ongoing attempts by church officials to build up the Catholic college at the expense of Prince of Wales. "It was a great day for St. Dunstan's when Prince of Wales' wings were clipped," he wrote, "but a tragedy for everyone else."[54]

There is little chance that supporters of St. Dunstan's College would be tap dancing at the prospect of its traditional rival's promotion. Prince of Wales was already monopolizing a field in which St. Dunstan's wanted an entry. Hundreds of Catholic students, men and women, had taken teacher training at Prince of Wales since its amalgamation with the Normal School. Starting in 1906, and for more than a decade after, the St. Dunstan's board of governors tried to persuade the provincial board of education to grant first-class teachers' licences to St. Dunstan's graduates with bachelor's degrees. The Catholic officials were refused. That meant continuing prestige for Prince of Wales, a further drain of Catholic students, and a probable loss of potential vocations to the priesthood.[55] Students could obtain Laval University degrees at St. Dunstan's, which had affiliated with Laval University in 1892. But McGill, Canada's leading university, was a much more prestigious institution than Laval. The affiliation would, in the short term, advance Prince of Wales only to junior-college status, but could well be a stepping-stone to degree-granting status, as was the case with colleges in Alberta and British Columbia. People of influence, including Alexander Anderson, had been ruminating about a "Prince of Wales University" since the college was founded. Inasmuch as one tiny province would have difficulty supporting two universities, even if only one was government-funded, any expansion ambitions at Prince of Wales would pose a threat. And prominent Catholics in the past had not shied away from attacking the "Protestant college."

At the same time, Catholic officials hadn't succeeded in the past in diverting government funds from Prince of Wales. In the development of St. Dunstan's, the Catholics had done it alone. There is no mention in Arthur Peters' surviving papers of any objection to the affiliation from Roman Catholics. Then again, there is no evidence in Peters' papers — aside from the premier's letters to McGill — of objections from farmers. Blaming it all on the farmers must have looked like a lame excuse to McGill officials. After all, they had discussed with Peters a plan to allow Prince of Wales graduates to obtain agriculture degrees at Macdonald College. That would not happen immediately, as the college was still under construction, and the faculty of agriculture would not be established until 1908.[56] But it's easy to imagine the word spreading that Prince of Wales was dropping agriculture altogether. To some Islanders, the college was already wasting an inordinate amount of energy on Latin and Greek. A memo filed with Peters' papers, possibly written by Samuel Robertson but identified only as "Proposed Affiliation of Prince of Wales College with McGill University," suggests that shortcomings in subjects such as French, physics, and Greek could be made up "by dropping agriculture and chemistry from the present course."[57] The memo adds that students "who do not intend to teach would not be required to take the extra subjects set down in the present Prince of Wales College curriculum." Does this mean Prince of Wales was ready to drop agriculture from its curriculum? It seems unlikely that such a controversial move would be contemplated. Agriculture, after all, was one of Sir William's favourite subjects, and the province needed to stay in his good books — especially when he had just spent $55,000 on a wing partly aimed at promoting agriculture. What is more reasonable is that it was proposed that agriculture could become an optional subject for *university-bound* students. Of course, reason never was any match for the Island's hyperkinetic rumour machine.

In any case, the premier's behaviour must have seemed bizarre to McGill officials. If he had received so many complaints from the farmers, why hadn't he paid attention to them until the last minute? In a sense, it was he who had courted McGill — right up until he heard the opening bars of the Wedding March.

Possibly a combination of forces was at work, as was the case when Vancouver College began its association with McGill. According to historian Stanley Brice Frost, several groups, including those supporting a Methodist college near Vancouver, tried to halt that project.[58] Opposition to the Prince of Wales affiliation could have come from Catholics, from farmers, from those who feared that affiliation would dilute the college's teacher-training efforts. According to Bagnall, even Alexander Anderson, who had long hoped for university status for Prince of Wales, was dubious about the affiliation idea, at least in the beginning. "Everyone I have spoken to here are very enthusiastic except Dr. Anderson," Bagnall reported after his return from Montreal in the summer of 1906. "He thinks it might interfere with supplying teachers for the country districts."[59]

Then there was the cost factor. That year, the government reported a deficit of $70,000. Education, by far the biggest cost item, ate up almost $124,000 a year, about a third of the provincial budget. Maintenance and salaries for six professors at Prince of Wales cost $11,125. The government had recently built a new $36,000 college building and had made improvements to the Hospital for the Insane. The province needed a new jail. The hoped-for increased subsidy from Ottawa hadn't yet come through. A provincial election was on the horizon, and Peters was vulnerable in his own riding. In the 1904 election, he and his Conservative opponent had received equal numbers of votes.[60] He could not afford to alienate too many voters. After six months of negotiations with McGill, Peters seemed to have no idea whether affiliation would, in fact, cost the province "a large sum of money." In a way, that's understandable, considering that the government would lose some of its control over Prince of Wales and its budgets.

And where was the money coming from? Sir William Macdonald's commitment to the project is unclear. He had given the Vancouver college $15,000 to support its affiliation,[61] and it is unlikely he would do less for his home province. But he was a taciturn man, and he wasn't giving much away in this instance. (The story is told that, after twice failing to respond to correspondence about a business deal, he received a third letter with the question: "Do you not answer your letters?" Sir William turned down a corner of the page, wrote "No," and returned it.[62]) Sir William customarily communicated through the principal of Macdonald College, James Robertson. Haszard apparently wrote to Robertson — or possibly to Sir William himself — in the spring of 1907. Sir William's reply, by way of Robertson, is enigmatic. Sir William "did not express any opinion on the definite point which you raised in your letter,"[63] Robertson reported. Sir William did disclose the opinion that affiliation with McGill would be preferable to attempting full university work alone, although the college's first duty lay in providing adequately for teachers in training and for students not intending to go on to university. Hiring more professors to fulfill the affiliation agreement "would no doubt be some advantage to the teachers in training and to the other students...."[64]

As far as can be determined, that was Sir William's last word on the subject. His gifts to Prince of Wales and the consolidated school were his last donations to Prince Edward Island. Never a man to encourage weakness, he may have been disgusted at the government's failure to grasp two golden opportunities to advance the Island's educational system. He was still sounding friendly in July 1907, but that was before his consolidation venture had foundered. He sent a message to Islanders, again through his mouthpiece, James Robertson. Robertson, addressing a Charlottetown audience on improving rural conditions through education, closed with "Sir William's thought of you." Not surprisingly, it was a sentiment with which Robertson concurred: "We like you, we wish you well, and ever rejoice when we hear of your happiness and prosperity."[65]

Samuel Robertson didn't have a James Robertson as a mouthpiece, and it is unclear what he thought of the proposed Prince of Wales expansion. Unlike Anderson, he was not on record as espousing university status for Prince of Wales. He did not mention McGill in any of his annual reports, and, if he ever breathed the name at convocation exercises, it was never reported. He did not appear to have much of a role in the negotiations. But that was standard procedure.

It was the premier, a man with a law practice on the side, who dealt with the academics. Not the principal, and not the board of education. Why? Aside from the possibility that writing letters to McGill was a welcome change from dealing with supplications from destitute Island widows, the answer is that Prince of Wales College had been run that way for more than twenty-five years. It was politicians who hired, fired, and decided who was going to be paid what. St. Dunstan's College may have been starving for government funds, but Prince of Wales was in bondage to them. The grants came with a price tag attached.

When you wanted a job at Prince of Wales, you didn't approach the principal. You wrote to the premier, as Harvard University graduate G. Douglas Steel did in 1909.[66] Steel was the son of a Methodist minister who had served in many charges in the Maritimes, and presumably knew how things worked on the Island. The premier, F. L. Haszard, responded four days later: "I have decided to appoint you on the staff of the teachers of Prince of Wales College at the salary of $900 for the first year, with an increase of $100 for the second year, providing your work and conduct at the school is satisfactory."[67]

J. G. Bennett, a twenty-eight-year-old Queen's University graduate from Alberton, took a more roundabout route. Bennett, vice-principal of West Kent School, had served as acting school inspector in Prince County for a year. He owned property there and therefore was eligible to vote in two places. Perhaps that is why he wrote to John Agnew, an Alberton meat and fish packer who was also Speaker of the House. Bennett wanted to know whether it was true that one of the professors at Prince of Wales, John A.

MacDonald, was leaving for the West. If so, Bennett wanted to apply for the job.[68] Agnew forwarded the letter to the premier. "If there are any vacancies I wish you would consider Mr. Bennett's application favourably," he wrote. Bennett followed up with a letter to Premier Haszard. After listing his academic qualifications and experience, he added, "I am a Liberal in politics and a property voter at Alberton...."[69]

Professor MacDonald did leave, in 1911, and Bennett joined the Prince of Wales faculty the next year to teach chemistry and physics. He remained on the faculty for another three decades. By the time he was hired, enrolment was up to 288 and climbing, and the college was acquiring a strong team of teachers. They included two Harvard graduates, Douglas Steel and Lily Seaman, a Prince of Wales alumna and the first woman on the regular faculty. Steel would remain on the faculty for forty years, and Seaman for more than fifty. The faculty also included two prominent Roman Catholics — J.-H. Blanchard, who had taught French for three years at St. Dunstan's, and James Murphy, a recent graduate of St. Dunstan's who eventually became a priest and later rector of the Catholic college.

As Prince of Wales matured, so did its mild-mannered principal. Samuel Robertson not only shared Anderson's ideas about education, he was starting to sound remarkably like his predecessor, giving advice to rural teachers, lecturing Islanders about the importance of staying in school. The high dropout rate was a constant sore point. Only about 200 of the 2,500 students who left school every year went on to Prince of Wales. It was not always for lack of desire. It was still tough to get into Prince of Wales, especially if you went to a rural school with an incompetent teacher in charge.

In the summer of 1912, Joseph Devereux of New Haven wrote the Entrance Examinations and failed, along with most of his class. The next fall, his parents sent him to school in Kelly's Cross, where the teacher had a reputation for getting pupils into college. In June, Devereux was among the 134 students who passed. Another 328 did not. Devereux enrolled at Prince of Wales, only to face another terrible set of exams at Christmas. It was "like trying the Entrance all over again."[70] The college had begun the practice of marking Christmas exams early enough to notify students before they returned from the holidays. Those who did poorly were advised to stay home and make a fresh start the next fall. "Our first session of the new year," Devereux recalled, "showed that a sizeable number had failed to make the grade — a tacit warning to the rest of us that we would face an even more searching challenge toward the end of another six months."

After a year at Prince of Wales, Devereux taught for a year, decided he was not cut out for that line of work, and planned to go back to college in the fall. But the winds of war were in the air. Instead of packing his books for college, he ended up in uniform. Other students would soon follow him.

On August 14, 1914, Charlottetown's big brass bell sounded, announcing that the First World War had begun. The next afternoon, the first Island soldiers marched to the docks in Charlottetown and sailed away in a potato boat.[71] Swept up in a wave of patriotism, and looking for adventure, more young Islanders soon followed. "When one considers how emigration has reduced the population of the province," Robertson observed, "so that none but the more profitable forms of labour can be prosecuted, one marvels that Prince Edward Island could have supplied so many recruits, and I rejoiced at her grand self-sacrifice."[72] His annual reports did not reveal how many Prince of Wales students were among the recruits, but he noted that the ranks of young male students were thinning out as early as the fall of 1914. Many former students had enlisted for service overseas instead of returning that fall for second or third year. Many more were missing from the college the next year. Edgar McInnis of Charlottetown, a future Rhodes Scholar, poet, and professor,[73] enlisted in the Royal Canadian Artillery in April 1916. Some students joined up in the middle of the college session, Robertson reported. "Many others are awaiting the completion of the session, or an approaching birthday, to get the opportunity to satisfy their wishes. Of those eligible for service abroad, scarcely one will be left to enter the teaching profession. The removal of the older men students from the classes, and the restlessness of the waiting period for the others, has greatly affected the quality of the students' work."[74]

The loss of male students changed the complexion of the college. Women had outnumbered men slightly for a number of years, probably because women were trying to achieve financial independence by teaching school. By 1915, there were almost twice as many women as men at Prince of Wales. It was also a year of record attendance: 309 in total — three times the enrolment the year Robertson became principal.[75]

That was not good enough for Robertson. Parents were making a grave mistake, he said, in allowing their children to leave school to work in offices, stores, factories, and on farms, where they made barely enough to survive and had little hope of advancement. "They surely must realize," he said, "that a very considerable education is required by the child that embarks on life in the 20th century."[76] At the same time, though, Robertson was clearly getting tired of the clamour for more scientific and practical courses at the college. Students should be taught how to live, he maintained in one report, not just how to make a living, to learn "what makes man more human, more safe to live with, more kindly to those with whom he lives."[77] Year after year he railed against the view that "there shall be only science, and lots of it," or that an education had value only when it led directly to a vocation: "How frequently one has to admit that the efficient, wealthy member of the community is not a good citizen, is unworthy of imitation ... Always keep in mind that the man is more than his vocation."[78] As the years rolled on, Robertson was sounding more and more like the preacher he may once have planned to be.

He *was* prepared to make a few sacrifices to the gods of Mammon. Great advances had been made in the teaching of agriculture, he reported in 1916. A federal grant had financed the salary of a full-time instructor, S. B. McCready, as well as equipment he needed for teaching in what now was called the "rural sciences department." There was even a demonstration plot where students could learn by doing. A piece of land south of the college, next to the greenhouse, was plowed and manured for a garden that would be used as a model for rural schools.

Like so many of the initiatives at Prince of Wales, this one was designed for future teachers. At that point, every student enrolled at the college was a potential teacher, and had to take school management and other normal training courses in first year, along with academic work.[79] Because there were no optional courses, many graduates thought they might as well make use of their training by teaching for a year or two. That kept the teacher supply fairly high for a number of years, and the salaries very low.[80]

Salaries remained low through the war years, even though good teachers were hard to find. The military claimed many potential teachers, even in the last year of the war. Male students at Prince of Wales, Robertson told a convocation audience, had been reduced "to scarcely more than a corporal's guard."[81] The first half-dozen who had enlisted when war broke out had returned, but many never would. In the last two years of the war, Prince of Wales closed two or three weeks early so that country students could go home to the farm and help put in the crops. Young able-bodied men were in short supply everywhere, including Island farms. The early closing, valedictorian Edward Aitken of Charlottetown noted in the spring of 1918, gave all students a chance to become "soldiers of the soil."[82]

By the fall of 1918, the war was over, but life was far from back to normal. In late September, a worldwide epidemic, the Spanish influenza, swept through the Island. The Charlottetown Board of Health closed down all schools, colleges, theatres, and churches on October 7. Soon even public funerals were forbidden. Prince of Wales did not reopen until late November. The flu raged on through the winter, and, by the time it had run its course, 900 people in Charlottetown had contracted the illness. Across the Island, 375 had died.[83] In his annual report for that year, Robertson did not mention whether he had lost any students, but he did complain about lost time. Never a man to waste a minute, he had tried to make up for the interruption by expanding the college week to six days, and cutting the Christmas holidays down to three days. That still didn't compensate for the shutdown of the college and the absence of individual students, he fretted. "Never in any recent years has our regularity been so much interrupted."[84]

By the end of the decade, life was finally settling down at the college. Robertson was back to scolding Island parents for failing to keep their children in school. "The people of this province fail to realize … that their children are going out to earn a livelihood in an educated world, in which their educational handicap will exact a tremendous toll."[85] Enrolment at the college was down, but the faculty was strong — as many as eight professors, four of whom had master of arts degrees in 1919. Robertson had just acquired an honorary doctorate from Dalhousie University. In his fifties, still a bachelor, he had spent three decades at the college, and was becoming as much of an institution as Alexander Anderson.

Along the way, another institution had left the scene. John Caven died in August 1914, and, on his passing, he got a better send-off than he had on his departure from the college. *The Guardian* described him as Charlottetown's "most highly cultured citizen." The Bishop of Charlottetown and numerous priests from across the Island attended his funeral service in St. Dunstan's Cathedral, and the leading men of the city — including the chief justice and former premier, Sir William W. Sullivan; a former lieutenant-governor, D. A. MacKinnon; and the current premier, J. A. Mathieson — carried his remains from the church.[86]

By the end of the decade, Caven was gone, Anderson had retired, and Robertson had travelled over a bumpy road at the college. In addition to wartime travails, a major epidemic, lost work time, and interminable complaints about the curriculum, Robertson had to watch, from the sidelines, the unfolding of the McGill affiliation fiasco. That issue represented a lost opportunity of incalculable dimensions. In the West, other colleges had gone ahead with affiliation plans, and were on their way to degree-granting status. In 1915, the University of British Columbia was inaugurated. In a letter of gratitude to Peterson, its chancellor wrote, "The benefit our Province has derived from your University's connection with it would be impossible to estimate. Many young people have received a university education for whom otherwise it would have remained an unaccomplished dream."[87]

As if the advancement of the western colleges were not enough, Prince of Wales was overtaken on its own turf. In 1917, St. Dunstan's won the right to grant degrees. In contrast to the McGill episode, there were no nasty surprises when the Conservative-dominated Legislature voted on a draft bill prepared by the St. Dunstan's board of governors. Of course, this proposal didn't cost the government any money — at least, not at the time. And Bishop Louis O'Leary had smoothed the way by asking A. E. Arsenault, minister without portfolio, to pilot the bill through the House, and enlisted the sympathy of a Catholic member of the Opposition to ensure that the Liberals would raise no objection. The bill passed on a voice vote on April 20, 1917, with only minor amendments. It allowed St. Dunstan's to grant degrees on its own — although it wouldn't exercise that right for another twenty-four years — as well as the power to expand as and when it wished.[88]

Meanwhile, Prince of Wales would not be able to expand appreciably for another sixteen years — and then only through the generosity of a private corporation. As Frank MacKinnon remarked, the public college had had its wings clipped. Whatever the motives were — and the final chapter on that issue has yet to be written — the political bosses had wielded the hatchet. And, in days to come, they would brandish a blunter instrument to let the academics know who was in charge. This time, in contrast to the McGill fiasco, everybody in the province would be only too aware of what was happening to Prince of Wales College.

Chapter Six

"A Great Teacher and a Great Soul"

6

"He lived for Prince of Wales College and gave his life for the welfare of its students. Their problems were his problems."
—*The College Times,* December 1937

In the packed assembly hall at Prince of Wales College, Samuel Robertson broke the news to a sombre audience of faculty and students: this was probably the last time, he said, that he would ever address them as a group. He was very sorry about the way things had turned out. Although he was no longer their principal, he would always be interested in their welfare. Some of the students wept.

The date was October 5, 1920. A few days earlier, the unthinkable had happened. All the professors at Prince of Wales College had resigned, and now the college was closed. The issue was salaries. The war had brought a measure of prosperity to the Island, as elsewhere in Canada, but inflation had pushed up the cost of living tremendously. Prices for consumer goods in Canada had risen 225 per cent since the outbreak of the war.[1] Times were especially hard for wage-earners. The long-suffering district school teachers, the lowest-paid in Canada, had formed a union in 1918. So many teachers were heading for better-paying jobs in Western Canada, there was a shortage of qualified teachers on the Island. Even the superintendent of schools, Col. R. H. Campbell, had resigned to take a teaching job in Saskatchewan. In 1919, when the teachers threatened to strike, the government caved in, promising to raise salaries by as much as 60 per cent. Now it was the turn of the college professors to get tough. Compared with the district teachers — and many other Islanders — the professors were well-paid. Salaries at the college ranged from a low of $800 for the art teacher to a high of $2,100 for the principal. Even the premier was making less than $1,800 a year. But most of the professors held bachelor's or master's degrees, qualifications that were uncommon in those days. They had been asking for a raise for a long time. They didn't think their demands were out of line: a raise of 33 1/3 per cent, at a time when other salaries had recently doubled or trebled.

The college faculty began to campaign in earnest in December 1919. Robertson and two of his staff, J.-H. Blanchard and Douglas Steel, paid a visit to the new premier, John Howatt Bell, a seventy-two-year-old Summerside lawyer who had led a Liberal sweep to power five months earlier. The premier seemed sympathetic, but asked the delegation to wait for a couple of months. To supplement provincial revenues, the government had just raised land taxes, changed the system of assessing the provincial income tax, and introduced a poll tax of $3 on every male over age 21.[2] Before making any commitments, Bell wanted to see how this would affect the bottom line.

Two months later, Steel and Blanchard again called on the premier, who again asked for patience. In the spring, yet another college delegation went to the cabinet. Members of the Legislature had just voted themselves raises of 150 per cent — to $500 from $200 — and approved $1,000 for the leader of the opposition. *The Guardian,* sympathetic to the professors but no friend of the Liberals, reported that the Bell government had also "appointed several hundred kindred spirits" to jobs throughout the province, and created a number of new government positions. "In fact," *The Guardian* remarked, "they had money to burn."[3]

At the close of the legislative session, and several times during the summer, Robertson knocked on the premier's door. Bell expressed sympathy and good will, but again called for patience. That was a quality that was becoming very scarce at the college. Robertson was trying to make peace, but was having trouble getting his staff back to work. He told the premier he had to have an answer before the college opened in the fall. "I explained that no principal could carry on successful work with a staff that was so dissatisfied," he said later. Bell again pleaded for time. "I promised we would stay on for a few days," Robertson said, "making it plain to him that I could not wait longer than until the end of September for a definite answer. The teaching staff, indeed, were unwilling to work at all under these conditions. I personally begged them to wait." Robertson then went back to the cabinet. "They assured me of their good will and told me that it certainly would be looked into."[4]

The college opened as usual in early September. When the paycheques arrived on Thursday, September 30, the faculty realized that nothing had been done. The professors wrote out their resignations that day and marched to the office of the provincial secretary-treasurer in the afternoon. Their display of bravado ended with the anti-climactic discovery that the office was closed that day. The next morning, they had more success. The strike was on. On Monday, the cabinet decided to close the college for two weeks, "in order to give time to the Government to ascertain if other teachers could not be had to fill the vacancies."[5] At that meeting, the cabinet drew up an advertisement that would be published in newspapers in Charlottetown, Summerside, Halifax, and Saint John:

"PRINCE OF WALES COLLEGE — TEACHERS WANTED
Applications will be received by the undersigned, to fill vacancies on the Teaching Staff of the Prince of Wales College, Charlottetown. Applicants must state qualifications and experience.

(Signed) Arthur Newbery, Asst. Provincial Secretary. 5th October, 1920."[6]

Editors of the Charlottetown newspapers were apoplectic. The very existence of Prince of Wales College was in jeopardy, they warned. In fact, the entire educational system of the Island could collapse! At the very least, the 240 students who had begun work in September and, in the case of country students, had settled into boarding houses, could lose a year's work. *The Guardian* placed the blame squarely on the shoulders of the Liberal government for treating the professors "with silent contempt," ignoring their requests and making false promises. "It is humiliating," the newspaper lamented, "to be obliged to admit that we have in this province ... a government so hopelessly imbecile as to permit such a calamity as this to fall upon its leading educational institution, an institution that for several generations has been our pride and boast and hope...."[7] *The Patriot,* loyal as ever to the Liberals, was equally indignant. The professors were both selfish and unpatriotic, the paper declared. "The Government did not close the college. The blame must rest with the teaching staff. They could beyond all question continue to carry on until the Government was in a position to meet or partly meet their demands."[8]

As the week went by, the war of words between the competing newspapers took on a life of its own. Each accused the other of lying. *The Guardian* charged its rival with "bluff and humbug" and "gross misrepresentations" of the position of the teaching staff.[9] *The Patriot* sputtered that the columns of *The Guardian* reeked, as usual, with slander and abuse of the Liberal government. Truth was "as foreign to the Guardian as decency is a stranger to its columns."[10] Furthermore, any newspaper that would try to justify a strike was "a menace to the peace and harmony of the community."[11]

In the torrent of daily insults between the two papers, the plight of the students — ostensibly the reason for such indignation — lay buried and almost forgotten. In spite of the dire predictions of the newspapers as to the future of education, the students' sympathy generally remained with their teachers. During the meeting in the assembly hall, when Robertson explained to students the professors' position, there were tears, cheers, and prolonged applause. Later in the week, third-year students wrote a long letter to *The Guardian,* praising Robertson's efforts on behalf of the college over many years, and defending the decision to strike. No teacher on the Island was qualified to replace the present staff, the students said, and nobody from the mainland would take the job of the principal, whose good reputation had spread far and wide. "Therefore, we feel that if any men are secured, they will be men of little scholarship and of no sense of honour."[12]

The students may have been right about the difficulty of finding suitable replacements. In any case, the two sides reached a settlement within the week. On Thursday, October 8, the professors asked permission from the premier to withdraw their resignations, "as we believe that it is in the best interests of the province that the students should again take up their class work at the earliest possible date."[13] Arthur Newbery, clerk of the executive council, informed Robertson immediately that the cabinet, "after due consideration," agreed to reinstate the teachers, and promised that the issue of salary increases "will receive their prompt attention."[14] The professors didn't get all they were asking for, but they did get a raise. Robertson's salary rose immediately to $2,400 from $2,100; Steel's to $2,000 from $1,700; Blanchard's and Bennett's to $1,700 from $1,400; and those of Russell Smith, Lily Seaman, and Annie McGrath to $1,400.[15]

The college reopened for business as usual on Tuesday, October 12. It had been closed for just over a week. The next spring, when Robertson was reviewing the year at the commencement exercises, he observed tactfully that despite "interruptions from various causes," work that year had been up to the usual standard.[16] After all the melodramatic pronouncements in the newspapers, the first and last strike at Prince of Wales had ended with hardly a whimper. It certainly could not be compared with the real disasters that would befall the college in the next two decades.

Still, the strike was memorable if only because it was so out of character for staid Prince of Wales College. Samuel Robertson was the most unlikely of revolutionaries. A somewhat shy, retiring man, he lived for his college, his church, and his books, and, aside from temperance work, had little to do with the rest of the community. His rebellious staff included the exceedingly proper Douglas Steel, the self-declared Liberal partisan Garfield Bennett, and young Miss Lily Seaman, so shy she taught all her classes with her eyes fixed on a corner of the room, or on the ceiling. And this odd band of renegades was operating in a conservative province with few labour unions and a very short history of strikes. The population was composed mainly of independent farmers who did not have much sympathy for either. *The Patriot*'s outrage over the college strike apparently stemmed not only from its affiliation with the Liberal Party but also from its horror of labour disputes in general. A strike, the paper said, was "the greatest weapon which agitators and revolutionists of the day, all over the world, are utilizing to hamper and destroy the governments of the nations."[17]

Of course, strikes were not the only modern phenomena that made *The Patriot* nervous. The post-war era, the paper observed, was a period of "vast unrest and dangerous instability," in which "dangerous agitators" had been brought to the shores of Prince Edward Island — presumably a reference to a visit to the Island by an organizer for the United Farmers of Prince Edward Island, one of the many political protest movements that sprang up after the war. Some of these organizations had even stolen Liberal stalwarts from the fold: in the 1921 federal election, Walter Jones and Horace Wright ran, unsuccessfully, for the Progressive Party based in Western Canada.[18]

There were other signs of the intrusion of the alien outside world into the Island's insular life. Battle-scarred young war veterans, sadder and wiser, were returning to school and work. Hemlines were rising to dangerous heights. Women were voting in both federal and provincial elections. Radios were bringing the voices of strangers into Island kitchens. Expatriates were arriving home from the Boston states for their summer vacations, driving automobiles, wearing American cottons, and showing off their newly minted Yankee accents.

Throughout all of this, Prince of Wales College remained as safe and comforting as a church. True, the country boys and girls who came to board in Charlottetown tended to be a bit giddy about their new-found freedom. “The first thing the girls did when they came to the college,” former art teacher Eleanor Lowe observed, “was to get a pair of earrings. And then they would colour their fingernails. The boys would get riding breeches. Sometimes their socks weren’t quite long enough to meet the breeches.” But in the college, even these fashion plates had to observe the strictest decorum: no smoking, no gum-chewing, no boisterous behaviour in the hallways. No skipping classes. No tardiness. No neglect of studies. No mingling of the sexes on the stairs.

For boys and girls from the country — in an era when cars and trips to town were few — Prince of Wales College was a long way from home. Fortunately (or unfortunately, depending on one’s point of view), they could hardly have found a more conscientious guardian than its upright, Bible-quoting principal. He was strict, firm, and often stern — and absolutely devoted to his charges. Robertson was a worrier. Were his students studying hard enough? Were they achieving “regularity” in their health habits? Were they dressed adequately for bad weather? “I remember one day he was at the door to check on latecomers,” said Lester Sellick, who enrolled in Prince of Wales in the late 1920s. “Some female students arrived dripping wet from the snow and the rain. He wanted to know what they had on underneath to keep them dry.”[19] Robertson encouraged male students to play football. At the very least, he wanted them to go for long walks and practise deep breathing to ward off tuberculosis, at that time a widespread and often deadly disease. He was greatly relieved when the college adopted a six-day week in 1924. Not only did it dispense with the two-day weekend interruption, with “its dissipation of time and energy,” but it also gave students time off in the afternoons. After classes were over, generally at 12:15 P.M., they could exercise out of doors and finish their homework early in the evening. Presumably he hoped they wouldn’t be tempted to use the rest of the day to have too much fun.

Robertson did not approve of social butterflies. For years, the students begged to be allowed to use the college auditorium for their Saturday evening socials. They were apparently innocent affairs, sponsored by the

Student Christian Movement, where young folks played games, sang, ate a lunch. Robertson refused. Instead, students had to gather on the third floor of the YMCA, or rent another hall downtown. "There was a fair bit of grumbling among the students," Helen MacKie MacDonald recalled. "Why was Dr. Robertson so strict?" Once, in an attempt to change the principal's mind, some students invited him to a party at the YMCA. As the evening got under way, they heard heavy footsteps on the stairs. "There, I told you the Doc was a good sport," someone said. "Now he's come to prove it!" Robertson stood in the doorway, arms akimbo. "I just wanted to see how many of you were up here wasting your parents' money, when you could be home studying," he said. Then he wheeled around and went back downstairs.[20]

Robertson was equally unimpressed by a Halloween tradition at Prince of Wales. Every year, students paraded through the streets on Halloween night and stopped by the homes of all the professors, shouting and singing. If the professors dared to come to the door, a group of boys would try to grab them and throw them in the air — an old Island tradition known as "bouncing." One year, some reckless students stood outside the principal's house on Upper Prince Street, chanting, "Come on out, Dr. Robertson!" The chanting became louder. Robertson finally appeared in his nightshirt. "You should be ashamed of yourselves, destroying the peace of the neighbourhood," he told them. "You're a disgrace to Prince of Wales College!"[21]

It is unlikely that anybody ever dared try to bounce Robertson, but Professor Blanchard, a rotund, genial, and extremely popular teacher who lived across the street, was fair game. "I can still see them bouncing Professor 'Peggy' Blanchard," Helen MacKie MacDonald said, "as he loudly protested, 'It's not funny, eh, boys? You're liable to break some of my bones, eh?'" One day, a few daredevils seized another professor in the college hallway, right under the principal's nose. The new mathematics professor, J. G. Paterson (nicknamed "Pansy" Paterson), had just dismissed his class, and was standing by the door when a group of boys picked him up. The classroom happened to be next door to the faculty office. "There was quite a hubbub," said Lloyd Lockerby, a farm boy from Hamilton who witnessed the crime. "Dr. Robertson came out of his office, and, just as he came out the door, Paterson was going up in the air." Fortunately for the young offenders, there was such confusion in the hallway, with students milling about to change classes, nobody was caught.

Part of Robertson's reputation as a strict disciplinarian stemmed from his belief that the goal of education should be to mould character as well as minds. That meant nurturing such virtues as responsibility, clean living, self-discipline, industry, and co-operation. "We hear talk about practical things," he observed in one convocation address. "People now know how to manufacture bombs and poison gas for the purpose of destruction; people have solved the problem of procuring food and clothing, but they have not learned how to live together. This is the work of education."[22]

At Prince of Wales, the logic of the rules for living together was not always obvious to the naked eye. Male and female students shared the same classrooms, yet were compelled to use separate stairways and entrances.[23] Skipping classes was an offence; yet, being a minute late could mean banishment for an entire period. Before classes began in the morning, Robertson would stand at the front door of the college, watch in hand. Only students who made it through the door on time were allowed to enter. As soon as the minute hand reached the 8:15 mark, he would shake his head and close the door. "He turned me back once," recalled Neil Matheson, a newspaper columnist and politician who attended Prince of Wales in the 1920s. "The chap just ahead of me got in. But I knew a back door we used in autumn for football practice, and I went to the back of the building and made the first class as though nothing had happened."[24]

Robertson was as dogged about tracking down truants as he was about catching latecomers. According to Matheson, two classmates, Steve Connolly and George Ayers, skipped second period — geometry — one morning, and hid in two large barrels in the basement. Robertson tracked them down, ordered them out, and led them upstairs "for the traditional lecture."[25] On another occasion, a chronic male truant hid in one of the lockers. "Dr. Robertson opened the locker and commanded, "Lazarus, come forth!" That student, Eleanor Lowe said, was known for the rest of his days as "Lazarus."

Apparently, Robertson did have a sense of humour. And he definitely had a soft side. He was always willing to help the underdog. "Although he was an ardent prohibitionist," Helen MacKie MacDonald wrote in her memoir about college days, "he never turned a drunk away from the door hungry. He was also known to have helped many a student." One day, he summoned one of MacDonald's friends to the principal's office. Robertson, noting that she was one of his brightest students, told her he hoped she planned to go on to university. She replied that, unfortunately, that was impossible. "I don't have a great deal of money myself," Robertson said, "but I'd be glad to help you out."[26] His acts of charity were not limited to high achievers. A former colleague, Theodore Ross, once told a story about a student who had failed his year at Prince of Wales. Robertson, hearing that he wanted to go out West, gave him the money to travel, never asking whether it would be repaid.[27] Many new students were intimidated by him at first, but later found him to be approachable and kind. Yet he was "merciless," as one of his faculty once remarked, when it came time to mark exams. And he wasn't above reprimanding his staff. Once he rebuked two of the young female professors, Eleanor Lowe and Lily Seaman, for setting a bad example by using the boys' stairs. But he never interfered with their teaching, and he worried about them as well as the students. When times were hard, he would order a carload of coal to distribute to the staff at rock-bottom prices. One of the Model School teachers used to call him "Saint Samuel." It is not clear whether this was a reference to his piety or to his genuinely charitable nature.

In any case, "Saint Samuel" had a few surprises up his sleeve. At the age of fifty-three, when it was widely assumed he had settled down to comfortable bachelorhood, he married Annie Laura McGrath, the forty-one-year-old English and botany professor. The marriage was quite a shock to his colleagues, who shared an office with him. Eleanor Lowe, for one, hadn't noticed any romantic sparks flying. Then there was the matter of religion. Robertson was an elder and Sunday school teacher in the Church of Scotland. Annie Laura was a staunch Roman Catholic from a family of twelve, raised on a farm in Norway, near Tignish. Two of her sisters were nuns; one brother was a priest. Annie Laura was a plain, dark-haired woman, exceptionally tall and thin. But she was also exceptionally bright and, according to a nephew, John R. McGrath of Norway, "a lovely person, kind and nice." He remembered hearing Robertson teasing her by saying, "I didn't marry her for her beauty — I married her for her knowledge." In fact, she was highly educated for her time: after graduating from Prince of Wales in 1911, she studied at Dalhousie, where she earned a bachelor of arts degree. She came from a family of achievers. Besides the siblings who had religious vocations, there were two doctors, a sea captain, and another teacher, Ella Mae McGrath, who taught commerce at Prince of Wales. For Samuel and Annie Laura, religion apparently was not an issue. There were no children to think about. He went to his church; she went to hers. "I remember him making sure that she got ready in time to go to church in the morning," McGrath said. "He'd put her in a taxi and send her off to the Basilica. And he paid to her church, too, as well as his own." Because Robertson was so highly respected, the marriage was not an issue for the McGrath family. (Religion did become an issue when Annie Laura died in 1953. She had insisted on being buried next to Samuel in the Sherwood cemetery. A priest who was a friend of the family said the funeral mass at her church, but there was no service at the graveyard. John McGrath, who was one of the pallbearers, recalled, "We just had five minutes of silence, and then they pressed a button and lowered the casket gently into the grave."[28]) Annie Laura resigned from the college when she got married. She and Samuel lived together on Upper Prince Street for fifteen apparently happy years. She brought out his softer side. Beatrice Blanchard, a neighbour who frequently visited the Robertson house as a child, once walked into the kitchen to find Robertson in the rocking chair with his wife on his knee. He was rocking and singing her a lullaby.[29] Samuel Robertson was, indeed, full of surprises.

A man with a supposedly narrow devotion to Latin and Greek, Robertson did some trail-blazing in fine arts at the college. One of his students was Eleanor Lowe, a talented artist who graduated from Prince of Wales in 1919. Robertson was a friend of her father's, Samuel Lowe, who had built the addition to the college in the early 1900s. Robertson persuaded Lowe to send his daughter to art school with a view to developing an art program at Prince of Wales. After a year at the Montreal Museum of Fine Arts and a few months at the Ontario College of Art, Eleanor began teaching drawing to pupils in the Model School. When Robertson saw what her pupils were accomplishing, he asked her to begin teaching first-year students. Art instruction was in its infancy in those days, and Eleanor had to devise her own program. But the art course at Prince of Wales gradually expanded. "Dr. Robertson had the feeling that you couldn't be a whole personality," Miss Lowe said, "unless you had something creative to do." The year the art classes began, Robertson also revived the music program under W. E. Fletcher. "No subject can add greater brightness to the schoolroom," Robertson commented in his annual report that year.[30]

There were a few other changes in the curriculum and organization of the college in the 1920s. In response to popular demand, the college added a commercial course in 1924, and later revamped the teacher-training program. In 1927, Robertson separated the first-year students for the first time into two streams — one for those who wanted a general education, and another for students who planned to become teachers. Robertson thought that this change would enhance both programs. The curriculum for university-bound students could be upgraded to ensure that they got full credit for their three years at Prince of Wales, and a reduction in the size of teacher-training classes would make it easier to organize practice-teaching sessions in the Model School.

In those days, Prince of Wales was still primarily a teacher-training school. When the classes were first divided into two streams, fewer than ten per cent planned to follow a strictly academic path. Teaching was increasingly becoming a profession for women. Partly for this reason, women still vastly outnumbered men at the college — two to one by 1931. And country students outnumbered those from town. Of an enrolment of 237 in 1920, for instance, only 58 were from Charlottetown. Most of the country students had to board in town.

At Prince of Wales, there were limits to how closely these students could be shielded from the temptations of the city, even for a patriarch as vigilant as Robertson. Students in residence at St. Dunstan's College lived a sheltered life twenty-four hours a day. They received religious instruction daily, were obliged to go to Mass every morning, and were prohibited from going to town, except on Thursday afternoons, without permission.[31] The only comparable situations for Prince of Wales students were church-run residences off-campus. Roman Catholic girls lived at Notre Dame Convent, which had its own strict rules. And a few of the luckier Protestant girls were housed in one of Charlottetown's grandest residences, Henry Cundall's old home near Victoria Park (later known as Beaconsfield). Run by an Anglican Church deaconess, it provided a sheltered environment that complemented the atmosphere at the college. Elizabeth MacDougall Brown, the daughter of a schooner captain in Belle River, lived at the Cundall Home with about twenty other residents when she attended Prince of Wales in the mid-1920s. The church officials imposed a curfew, gave lessons in etiquette, organized religious services. Occasionally, a couple of the girls rebelled and slipped out the window after curfew. Elizabeth wasn't one of them. She didn't mind the restrictions at the Cundall Home; she didn't get out much in Belle River, either. Every evening after supper, the young ladies gathered in the common room for a religious service. "We sang hymns we never heard before," she recalled. "'The Day Thou Gavest, Lord, Is Ended' — that was one. It was the most wonderful opportunity for country girls who had never been anywhere and never been exposed to anything on the outside. But we were just ignorant country girls, and we didn't realize how lucky we were compared with others living in boarding houses."

Wallace and Isobel Andrew of East Royalty lived close enough to town to travel there by car in summer or horse and sleigh in winter. They used to tie up the horse behind the MacLean Funeral Home on King's Square. Taking a shortcut to the college, they would go in the back entrance of the funeral home, walk through the embalming room, and leave by the front door to King's Square. In Wallace's third winter, 1931, he boarded at the funeral home. The family lived on the second floor. "They were wonderful people," he said. "There was only one person on duty at night, so if they were short of help during the evening and needed to go get a body, I frequently would volunteer to go with them."

Few students had such unconventional boarding arrangements. Georgia Matheson of Albion, who later married Wallace Andrew, was more typical. During her first year, she lived with her uncle, a rather strict clergyman, but had much more fun the next year when she moved to a boarding house with a group of other female students. Room and board cost $3.50 to $6 a week, which made sending a young person to college a considerable hardship. In the early 1920s, two sons of Peter and Elizabeth Brehaut of Guernsey Cove were at Prince of Wales at the same time. Money was so scarce, Cecil and Roy Brehaut shared a navy serge suit, which they sent to their mother periodically to be cleaned. She would send the suit back with a few coins in the pocket for emergencies.[32] In the Depression years, when farm prices plummeted, it was no wonder that some students had to accept the cheapest possible living arrangements. According to *The College Times* issue of March 1931, as many as six girls were packed into a room at one boarding house. "One can imagine the confusion in that room when studying time came," *The Times* commented.

In theory, the college administration scrutinized all boarding houses. "All students shall live in approved houses of lodging," the 1932–33 college *Calendar* noted. "They will be visited from time to time by a member of the teaching staff." In practice, there was little Robertson could do — except worry. "Each session," he wrote in the mid-1930s, "there occur failures of capable students definitely attributable to this cause. In selecting residences for the session, parents must see to it that their children are properly guarded from lurking disease, and from the many disturbing factors that make impossible the peace and quiet so necessary for study."[33]

It was a wonder that parents were able to send their children to college at all. In the fall of 1930, prices for farm products plummeted, setting off reverberations throughout the entire Island economy. By 1931, the economic crisis was so bad, the new premier, J. D. Stewart, noted that delegations of Islanders were calling on him daily for help for destitute rural residents.[34] Oddly enough, enrolment climbed to 380 in 1930–31, and to 477 in 1931–32. Robertson attributed the marked increase to a greater appreciation of education by Islanders — a theory that must have cheered him, considering his longstanding despair over the public school dropout rate. Possibly, though, some of the increase might have been due to the Depression: if you can't find a job, you might as well go to college. (In the same period, enrolment at Mount Allison University stayed at about the 400 mark; Dalhousie University enrolment increased both years, although it began dropping in the mid-1930s.)[35]

The increased enrolment made the college uncomfortably crowded. And, despite Robertson's frequent complaints, there still was no reference library. In his annual report for 1931–32, however, he was sounding positively cheerful. Many renovations had been carried out. There were two new classrooms, one on the third floor and another on the second; the typing room in the commercial department had been enlarged; the college had new hardwood flooring, new furniture in two of the classrooms, and a new coat of paint. "Possibly never was the building in better form or condition to do its intended work than it was to begin the present session," Robertson wrote. "Never in a larger measure did it command the respect and loyalty of the students and teachers."[36]

Never was a principal's report more destined to haunt its author.

In the early morning hours of Saturday, February 6, 1932, fire broke out in the central section of the college. The alarm was turned in about 3:20 A.M. By the time firemen arrived, flames were belching from the windows and soaring upward. Nothing could stop this fire. As it progressed, rafters, walls, and masonry tottered and crashed. Moments before the central stairway was engulfed in flames, the janitor, Patrick Ryan, and his family fled in their nightclothes. Two firemen aiming hoses at the northwest wall narrowly escaped injury when the wall collapsed, sending down a shower of bricks. Even in sections of the building not yet ablaze, the heat was so intense, it was impossible to enter the building to save anything. Everything was lost — irreplaceable records, books, furniture, laboratory equipment.

The fire lit up the night sky for miles around. Eleanor Lowe awoke in the middle of the night. Through her bedroom window, she saw a red reflection in the sky. She went to the phone and called the telephone operator. "I said, 'Is that the college?' 'Yes,' she said, 'I'm afraid it is.'" In the morning, Miss Lowe walked over to Weymouth Street. Nothing was left of the college but a gaunt chimney and piles of black, smoking rubble. She was devastated. Prince of Wales College was home to her. She had gone to the Model School as a child, had studied at the college, had embarked on a career there. "What is going to become of us?" she asked herself. While she was staring at the ruins, a group of boys came up Cumberland Street. "It was all new to them. They had never heard anything in the night, had never read *The Guardian* or anything. They just stood there, stupefied, at those bits of ruins. At last, one of them found his voice. He said, 'Perhaps there won't be any classes this morning.'"

Some of the country students made plans to go home, thinking that classes would not be held for a week or more. "We were all nonplussed as to how we were to continue with our work," recalled Horace MacEwen, then a third-year student. The board of education didn't waste time figuring that out. On Sunday, the board decided that all college classes would be held in the afternoons in two city schools: first-year students at Prince Street School and second- and third-year students at Queen Square School. Classes began Monday afternoon. "Poor Dr. Robertson looked like a wreck that day, for the blow was a heavy one to him," MacEwen said. "He had taught in that building since its construction." Robertson and other professors had also lost their personal libraries, as well as irreplaceable notes from years of study.

The new arrangement was inconvenient for everybody, including the teachers and pupils at Prince Street and Queen Square, who had their schedules disrupted. "The teachers there didn't like the visitors much at all," Eleanor Lowe said. Professors had to scurry between Prince Street and Queen Square between periods. Somehow, though, it all worked out. St. Dunstan's College agreed to share its chemistry laboratory at the end of the term, despite the fact that it was a male students' school and Prince of Wales would be sending young ladies. Convocation exercises were held that year in the auditorium of Rochford Square School. Students adapted to the new regimen, but mourned their loss. In its April 1932 issue, in an article entitled "The Great Disaster," *The College Times* wrote, "A deep sense of loss was universal in the student body.... The building like a staunch old friend had ever been taken for granted.... Nor was regret arising from attachment confined to the student body alone. Men and women, former students, and in various parts of the world, and in various walks of life, heard with peculiar sorrow that Prince of Wales College was no more."[37]

There were at least two silver linings in that cloud. One was that former students, perhaps motivated by that sense of loss, decided to form an alumni association. That spring, C. H. B. Longworth, a prominent Charlottetown businessman, was elected president of the new Prince of Wales College Alumni Society, which included in its executive committees such luminaries as Dr. Cyrus Macmillan, head of English at McGill; Roman Catholic Archbishop J. C. McGuigan; and L. M. Montgomery. *The College Times* was especially cheered by Longworth's election. "He is much in favour that the students should have the College Hall for their social functions," the student newspaper reported, "and has made efforts in that direction."[38] While sad about the loss of the college, Lloyd Lockerby gave thanks for a blessing on a personal level: the results of his algebra exam had gone up in smoke. "I never was proficient in algebra," he said many years later. "I didn't pass Entrance in algebra, and I was slated to write the exam later at Prince of Wales. But they lost track of my failure in algebra, so I never did have to write it."

For the provincial government, the fire could hardly have occurred at a worse time. Two months earlier, the Falconwood Insane Asylum had burned down. With farm prices in freefall, many taxpayers were going in debt. The government had been trying desperately to balance its own budget, even refusing to borrow from Ottawa to finance relief programs.[39] The monetary loss of the Prince of Wales building was estimated at $250,000. There was $150,000 of insurance on the building, and another $10,000 on the equipment.

In spite of the hard economic times, the Conservative government of Premier J. D. Stewart decided to replace the college immediately. In contrast to previous construction projects at the college, the government hired off-Island architects and an off-Island general contractor. This did not sit well with some Islanders. A Toronto firm, Marani, Lawson and Morris, won the design contract, for which it was paid $14,863.[40] Charlottetown architects James E. Harris and E. S. Blanchard protested that the competition had been unfair and the hiring unwise. Putting local people in charge of construction not only would circulate money at home, they argued in a letter to *The Guardian*, it would also keep costs down. "What does the Government know of the materials that the Toronto gentleman employed may specify for our building, where conditions are so radically different from those which he has been used to work in?" they asked.[41] A Sherbrooke, Quebec, firm, the Stewart Construction Company, won the contract to build the college, submitting the lowest bid of $249,814. The Quebec company beat out twenty-one others from across Canada, including two from Charlottetown — McDougall and MacAulay, and Phillips Clark and Fitzgerald.[42] Off-Island firms also won many of the subcontracts. Every step of the way, *The Guardian*, faithful as always to the governing Conservatives, defended the process. Of the 149 men employed on the job, the paper pointed out, 121 were Islanders, in accordance with the government's desire to provide local employment. Local bricklayers were passed over only because they lacked the required experience. The project was not behind schedule — contrary to reports in "The Evening Liberal Organ" — because of delays in obtaining steel. The new building would be open for business, as scheduled, after the Christmas holidays.

On the last point, at least, the paper was not far wrong. In late January 1933, students moved into the new building, a two-storey, Georgian-style structure of red brick and stone. The new college was about a third larger than the old one, and had a larger playing field, as the site was between Weymouth Street and the foundation of the old building. Inside, there were four laboratories with modern equipment, twenty-three bright classrooms, two libraries (one for students and the other for a provincial library system), an auditorium with vaulted ceiling, a Model School with five classrooms, four stairways, washrooms, storage rooms, offices, cloakrooms, and a domestic science department and storage room in the basement. Showing admirable restraint, *The Patriot*'s editor observed, "We will not at present enter into a discussion as to whether the enlarged and improved accommodations now being provided in the Prince of Wales College could have been provided at less cost with the same measure of efficiency. That will be a matter for further consideration when the full details of the expenditures are made known later."[43] The final cost of about $275,000[44] would indeed be subject of "further consideration": two years later, the Conservatives were wiped out, partly on the issue of government spending.

For the time being, though, there was great excitement over the new facility. When the college reopened, with much fanfare, on February 16, *The Patriot*, swallowing its political bias, heralded the government's newest creation with a screaming headline on the front page: "Magnificent New Temple of Learning Opened; New Epoch in the Educational Annals of Our Province Ushered in Last Evening."[45] As in the opening of the old building three decades earlier, the audience overflowed the auditorium. The chairman was Dr. W. J. P. MacMillan, who, as minister of education, had overseen the construction. He read a message from the current Prince of Wales (later Edward VIII), who must have wondered where Charlottetown was, but said he was glad to hear about the new building: "I send my best wishes on the occasion of this re-opening ceremony for the successful program of the Institution which bears my name." The guest speaker was the head of the McGill English department, Cyrus Macmillan, a native of Wood Islands who had studied and taught at Prince of Wales, and later served as a federal cabinet minister. "Tonight in this building," he told the audience, "we have a renewal of our educational faith — a realization of our pioneers' dreams. It is another of what the poet would call 'God's lamps' in a sorely perplexed and blindly groping world. Its splendour soon or late will help to pierce the gloom with the light of attainable truth...." On the platform, decked out in evening dress and academic gowns, were the leading men and women of the province and beyond, including the Roman Catholic Bishop of Charlottetown, the lieutenant-governor, members of the cabinet and the judiciary, and the college faculty. One important person was absent: Principal Robertson stayed home, pleading illness. Some of his students, including Horace MacEwen, were skeptical about his excuse: "He did not like public celebrations, so there was some doubt as to the validity of this affliction."[46]

There was no doubt about Robertson's delight in the new quarters. "The building is satisfying all expectations," he wrote in his report for the 1933–34 school year. He praised the wide corridors, the well-ventilated classrooms, the enlarged chemistry laboratories, the new physics and biology labs. Most satisfying of all, from Robertson's point of view, was the fulfilment of two

Historic roots. At a 1967 open house highlighting plans to expand Prince of Wales College (recently elevated to university status), Dr. Frank MacKinnon, PWC Principal, examines the 1834 Royal Charter for the college's forebear, Central Academy. [Photo album compiled by Prince of Wales College publicity office, late 1960s] UPEI Archives: *PWC Scrapbook #3*

Sir William C. Macdonald. A student at the Central Academy in the late 1840s, Macdonald went on to wealth and fame as "Canada's Tobacco King," and established himself as one of the Canada's leading educational philanthropists. Best known for his extraordinary generosity to McGill University, he also supported PWC, funding a new wing for the college building in 1907. PEI Public Archives and Records Office: *Acc. # 4170/26*

HRH Edward, the Prince of Wales (1841–1910). [From a painting by Jane E. Reagh, donated to the University of Prince Edward Island by the PWC Class of 1938, on the occasion of their 50th reunion.] UPEI Art Collection: *Acc. # 242*

Dr. Alexander Inglis, first Principal of Prince of Wales College (1860–1868). [From a pen-and-ink sketch donated to UPEI by Royal Roads Military College, 1980] UPEI Archives: *Special Collections Photo/Art Drawer—Prince of Wales College*

"The Lion of Prince of Wales": Dr. Alexander Anderson, PWC's second Principal (1868–1901), was widely praised for his work as a professor and administrator, and as a tireless advocate for improvements at the college and in the Island's public school system. After his long tenure at PWC, Anderson became PEI's Superintendent of Education. PEI Public Archives and Records Office: *Acc. # 3381/4*

Jacob Gould Schurman. Born on a farm near Summerside, Schurman won a scholarship to attend PWC in the early 1870s, marking the start of a brilliant career in academia—culminating in his presidency of Cornell University (1892–1920) and in the US diplomatic corps. Schurman once remarked, "I have sat under many instructors ... but I have never yet met such a great teacher as Prof. Anderson." Cornell University Archives

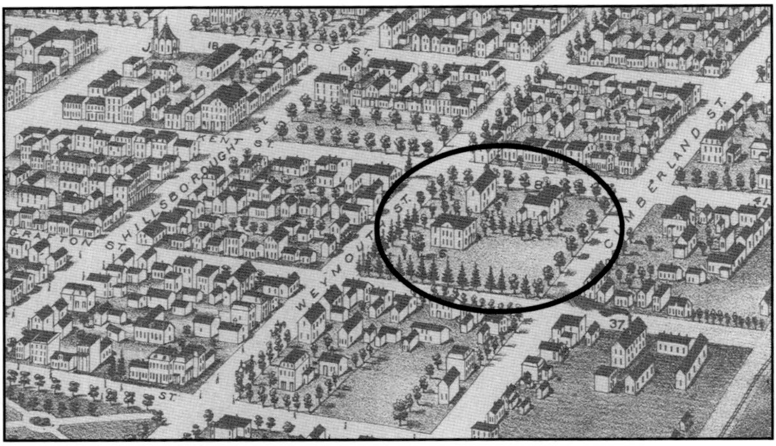

This detail from a reprint of an 1878 panoramic sketch of Charlottetown shows the PWC building on its campus near the intersection of Weymouth and Grafton streets, a site the college occupied until its demise in 1969, and which went on to become the main city campus of Holland College. UPEI Robertson Library: *PEI Collection Map Gallery (# 6)* [Used with the kind permission of the PEI Museum and Heritage Foundation]

Sir Andrew Macphail. After attending PWC on scholarship in the early 1880s, Macphail went on to win national renown—and a knighthood—as a physician, scholar, and writer. Like other distinguished PWC alumni, such as J. G. Schurman, he would later praise Dr. Anderson as the best teacher he had ever known. [Detail from a painting by Alphonse Jongers, 1924] UPEI Art Collection: *Acc. # 118*

In the earliest known photograph of a PWC class, Dr. Anderson poses with his first-year students in the autumn of 1888. UPEI Archives: *Prince of Wales College—Photographs—Vertical File #1 (#10)*

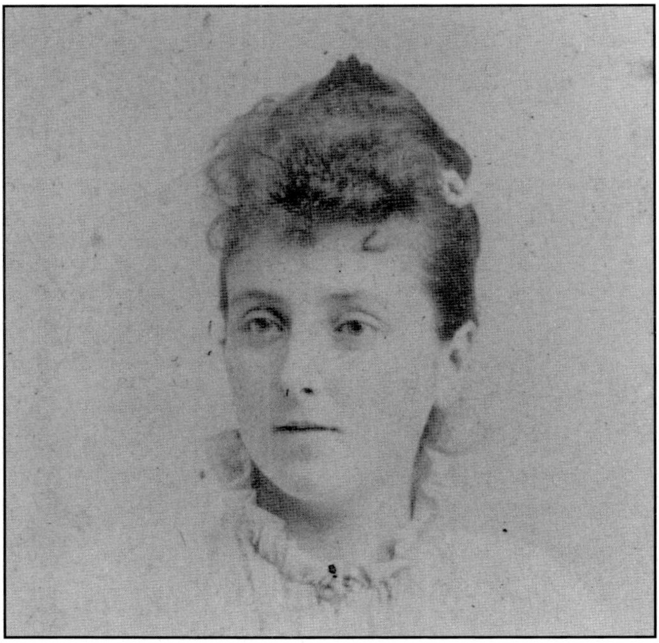

Lucy Maud Montgomery. Years before achieving international fame as the author of *Anne of Green Gables* and scores of other novels, stories, and poems, eighteen-year-old Montgomery attended PWC in the 1893–94 school year to study for her teacher's licence. Montgomery later described her time at the college as "the happiest year of my life." PEI Public Archives and Records Office: *Acc. # 2320/38-1*

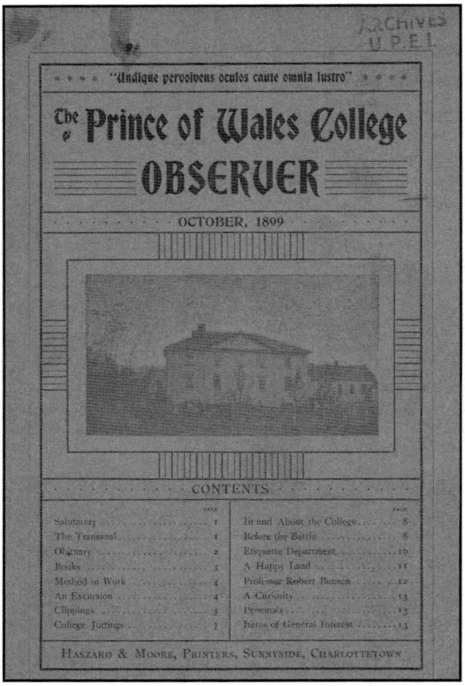
"Undique pervolvens oculos caute omnia lustro"

The Prince of Wales College OBSERVER

OCTOBER, 1899

CONTENTS

	PAGE		PAGE
Salutatory	1	In and About the College	8
The Transvaal	1	Before the Battle	8
Obituary	2	Etiquette Department	10
Books	3	A Happy Land	11
Method in Work	4	Professor Robert Bunsen	12
An Excursion	4	A Curiosity	13
Clippings	5	Personals	13
College Jottings	7	Items of General Interest	13

HASZARD & MOORE, PRINTERS, SUNNYSIDE, CHARLOTTETOWN

In introducing this early issue of PWC's first student periodical, the editor noted, "In every enterprising college, it is customary for the students to publish a paper edited by themselves." UPEI Archives: *Prince of Wales College—Newspapers—*The Prince of Wales College Observer*—Vertical File*

PWC Hockey Team—Intercollegiate Champions, 1901. *Back row, left to right*: F. Sterns, G. Sutherland, E McLean. *Middle row, left to right*: J. Brehaut, Lester Sharp (Captain), C. J. McMillan (President), R. Holman. *Front*: S. McArthur. From modest beginnings in the late 1800s, PWC developed a strong tradition of student athletics, with ice hockey a particular favourite. This photo attests to an early victory over local rivals, the St. Dunstan's University "Saints." UPEI Archives: *Prince of Wales College—Photographs—Photo Drawer (#7)*

This photograph, presumably taken in 1899, shows the much-maligned original PWC building in the foreground, with its long-awaited replacement under construction behind. PEI Public Archives and Records Office: *Acc. # 2301/76*

J.-H. "Peggy" Blanchard, a popular and long-serving PWC professor, in front of the second college building in 1922. UPEI Archives: *Prince of Wales College—Photographs—Vertical File # 2 (# 10c)*

One of the earliest known group photographs of PWC teaching staff, taken ca. 1900, showing Dr. Anderson (*seated, middle right*) near the end of his tenure as principal, and Dr. Samuel Napier Robertson (*seated, front right*) as he was about to begin his. Also shown is John Caven (*standing, back right*), a long-serving professor at PWC, who would, like Anderson, leave the college shortly after this photo was taken. The identity of the others is uncertain, although the woman is likely Alexandra Scott, teacher of the "Infant Department" at the Model School.
UPEI Archives: *Prince of Wales College—Photographs—Photo Drawer (#8)*

"A great teacher and a great soul": Dr. Samuel Napier Robertson, PWC's third principal (1901–1937), and the first born on PEI, took a more understated approach to his work than his predecessor, but still inspired great affection and respect in his students and colleagues, building on the high academic and disciplinary standards set by Anderson. UPEI Archives: *Prince of Wales College—Photographs—Vertical File #1*

Annie Laura McGrath, BA, professor of English and botany at PWC, posts she resigned when, at the age of 41, she married Dr. Robertson. Despite the circumstances of their meeting, and the fact that Robertson was an elder in the Church of Scotland while McGrath was a devout Catholic, the marriage seems to have caused no scandal, perhaps reflecting the esteem in which both were held. UPEI Archives: *Prince of Wales College—Class Photographs Gallery (1918–1919)*

PWC's second building was a handsome edifice of brick and stone, further enhanced by a sizable 1907 addition, financed by William Macdonald. This photograph was taken ca. 1930, shortly before the building's destruction by fire. PEI Public Archives and Records Office: *Acc. # 2301/90*

"The Great Disaster." This snapshot shows the destruction wrought by a massive fire at PWC on February 6, 1932: fortunately, there were no injuries (the blaze broke out in the early hours of a Saturday morning), but the building and its contents were lost. Incredibly, college classes resumed two days later, in temporary quarters at nearby city schools. [from a scrapbook compiled by PWC Class of '32, on the occasion of their 50th reunion] UPEI Archives: *PWC Scrapbook #4*

"Magnificent New Temple of Learning." PWC had better luck with its third, and final, building. Despite political wrangles over contracts and costs, it opened to students in January 1933, less than a year after the great fire. A third larger than its predecessor, this building continued to serve PWC until 1969. PEI Public Archives and Records Office: *PEI Museum and Heritage Foundation Collection Acc. # 3466 HF 70.2933.8*

"... you had to respect him." A long-serving professor and vice-principal at PWC, Dr. G. Douglas Steel became the college's third principal (1937–1949) following Dr. Robertson's sudden death. Although sometimes criticized as overly strict, he was well-liked by many of his colleagues and students, and respected for his firm and fair enforcement of the high academic and disciplinary standards set by his predecessors. UPEI Archives: *PWC Scrapbook #6 [Ivan Mitchell album]*

Wearing a blood-stained sword, and carrying a bulging sack labeled "The Army," the God of War reaches greedily for PWC in this editorial cartoon from the December 1943 issue of *The College Times*. Dozens of PWC students enlisted in the armed forces during the Second World War, and by 1942 virtually every able-bodied male student was taking some form of military training. UPEI Archives: *Prince of Wales College—Newspapers—*The College Times *(vol. 20, issue 1, p.55)*

With so many young men in the military, PWC and St. Dunstan's were unable to form their own hockey teams for the 1944–45 season and so created a joint squad, "The Collegians." An amalgam of two teams with a long-standing rivalry, and comprised mainly of small, very young players, "The Collegians" were greeted with some scepticism, but led the tough Summerside/Charlottetown league in scoring and finished the season in second place. Nick Nicolle Family Collection

Left to right): Students Mary Sigsworth, Joan Sherren, and Michelle Raymond outside PWC, ca. 1948. Following its 1879 amalgamation with the provincial Normal School, only PWC offered higher education to women on PEI (St. Dunstan's University was not co-educational until 1942). There were soon large numbers of female students at the college, and, as early as the 1890s, they were sometimes in the majority. By the time of this photo, teaching was only one of many fields of study pursued by PWC women, and they were active in all aspects of campus life (including ice hockey). UPEI Archives: *PWC Scrapbook #6 [Ivan Mitchell album]*

"... a man of vision and action." Dr. Frank MacKinnon was only 30 years old, but already a distinguished scholar when he was invited back to the Island to serve as PWC's fifth principal (1949–1968). MacKinnon's bold and ambitious style attracted both fierce criticism and deep loyalty, but his passionate dedication to PWC and PEI was never in doubt, and he would see his school elevated to university status in 1965. PEI Public Archives and Records Office: *Acc. # 2320/37-6*

This picture, taken ca. 1950, likely shows one of the last occasions when the PWC faculty was small enough to be photographed as a group. In the years ahead, demographic forces and MacKinnon's energetic leadership would drive considerable growth in all elements of PWC, including its teaching staff. UPEI Archives: *Prince of Wales College—Photographs—Vertical File # 2 (# 14)*

In a posed publicity photograph, students "relax" in the library of PWC's Montgomery Hall, a four-storey dormitory with adjoining library, dining hall, and common room, opened in the fall of 1961. The name was a tribute to L. M. Montgomery, PWC's most famous alumna and just one of the many who had, in years past, been forced by the college's lack of a residence to rely on unsatisfactory housing off-campus. [Photo album compiled by Prince of Wales College publicity office, late 1960s] UPEI Archives: *PWC Scrapbook #3*

This architect's model, displayed at a 1967 open house, shows some of the ambitious expansion plans contemplated by PWC following its elevation to university status. The grand concourse across Weymouth Street and other new buildings—modeled here in dark wood—were never constructed, although the existing PWC buildings served as one of two UPEI campuses during the 1969–1970 academic year, and then became the main campus for Holland College. [Photo album compiled by Prince of Wales College publicity office, late 1960s] UPEI Archives: *PWC Scrapbook #3*

In September 1967 PWC awarded its first university degrees—albeit honourary—to a number of prominent figures, most notably former principal G. D. Steel and Prime Minister Lester B. ("Mike") Pearson. After the ceremony, jubilant PWC students pulled Pearson and his wife through the streets of Charlottetown in a buggy. [Photo album compiled by Prince of Wales College publicity office, late 1960s] UPEI Archives: *PWC Scrapbook #3*

T. M. Lothian, MA, PWC's interim principal (1968–1969). After Dr. MacKinnon's resignation in 1968 (the resignations of sixteen other PWC faculty soon followed), the unhappy task of overseeing PWC's final year of operation fell to Lothian, a biology professor who had also served for several years as chair of PWC's Science faculty. UPEI Archives: *Prince of Wales College—Yearbooks—The Welshman (1968–59)*

On May 16, 1969, PWC's final convocation procession leaves the Confederation Centre of the Arts (established only a few years earlier, largely through the efforts of—ironically enough—Dr. Frank MacKinnon), after more than sixty graduates received the college's first and last Bachelor's degrees. One year (less a day) later, the first graduates of the new University of Prince Edward Island would, quite literally, follow in their footsteps in a ceremony held at the same site. UPEI Archives: *Prince of Wales College—Yearbook—*The Welshman *(1968–69)*

long-standing desires. One was the addition of a fourth year and three new subjects: biology, sociology, and economics. The college had come within a hair's breadth of attaining junior college status in 1907, when affiliation with McGill was being proposed. Now the fourth year, providing the equivalent of the second year of university, was possible, thanks to a grant from the Carnegie Corporation of New York, which had long been interested in education in the Maritimes.[47] During the planning stage for the new building, the minister of education had asked the corporation's president, Dr. F. P. Keppel, to come to the Island to discuss the possibility of financial help. Carnegie officials had already talked to Robertson and the rector of St. Dunstan's, Dr. James Murphy, about financing shared science facilities. That idea had fallen through, partly because of the two-mile distance between the two colleges. Keppel's visit produced better results. Three months later, the corporation announced grants of $4,500 to Prince of Wales and $1,800 to St. Dunstan's, spread over three years, for their respective libraries. The corporation also promised $60,000 (which later was increased to $110,000) to set up a circulating library system for the province, and $75,000 to endow a chair of economics and sociology at Prince of Wales, with the understanding that the college would share the new professor with St. Dunstan's.[48]

The new man was John T. Croteau, a tall, portly American fresh out of graduate school at Clark University in Worcester, Massachusetts. Croteau and Robertson did not see eye to eye. For one thing, Croteau disapproved of the "ruthless" examination system at Prince of Wales. It was not unusual, he complained, to see a third of the student body fail at the end of a semester. In the Entrance Examinations, the failure rate hovered around 50 per cent. Many Islanders would have agreed with Croteau. A royal commission in 1930, headed by Cyrus Macmillan, found that the failure rate was what people criticized most about the college. The commission blamed an inadequate public school system. Even when students passed the Entrance Exams, it said, they often did so by simply memorizing specific texts, and were ill-prepared for the rigours of first-year work at the college. Croteau blamed the rigid standards at Prince of Wales, which he said stemmed from a deliberate policy of reducing the population pressure on the Island by preparing a few young people for life elsewhere. "It was true that those who were successful at Prince of Wales were pretty sure to succeed anywhere else," he wrote in a memoir of his stay on the Island, "but the culling process led to a waste of good material. I always suspected that Dr. Robertson was influenced by a religious belief in predestination; those who succeeded under such a difficult system were the elect. Personally he was one of the most charitable men in the community. He paid many a poor boy's way through college, and gave quantities of food and coal to poor families in the town. Yet when it came to marks and grades he was merciless."[49]

In Croteau's opinion, the system at St. Dunstan's was more humane. The rector, Dr. James Murphy, had taught at Prince of Wales before he became a priest, but he differed sharply from Robertson in both temperament and philosophy. Murphy was a convivial public-relations man who easily cultivated useful connections in the community; Robertson had none of those skills.[50] Croteau preferred Murphy's educational philosophy: "Dr. Murphy did not believe so much in the exclusive education of an elite, but wanted to broaden the base of education and to make the influence of his university felt in the community at large, rather than among a highly-educated student body."[51]

To be fair, Robertson, like Anderson, had always pleaded for improvements to the district school system, complained constantly about the high dropout rate in the schools, and insisted that Island children were entitled to better-qualified and more mature teachers. His route to the salvation of the community lay in upgrading the schools, maintaining high standards in higher education, and providing decent libraries. He was particularly enamoured of the circulating library located in the basement of Prince of Wales. It was, he wrote in 1935, "the great implement to accomplish the education of the people of this province." Once out of school, Islanders who used the library could continue their education for their entire lives. "Then only," he wrote, "shall one know the meaning of 'Adult Education' and its method."[52]

Croteau had quite a different vision of adult education. It involved fundamental changes in society. A couple of years after he arrived on the Island, he went to St. Francis Xavier University in Antigonish, Nova Scotia, to study a social-reform movement that had originated there. It promised to promote economic development by teaching adults, mainly through study groups, how to improve their lives by forming self-help groups such as credit unions and co-operatives. Croteau was an enthusiastic convert. He began organizing study clubs on the Island and broadcasting lectures on adult education over the Charlottetown radio station. When it came time to finance and broaden this program, the government, St. Dunstan's College, and the Bishop of Charlottetown, J. A. O'Sullivan, were supportive, as were a few of the Protestant churches. Robertson was not. "The whole idea of the movement, to inaugurate an adult education programme which would enable the common people, themselves, to better their economic circumstances, was foreign to Dr. Robertson's philosophy of education," Croteau said.[53] Nevertheless, Croteau continued to teach at both colleges. In the evenings, he and the regional librarian, Bramwell Chandler, travelled the Island's red-clay roads to hold meetings with farmers and fishermen. By the end of 1937, there were 338 study groups across the province, with 4,300 members. Credit unions and co-operatives sprang up like dandelions in the spring. In a dark time, they gave people hope.

As the co-operative movement blossomed, so did St. Dunstan's. The Catholic college — hamstrung as always by lack of funds, suffering now from dropping enrolments, and conscious of the need to upgrade its teaching staff and facilities — finally found its feet. When the co-operative movement began, the college had quietly helped expand the adult education program. The extension department, formed in 1937, gradually became more and more pivotal in the field work of the movement. The department's role enhanced the status of the college among both Catholics and Protestants, and boosted its own self-esteem. "Size and shortcomings notwithstanding," historian Edward MacDonald has observed, "the College could pride itself as being on the cutting edge of an exciting new philosophy of adult education."[54]

Prince of Wales College, on the other hand, remained detached. While one of its professors was energetically preaching the gospel of social reform, the college clung to its traditional role, and its usual standards. As this anonymous submission to the December 1936 issue of *The College Times* indicates, Christmas was still more of a trial than a celebration for some people at Prince of Wales:

Too Bad! Very Sad!

Boy in college
Not for Knowledge
No one misses

After Christmas:
Boy who lays
Away his days
Smiling at girls
With pretty curls.
So take heed
And boy'll not need
To heave a sigh
When others pass by
To College
For Knowledge.

But even at Prince of Wales, change was inevitable. As the Depression deepened, enrolment dropped. The record enrolment in 1933–34 of 570 fell the next year to 461, and the year after that to 401.[55] The college continued to turn out 150 to 200 new teachers every year, despite a new regulation that had raised the pass mark for student teachers to 65 per cent. Their job prospects were grim; as teaching jobs evaporated off-Island, teacher shortages turned into teacher surpluses.

As if the deprivations of the Depression were not enough, rumours of war were again drifting across the Atlantic. If the pages of the college newspaper are any indication, the naivety and blind patriotism of pre-1914 days had been replaced by caution, if not outright pacifism. "Many believed the last war was the war to end war," the lead editorial in the May 1934 *College Times* said. "This time the response might not be so good. Many young men are not willing to go to war. If 'war is hell' as a great American soldier has said, then we should keep ourselves and our country out of it." The March 1936 issue of the *Times* reported that Rev. John Copp, the Maritimes representative of the Student Christian Movement, had talked to students during the regular song service at Zion Church, and warned them not to rush into another war. "He was absolutely convinced that war was never justifiable," the paper said. "His opinion is shared by many thinking people in the world today."

There were subtle changes in students' attitudes toward life at the college as well. Moving pictures and radio had opened doors to the outside world, and this generation was more sophisticated than previous ones. At least, its members thought they were. Many had worked at teaching or other jobs to make enough money for college. They were men and women, and they tended to chafe at the confines of the college cocoon. For generations, male and female students at Prince of Wales had dutifully used separate doors and separate stairs. Now they were rebelling, at least in the pages of *The Times*. "Why all this foolish fuss when a student is caught 'sneaking' in the wrong door, perhaps to make up for lost time?" asked "Disgusted Student." In another letter in March 1936, "Eve" complained about the rule on female attire for physical training exercises in the gymnasium. "I'm sore! Mighty sore!" Eve announced. "I came to PWC last fall for the first time, without the least suspicion of what an out-moded old dump it was. To prove my innocence, I went down to Moore and MacLeod's and bought a pair of gym shorts for PT. To my horror, I was informed that only black bloomers were allowed on the floor, and that they must conceal the knees! Any idiot knows that bloomers large enough to come comfortably down over the knees will assume the girth of a circus tent and give it at the same time all the comfort and freedom of a bean bag. When God gave us our knees he didn't say to cover them up...."

Even the Saturday night socials organized by the Student Christian Movement, for years a mainstay of student entertainment, were being viewed with a critical eye. In an unsigned article in the May 1935 issue of *The Times*, the writer sneered that the gatherings were a "Sunday school picnic type of social," not at all interesting "to more mature minds." Roman Catholic students had formed a Catholic Christian Club at the college in 1932, and apparently were having more fun than the Protestants. The Catholics were dancing every week at the Knights of Columbus Hall. If the SCM would follow their example, "it would receive the support it deserves," the paper declared.

There were other signs that students were asserting their independence. For years, they had complained about the lack of organizations to represent them. Finally, in the fall of 1936, the timing — and the mood — was right. First, an athletic association was formed in hopes of improving the sports scene at the college. For various reasons, Prince of Wales had never shone in athletics. There were constant complaints in the college paper that the players didn't get enough practice time; that neither the students nor the faculty gave the teams enough support; that athletics didn't get the respect it deserved. The boys won some hockey and football games (the girls' hockey teams seemed to do better), and even took home a trophy or two, but the sports news was often bad, as this brave little piece in *The Times* illustrates: "'Defeated but not disgraced' is perhaps the best explanation which may be submitted on behalf of the PWC hockey team for the season..... Though defeated in every game, the boys always went on the ice full of fire and dash, and always gave the fans their money's worth. They were also noted for the clean brand of hockey they always displayed."[56]

The year the athletic association came into being, students organized their own council. Its first task was to tackle the irritating issue of Saturday night socials. Robertson had always refused to allow these apparently innocent events in the college auditorium. This wasn't quite as trivial an issue as it appears, because the rule sometimes meant hiring an outside hall, at a cost of hundreds of dollars a year. One of the many complaints about this rule came from Erma A. Patterson, a sports-minded Charlottetown student, who told readers of *The Times* that the hall was off-limits even to practise college cheers after class. "The modern age is lauded as one of democracy," she wrote, "but in Prince of Wales College the students ... are allowed no voice in any matter affecting us. These dictatorial refusals are altogether out of keeping with the modern age; the world is passing Prince of Wales — we are lagging behind in the Victorian era...."[57] Robertson was unmoved by such protests. In one of the weekly debates in the early 1930s, one class tackled the touchy subject of the college hall. The principal, who was supervising the debate, stood up and launched into a lengthy argument of his own. "His belief was that students were there for serious study and should have no time to waste," Horace MacEwen recalled. "He thumped the desk vigorously in his final declaration, and thus we were dismissed."[58]

By the mid-1930s, students were not so easily dismissed. In 1935, the third- and fourth-year classes sent a petition to the minister of education requesting the use of the college hall. The government rejected the petition on the ground that no parents had signed it. The next year, the students' council began work on a referendum that would be mailed to parents. By this time, Robertson was finally starting to bend a little. He promised that if the parents wanted students to use the hall, he would agree to it. In the spring of 1937, when the questionnaires were returned, 92 per cent of parents polled sided with the students. Robertson kept his word. He said students could use the hall for their convocation dance that year.

By fall, Robertson had mellowed even further. According to *The Times*, he remarked to one of the teaching staff one Saturday in early October that he thought that holding dances in the auditorium was an excellent idea. Furthermore, he planned to attend the Saturday evening socials there that winter. That did not happen.

On Saturday, October 2, 1937, Robertson was at his usual post at the college. The next morning, Eleanor Lowe got a phone call from friends who lived next door to the Robertsons. He had been stricken with a heart attack in the middle of the night, they told her. He had died Sunday morning at about 11 o'clock. He was 68 years old — not yet an old man, and apparently in reasonably good health, except for a chronic stomach complaint. Eleanor Lowe, along with most other people who knew Robertson, was shocked. "I thought, 'What are we going to do now?'" She had known Samuel Robertson all her life, had studied under him, had worked with him for sixteen years. He had been principal of the college for thirty-six years, and had taught there since 1893. It was impossible to imagine Prince of Wales without him. To Miss Lowe, his death was a loss even more profound than that of a relative. "It was like losing a future," she said.

In his years as principal, Samuel Robertson had steered the college along a course set by his mentor and predecessor, Alexander Anderson. Robertson had made some attempts to accommodate the various demands of a changing society, but he was not interested in trying to be all things to all people. He obviously believed that, above all else, it was important to preserve a beacon of high academic standards. He did so during a period in which the student population grew to 449 from 176, and the faculty to more than 20 from 5. Along the way, he oversaw the evolution of Prince of Wales into a junior college. Perhaps more significant was the gift he bestowed on generations of bright young Islanders, in the form of paternalistic, uncompromising devotion. One of his former students and colleagues, Cyrus Macmillan, called Robertson "a great teacher and a great soul." He added, "There was something very noble about him, his scholar's face, with the clear eye, the ready smile, the quiet humour, the friendly hand.....With the scholar's shyness of the crowd and its idols, he moved but little outside the world of learning. To his work he gave all his energy, and it was a great and devoted and earnest life he gave to our college."[59]

It was fitting that Robertson's funeral service would be held in the college that was the focus of his life. On Wednesday morning, Rev. Ewen MacDougall,[60] who was in charge of the Church of Scotland congregation on the Island, conducted a private funeral service at the Robertsons' home. Then, at 11 o'clock, the principal's body was brought to the college auditorium. His students stood guard beside the casket until the afternoon, when MacDougall and Rev. Theodore Ross, a graduate and former teacher at Prince of Wales, conducted the service. A massed choir from various city churches led the singing of "The Lord's My Shepherd," "Nearer, My God, to Thee," and "Peace, Perfect Peace." *The Patriot* reported that the funeral was one of the largest ever held in the province. The auditorium was packed, and the funeral procession, led by about 500 students who walked behind the hearse, extended for several city blocks.[61]

There were many tributes, from politicians, former students, other educational institutions, the newspapers. Probably none was more heartfelt and frank than the editorial in *The College Times*: "He lived for Prince of Wales College and gave his life for the welfare of its students. Their problems were his problems. We argued with him, criticized him as pupils always criticize their teachers. But what a shock to all of us when, on Sunday Oct. 3 we heard the woeful tidings. It was incredible. Prince of Wales without 'The Doc'.... On first attending Prince of Wales, students feared 'The Doc,' but on leaving, having completed their education there, it was with a feeling of sadness, a feeling of leaving one who had won their love and respect and whose friendship would always be cherished."[62]

The final tribute came later, from the student body at Prince of Wales. That year, they decided, there would be no dances in the college auditorium after all.

Chapter Seven

Memories of Old Prince of Wales

7

"We thought we were leading Peggy around by the nose and having the greatest time with him. It wasn't until years later that we realized that it was Peggy leading us and we didn't know it."
—Lawson Drake

Are we proud of Prince of Wales
Yes, it surely tops the scales
And we'll ever do our best
To make it outshine all the rest
Honour sportsmanship and truth
Are the things for which we root
And we ever will uphold the honour of Prince of Wales.

(College song *circa* 1940)[1]

In the fall of 1938, Frank MacKinnon of Charlottetown, then a nineteen-year-old arts student at McGill University, wrote an instructive and somewhat wistful letter to friends back home. MacKinnon, a son of former Lieutenant-Governor Murdoch MacKinnon, had taken his high school years at Prince of Wales, but had left for Montreal in 1937. With the clarity of vision of the sadder-but-wiser expatriate, MacKinnon told readers of *The College Times* that they should be proud of their province and of their college, which was "one of the finest of its kind in North America. And that's a positive fact." He continued, "It is only when we get away to other institutions and see drunkenness, vice, and wild women among the students that we really appreciate our good old PWC and wish that other colleges had as much common sense in them as Prince of Wales. At a recent dance, one of our co-eds at McGill fell on me, spilled a glass of champagne on me and collapsed in a drunken heap on the floor and before she got up again said, 'Shay, am I happy? Whoopee!' This wouldn't happen at a Prince of Wales College dance, at least, I hope not."[2]

It certainly would not. At least, not if G. Douglas Steel had anything to say about it. Steel had inherited the principal's job after Samuel Robertson's death in 1937. The job apparently had been offered to Professor J.-H. Blanchard, who had studied at both Prince of Wales and St. Dunstan's, had taught French part-time at both institutions, and had joined the Prince of Wales staff full-time in 1911. He turned down the offer, his son Francis Blanchard said, because he wanted to devote as much time as possible to working for the welfare of the Acadian community.[3] Instead, Blanchard took on the position of vice-principal, and acting principal when Steel was absent. Steel's appointment made the transition an almost seamless one. He had taught English and served as vice-principal for almost three decades, and, as principal, he carried on traditions of scholarship and comportment that went all the way back to Alexander Anderson and probably to Alexander Inglis. Under Steel, the academic standards remained high, the examinations tough. He continued the rigid rules about separation of the sexes: boys used the Grafton Street entrance and the stairs nearest the south side; girls used the Kent Street entrance and the north-side stairs. One morning, just as the bell was about to ring, Steel caught a young gentleman trying to take a shortcut through the ladies' entrance. Steel gave him a stern lecture and ordered him to walk around to the proper door. By the time the unfortunate wretch made it to that entrance, Steel was waiting for him with another lecture — this time, for being late.[4]

If anything, Steel was a sterner, sharper-tongued version of his predecessor. He was aptly named. He was always immaculately dressed in a steel-grey suit; he had steel-grey hair and, some would say, a steel-grey heart. The faculty liked him — some who knew him well thought he was the kindest of men — but he wasn't a stranger to sarcasm. He called it "gentle irony." Like Robertson, he was active in the church — he served as clerk of the session of Trinity United Church for many years — and the sins in his catechism included tardiness, sloth, boisterous behaviour, smoking, and gum-chewing. He called smokers "cigarette suckers." (Whether this was descriptive of the act or of the gullibility of the smoker is unclear. Perhaps both.) He once threw a female student out of his English class for chewing gum, giving her a lecture in rhyme as she left: "The gum-chewing girl and the cud-chewing cow are much alike, but there's a difference somehow.

Oh, yes, I have it now — it's the intelligent look on the face of the cow."[5] Steel usually didn't have to resort to such extreme measures. One glare — coupled with "Better late than never, but better never late" — was usually sufficient. His introductory talk at the start of the term included the rule that young gentlemen always took their caps off when they entered the college. It was one of the lessons from college that Don Anderson of St. Peter's Bay never forgot. "That is something that has stuck with me to this day, whenever I go into a store or another building. These were small things, but something that stayed with you. He was a strict disciplinarian, but you had to respect him."[6] And Steel was not entirely without a sense of humour. One day when on patrol, he scolded some male students for loitering in a ground-floor washroom. Later, he found the same boys chatting in a washroom on the second floor. "What is the difference between loitering on the first and second floor?" he asked them. "Well, sir," one cheeky fellow responded, "at least you have to admit this is on a higher level."[7] Steel laughed, turned on his heel, and left. In a way, he embodied the trite-but-sometimes-true image of the warm heart beneath the gruff exterior. One year, he learned that a bright female student was practically immobilized with fear when faced with writing examinations in the auditorium with hundreds of others. Steel arranged for her to write her exams in a classroom, with only a supervising teacher for company.[8] When Arnold Hiltz of Seaview lost a month of college because of a ruptured appendix and pneumonia, Steel postponed the final English exam, and lent Hiltz his notes and textbook.[9] It was a small act of kindness — but one that would colour Hiltz's memories of Steel for decades to come.

As Frank MacKinnon had observed, Prince of Wales College was quite a civilized place. And it was one that clung to a sort of Victorian gentility in the face of a world that was becoming more frightening by the minute. By the time Steel took over as principal, the newspapers were once again filled with talk of war in Europe. The difficult years of the Depression would soon fade into an era that was much worse. In the months leading up to the war, *The College Times*— at that time published in the form of a magazine three times a year — had taken a pacifist stance. In the March 1939 issue, editor George Burnett defended Britain's attempts to appease Nazi Germany. "To oppose the dictators means war," he wrote. "War means the loss of millions of young men and tens of millions of dollars. Some of the victims will be your own friends and acquaintances. You yourself may be called upon to face death.... Surely every expedient, within the bounds of honour and reason, should be tried before we bring such consequences as these upon ourselves."

The next September, Britain declared war on Germany. Days later, on September 10, 1939, Canada followed suit. When the noon bell rang the next day at Prince of Wales College, Alfred Blanchard walked to the Armouries and enlisted in the Canadian Army. Alfred was the eldest son of Professor J.-H. Blanchard and in many ways a chip off the old block. Short, stocky and dark — his nickname was "Blackie" — he had a multitude of interests. He was a second-year commerce student, played rugby, worked on *The College Times,* headed a debating team, served on the students' council. That evening, he told his troubled parents that he was leaving all that behind. He said he figured the war was going to last for a long time, and he might as well enlist first as last. He was eighteen years old.[10]

Alfred Blanchard's departure was a forerunner of things to come. That month, two faculty members, on the staff since the early 1920s, joined the Prince Edward Island Highlanders — W. J. "Billy Archie" MacDonald, then teaching French and Latin, and J. F. MacMillan, teaching botany and history. H. H. Court, supervisor of teacher training, enlisted in 1940.[11] More students, former students, and teachers would soon follow. For the next six years, *The College Times* would track their respective journeys in brief, sometimes chilling items that would provide a dark counterpoint to the safe, gentle college life the brand-new soldiers had left behind.

By 1941, George Burnett and his four brothers, Ian, Bill, James, and Niall — sons of long-time *Guardian* editor J.R. Burnett — had all enlisted in the armed forces. Niall, a much-loved, community-minded young man, had edited *The College Times* in the early 1930s. When he graduated in 1937, the heading on his biography hinted at the regard in which he was held: "*May He Live Long With Happiness.*" He was in Montreal when war broke out, studying for the Presbyterian ministry. In June 1940, after learning that France had capitulated, he joined the Royal Canadian Air Force, and was sent to England to train as a bomber pilot. A year later, about a week after his twenty-seventh birthday, he was killed in a training accident. [12]

The year that Niall was killed, the covers of *The College Times* magazine took on a decidedly patriotic air. The December cover featured a drawing of armed services men in front of the main door of the college, with the plumes and *Ich Dien* motto prominently displayed. "In these days when history-shaking events are taking place almost hourly, Prince of Wales students are living their motto, 'Ich Dien,' the lead editorial noted. "Nearly every issue of our daily newspapers tells the story of some valiant student who has laid down his life in cleansing the world of Nazism. Many of the boys have left the classes and corridors of PWC to take up the strenuous and serious training of the RCAF."[13]

In that issue of the magazine, amid the frothy items about college socials and rumours of romance, there were notices like this one: "Sgt. Observer Frank A. Tredenick, Sgt. Pilot Allison Boyce MacKie (Buddy), and Sgt. Pilot Charles O'Brien are missing after air operations overseas." Another item indicated that female alumnae had joined the war effort as well. Mae Heartz and Doris MacDonald were both nursing in England, the magazine reported. In 1943, it began a feature that continued all through the war — a list, edged in black, of former students who were not coming back. MacKie, O'Brien, and Tredenick were on the first Honour Roll, along with fourteen others.

Even without such grim reminders, it would have been hard not to pay attention to the war. In a way, Prince Edward Island was in the thick of things. Early in the war, recruitment and training centres were set up in Charlottetown for the army and navy, and, by 1941, three Island air bases were up and running. Planes droned overhead; rumours abounded about German submarines off the coast; servicemen in uniform were everywhere: in the restaurants, stores, and on the streets. Day after day, the war news was splashed across the front pages of the Charlottetown newspapers. "Nazi Shipping Crippled by RCAF Raids," the headlines screamed. "German Raiders Reported Off Southern England." Half-page advertisements shouted: "Buy Victory Bonds." "Take YOUR Place — Help Finish the Job!" "You Are Needed NOW For Active Service." By the fall of 1941, about 7,000 Islanders had heeded that call.

Ultimately, the war, and its aftermath, would have a profound effect on the college. But on one level, life went on much as it had in the past. Enrolment dropped in the first year of the war (to 478 from 522), and again in 1940–41, when 442 students were registered. Steel attributed the decline on enlistment by students and prospective students, and on "the general uncertainty." But the next school year, enrolment was back up to 492, possibly as a reflection of wartime prosperity. The size of the faculty increased as well, ranging between 24 and 31 during the war years, plus four teachers in the Model School. The core of the faculty helped give the college its sense of stability. Many of the professors had been on staff since the 1920s and early 1930s. Some, like Steel, Garfield Bennett, J.-H. Blanchard, Lily Seaman, and Eleanor Lowe, had an even longer association with Prince of Wales. The professors were Roman Catholic and Protestant, male and female, but they were almost all Prince Edward Islanders, and many were former students at the college. Their teaching methods probably had been handed down from their own professors.

The standard procedure was the lecture. The professors talked; the students took notes. To Willard Brehaut of Guernsey Cove, who later went on to obtain a doctorate in education, the classrooms at Prince of Wales, even in third and fourth years, were a poor preparation for university, where students were expected to do independent research.[14] Then again, the library resources at Prince of Wales were limited. R. B. Bennett, the former Prime Minister, had donated 1,000 books to the college in 1938, but that brought the total up to only about 4,000 volumes.[15] A student had to depend mainly on what the professors said. The professors were teachers, not researchers. A few had advanced degrees. Of 31 professors on staff in 1943–44, for instance, 9 had master's degrees, and 3 had doctorates (Steel's was an honorary degree from Mount Allison University). But their specialties did not always match the subjects they were required to teach. "One of the English teachers had a background in chemistry," Brehaut said. "He admitted he didn't know much about Shakespeare."

That criticism did not apply to Dr. Steel. He had a master's degree in English from Harvard University, and some thought he was a brilliant teacher. Others found him dreadfully dull. His obsession with the finer points of the literature awed some students and irritated others. He would examine a poem microscopically, word by word, line by tedious line. He made an exception, however, for certain passages. "Any place where there was sex mentioned he'd skip right over it without saying anything at all," Earl Wonnacott recalled. "He'd skip the dirty parts, and there are lots of them, of course, in Shakespeare. Not that he was a prudish fellow. He just didn't think he should get into that kind of thing in class."[16]

The French classes were more entertaining. Professor Joseph-Henri Blanchard, or "Peggy" — a nickname he picked up as a young rugby player at St. Dunstan's, where he was noted for being as solid as a peg — was short, round, and jovial. Despite the fact that his eyes were so bad that he had to correct papers with a magnifying glass, he was a prolific reader with many interests. He had obtained a certificate in botany from the Guelph Agricultural School and another in French language, history, and art from the Sorbonne in Paris, and in his early years on the Prince of Wales faculty, he taught physiography, botany, and rural science in addition to French. By the 1940s, French was his only subject — in theory, at least. His students soon learned that they could avoid too much exposure to the language by mentioning one of the many other subjects that fascinated Professor Blanchard. Once nudged off the track, he would expound for half an hour on botany, art museums in France, the origins of words, travels in Switzerland, the making of cheese. When exam time came, some students wished he had spent more time on French. In later years, though, some realized that they'd received something of more value — an appreciation of the world around them. "We thought we were leading Peggy around by the nose and having the greatest time with him," Lawson Drake observed. "It wasn't until years later that we realized it was Peggy leading us and we didn't know it."[17]

Bill Reddin ("Botany Bill"), a tall, lanky man who taught botany and agriculture in the 1930s and 1940s, conducted classes that were similarly unstructured and equally popular. One of his claims to fame was that he had paddled around the Island in a canoe in the early 1930s. He believed in teaching from real life: at least once, he had his class walk to his home in Tea Hill to study the local flora, and he would often arrive late for class, carrying an armload of goldenrod or evening primrose that he had picked along the railroad tracks. But, like Blanchard, he did not limit his lectures to the subject at hand. He veered off topic so frequently that he'd have to ask his class to come back for extra lectures just to get through the course. Besides his distractibility, he endeared himself to students by occasionally distributing chocolates from Zakem's store on Grafton Street. And sometimes, if pressed just a little, he would sing. "We'd say, 'Sing, Mr. Reddin,'" Zelda MacLeod MacNevin recalled. "He'd say, 'Oh, you don't want to hear me.' We'd say, 'Oh, yes, we do!' So he'd sing to us, the standards of the day. We loved to go to his class."[18]

There were neither sweets nor solos in James Brow's physics class. A tall, austere, and stern-looking bachelor, Brow was known as "the Gray Eminence." He was a loner who rarely mixed with the other teachers, partly because he had his own inner sanctum, an office off his well-equipped physics laboratory. He liked to teach by demonstration, one of the class favourites being the pinhole camera trick: when the blinds were pulled tight and a piece of plywood with an inch-and-a-half hole was mounted in a window, an inverted image of cars and people would be projected on the opposite wall. Earl Wonnacott, a student in the 1940s who eventually would follow in Brow's footsteps, had vivid memories of Brow's physics laboratory more than half a century later — the smell of pipe tobacco and cleaning agents; the constant din from electrically driven tuning forks, from the ice-crusher, from instruments used to measure the speed of sound in gases. "When a student finished his work, or thought he had, he or she would, with considerable trepidation, take his work to Mr. Brow's office, where the result was compared with a standard or 'accepted' value. Quite often, the student would be asked to go back to the lab and try the experiment again to improve the result. Each completed lab experiment had to be formally written up in a special report book and handed in promptly for Mr. Brow's perusal." Brow was a demanding teacher, Wonnacott recalled, hard on students who tried to bluff their way through his course, but helpful toward those who showed they wanted to learn.[19]Brow was probably the most creative enforcer of the unwritten rules. He believed in nipping tomfoolery in the bud. Once when he caught a male student spitting out a Weymouth Street window, Brow made him get down on his hands and knees and scrub the front step. Another boy, a repeat offender of various misdeeds, was made to sit on a metal stool in Brow's office, beside an alarming electrical apparatus, while a grim-faced Brow silently sharpened some equally alarming instruments. Finally Brow glared at the student: "We've been watching you, MacDonald." That was all. The prisoner fled, no doubt glad to be alive.[20]

In contrast to Brow's well-ordered kingdom, George Paterson's mathematics classroom was a place where you could expect the unexpected. Paterson was a slight, moustachioed man from Cape Breton with a hearing and speech impediment, the result of a First World War wound. His nickname was "Pansy," not because of his behaviour but for another obscure reason, possibly related to his once having appeared on the street with a bouquet of flowers. Students who liked math found his classes fascinating. One of them was Austin Bowman. "He was always introducing concepts in math. He would talk about the realm of the imaginary, for example. The phenomenon that parallel lines never meet. Well, where do they go? Negative square roots. Where are they? Paterson proposed that there was such a thing as the realm of imaginaries, and he used to say that you plot this on the other side of the blackboard. He was probably right, but at any rate some of us were inspired to think about these concepts."[21] Unfortunately, Paterson was not a great disciplinarian, and students with no interest in negative square roots or repeating decimals found other ways to amuse themselves, especially while he was working at the blackboard. A typical adolescent prank involved throwing an old sock with a string on it to the front of the class and hauling it back down the aisle. One day, one of the girls decided to leave through the window. A male student grabbed her by the ankle when she was half-way through. Just then, Paterson turned around. "It didn't bother him too much," Clive Stewart recalled.[22] That kind of behaviour probably annoyed the serious math students more than the professor. Once, they complained to Steel that Paterson couldn't hear their questions. Steel asked Paterson to buy a hearing aid. He did, but soon stopped wearing it. Steel asked him why. "I was hearing too much," he replied. [23]

It was the eccentricities, the quirks of behaviour, that made the professors memorable long after their words of wisdom were forgotten: "Shifty" John Connolly, who suffered from a nervous disorder that kept him in constant motion, but had the uncommon ability of being able to write over his shoulder on the blackboard; Art Woolner, a man with a weakness for poetic phrases — "the glory that was Greece and the grandeur that was Rome" — and for hurling small objects across the room in a fit of temper; Miss Lily Seaman, a portly woman of a certain age who never looked at her students while lecturing but knew everything that was going on anyway.

The female professors generally ran a tight ship. Tiny Eleanor Lowe, the art teacher, was shy, dignified, and soft-spoken, but had one of the quietest classrooms in the college. Edith Hugh, a math teacher, terrified some students, including Catherine Bethune Coyle: "My fingernails turned blue when she walked into the room. I didn't realize that she had an arthritic condition that made her feet hurt terribly. She was nice once you realized that it was her sore legs that were the matter with her, not that she didn't like you."[24]

If some of the professors were intimidating, the smallest denizens of the college — the Model School pupils — were worse. Catherine Coyle had attended the school as a child, and her mother once taught there, so she knew what to expect when her turn came for practice teaching. "I shuddered at the idea of going to the Model School because I knew that the kids were primed to ask the hardest questions, the stupidest questions. And these poor students — because the Model School teacher, Mildred Harrington, primed the kids to be as bad as they could be. Well, it sure broke you into teaching. Not much that happened to you afterwards could be that bad."

Aside from the Model School pupils and the twice-yearly examinations, the college was not a frightening place. For the most part, misdemeanours were minor and punishment light — banishment from a class for a day, a lecture from Dr. Steel, or an enforced visit to the library, a place as quiet as a tomb. Miss Letitia Passmore, the librarian, saw to that. She also kept an eagle eye on the reading material. If you wanted something racy, like *Canterbury Tales,* you had to ask for it. Miss Passmore had taught in the Model School in the 1930s, and she supervised her college-age students with much the same diligence she had exercised with young children.

Of course, some Prince of Wales students *were* still children. In those days, bright public school students were often encouraged to skip grades; it wasn't unheard of to write Entrance exams as early as age thirteen. Dozens of young teenagers would land on the doorstep of Prince of Wales every fall, fresh from the rough-and-tumble world of the farm. Some had been to the city only once or twice in their lives. Many had rarely encountered a person with a university education, aside from the local clergyman or doctor. To Bryer Jones, a farm boy from Crossroads, the professors at Prince of Wales were "great people, endowed with a wisdom and knowledge that astounded us." A young teenager would find himself or herself addressed, probably for the first time ever, as "Mister" or "Miss." There was an arm's-length formality about that — the professors had no intention of being pals with their students — but also a sense of respect that seemed to demand grown-up behaviour. "It was a wonderful place," Jones said. "You felt a wonderful sense of security. It was always so clean and orderly. There was that lovely, quiet library and the good manners and standards of dress. It was a kind of sophisticated family."[25] It was a family that encouraged excellence. Exams were tough, and the marks, in keeping with a tradition that dated back to Alexander Anderson, were kept low. One graduate was denied entrance to Harvard because of her final marks at Prince of Wales — until she pointed out that 71 was the highest mark in her class.[26] Poor students fell by the wayside, but bright ones were encouraged to excel, perhaps for the first time in their lives. Zelda MacLeod MacNevin had been the only member of her class of Murray River. At Prince of Wales, the teacher-training supervisor, William Angus MacPhee, told her one day that she had real potential as a student. "Nobody had ever let me know that I had any particular ability. That was my first realization that maybe I should work a little harder."

For Ruby MacMillan Matheson, Prince of Wales was the portal to adulthood. She was only fifteen when she left the farm in Wood Islands to take teacher training. "From the day I entered Prince of Wales I became an adult. There were all these new experiences, having to think for yourself, look after yourself. And all of a sudden, you had to have money for everything. This was something I never had to worry about as a child. Our clothes were all made at home, and our food came from the farm we lived on." At home, her neighbours were mostly other MacMillans, and all Protestants. On her first day in class, she turned to ask a question of the girl in the seat behind her. Ruby was astonished to notice that her classmate had written "Roman Catholic" on a form the class had been asked to fill out. "I had never met a person that I knew to be Roman Catholic. That was something you might read about in the newspaper. I was amazed. She was the same colour as I was, and a very nice person. So that gives you an idea of the change in lifestyle when I went to Prince of Wales."[27]

In her first few weeks at Prince of Wales, Ruby MacMillan Matheson was so homesick, she used to walk to the railway station every Saturday in hopes that she'd spot a friendly face from Wood Islands. Like most young people from the country, she soon adapted to town life, became immersed in studies, and made friends. Her boarding situation helped. Her landlady, Mrs. R. W. Stevenson, moved to town from New Glasgow every fall to provide a home for her own five children while they were going to college. To finance the move, she rented half a duplex on Cumberland Street and took in boarders. Ruby was one of ten students at the boarding house. It was a home away from home. The boarders called Mrs. Stevenson "Granny," and she made sure that they ate well and studied hard. Like Prince of Wales, the boarding house observed a strict separation of the sexes — girls on the second floor, boys on the third. Everybody met in the dining room for meals. Like many other boarding houses, this one provided instant access to a social life.

But it was a social life outside of the college. Students who boarded at the same place tended to travel in packs. For 11 cents, they could see Alice

Faye, Don Ameche, and Carmen Miranda in *That Night in Rio* at the Capitol Theatre. They could buy a smoke for a couple of cents at Zakem's store on Grafton Street, or nurse a cherry coke for an hour or two at the Old Spain restaurant on Kent Street. But there were no student residences; the college library shut down by 5:30 in the afternoon, and there was no place at the college where students could gather after hours. Even the auditorium was unavailable much of the time. Students had fought persistently in the 1930s for use of the hall, but their victory turned out to be a rather hollow one. Being one of the few decent auditoriums in the city, it was constantly in demand for plays, concerts, music festivals, and other events. Aside from the college socials, held about three times a year, organized extracurricular activities consisted mainly of sports (football, boys' and girls' hockey, boys' and girls' basketball, track and field, and sometimes baseball and boxing), the students' council, *The College Times,* the Student Christian Movement, the Catholic Collegiate Club, a social committee, and a glee club. All of the non-athletic groups seemed to have trouble attracting and keeping active members.

During the war years, military training requirements cut down further on the time students could spare for social life. At the beginning of the war, the Canadian government had decided that students could best serve their country by finishing their education. In 1940, the National Resources Mobilization Act gave the government authority to impose conscription for service on the home front. By 1942, almost all the fit male students at Prince of Wales were taking some form of military training, mainly sea, air, or army cadets. For women, there were courses such as first-aid, military law, office administration, nutrition, home nursing, and motor mechanics.[28]

Many of the older students took part in a Canadian Officers Training Corps (COTC) program at St. Dunstan's University. The corps, restricted to students over seventeen-and-a-half years of age, consisted of about 100 students, about 30 of whom were from Prince of Wales. Drills and lectures on such topics as gas, small arms, and military law were given two afternoons a week, and trainees attended a two-week camp at the end of the term.[29] In March 1943, *The College Times* pointed to the COTC program to dispel the notion of the student as draft dodger. "As you can see, the students of PWC and SDU are by no means shirking their duty to their country. Those who do not take military training are either too young or are not medically fit...." At Prince of Wales, as in other post-secondary institutions, increasing numbers of students were taking science and pre-medical courses, partly because of perceived job advantages, partly because the government was encouraging them to do so as part of the war effort.

But as the war progressed, and the shortage of men and women in the military became more acute, the pressure to enlist mounted. By the end of 1942, the National Selective Service Authority had ruled that any student of military age who refused to join the COTC or equivalent would immediately become liable for the draft, as were students who failed to do well in yearly or mid-term exams. In his annual report at the end of the year, Steel noted that he had been obliged to report two students to the military authorities.[30] Steel approved of the new government policy. "High schools and colleges could accomplish more," he observed, "if the work of the classes were [*sic*] not continually impeded by students who are failing to profit by the opportunities society has provided for them."[31]

Some students apparently suspected that college men of military age were simply trying to avoid the draft. "Where would our country be today if the entire male population of Canada thronged to colleges and universities at the outbreak of war?" Nancy Simpson and Helen Muttart asked in a letter to *The College Times* in March 1943. "Please understand we are not against boys taking courses such as medicine, dentistry, engineering, chemistry, which, in their own way, are vital to the war effort. What we do object to is the boys who are attending colleges because they feel too superior to use their minds and bodies on the battlefields in the cause of justice...."

In the May issue of the magazine, editor Gerald Foster pointed out that the government policy of weeding out poorer students left only those who were diligently pursuing their studies. "Why, then, must the student be constantly defending his cause against those supposedly war-conscious people who scorn his attempts to fit himself for a useful purpose in our war effort? The forces are in need of doctors and engineers; and factories, war plants, etc., need physicists and engineers. Those can not be plucked out of the magician's hat or the proverbial thin air.... We are working now to equip ourselves that we may bring this war to a rapid conclusion; we will work much more competently if we are unhindered by the expressions of disapproval that overburden us at present."

The next December, *The College Times* announced that Gerald Foster was a first lieutenant in the Canadian Army. The Honour Roll in that issue contained 26 names. Among them was Alfred Blanchard's. A telegram had been delivered to Professor Blanchard at the college on the morning of December 2, 1943: *"Regret deeply that Lieutenant Alfred Blanchard officially reported missing in action November 23 1943 Stop Further information follows Stop Director of Records."* The next month, another telegram arrived. Lieutenant Alfred Blanchard of B company of West Nova Scotia Highlanders Regiment had been leading a platoon into the enemy stronghold in the Appenine Mountains of Italy when he was killed by machine-gun fire. He was buried in the mountains of Italy. "If ever an officer was worshipped by his men," Major Allison Rogers of Charlottetown wrote to Alfred's parents, "your son certainly was. He had that gift of leadership mixed with a grand sense of humour that commands the love and respect of a Canadian soldier...."[32]

As the war progressed, there were other obituaries in *The College Times* — items in grotesque contrast to the sometimes thoughtful, sometimes endearingly silly preoccupations of college life. While some young men and women were marching off to war, or thinking about it, others were agonizing over the issue of "college spirit" — a subject that had tortured young minds at Prince of Wales since the 19th century. There was always somebody grumbling in the student publication that people were failing to cheer for the home team at football and hockey games, failing to show up at assemblies, failing to pull their weight on student council. Sports events were a perennial sore spot. "It was really heartbreaking to see the few PWC supporters at St. Dunstan's field on Oct. 29, the day of the opening game between the old rivals, PWC and SDU," a sports writer remarked. "They were outnumbered and outcheered by supporters from a seat of learning which is only half the size of PWC. What is the matter with us? It would seem rather obvious that we don't care who wins."[33]

Perhaps, as one editorial writer observed, "The college spirit never gets into a person until he has left PWC, then if somebody says something against it — wow."[34] Perhaps it took a little longer for the spirit to enter the country students, who were in the majority. The townies tended to dominate college committees, partly because many of them were friends from public school, knew how to play team sports, had already learned the fox trot, and generally had a bit more confidence. "You could pick out the town students after you were there a little while," Ruby MacMillan Matheson said. "They'd saunter into the classroom with their books under their arm. You could tell they were just 'man about town.'" The country students tended to be more studious. They were probably more afraid of failing, too. Tuition fees were still low for the high school and teacher-training classes ($5 for rural students and $10 for Charlottetown students) and steeper for the university-level courses ($50 and $75 in third year and $100 and $150 in fourth). But the major expense was for room and board, which represented a great sacrifice for many parents. There probably would be no second chances for failing students. "They knew there was a pitchfork and a shovel waiting for them at the end of the barn," Roy Campbell observed.[35]

It took town-connected girls like Helen Grant Killorn to keep things hopping at Prince of Wales. Helen had gone to school in Montague, but she was no country bumpkin. Her father was a physician and Member of Parliament, and she had lived in Ottawa. Moreover, she was a friend of Mac Beck, a Montague boy who was also a star athlete on the hockey, football, basketball, and track teams, and was considered part of the town crowd. Helen later remembered her Prince of Wales years as "one of the most fun times of my life." As one of three members of the cheerleaders' squad, she kept the old "Boomalacka" cheer alive:

Boomalaka boomalaka boomalaka — B
Chikalaka, chikalaka chickalaka chee
Boomalaka chickalacka Ziz Boom Bah
Prince of Wales, Prince of Wales, rah rah rah!

Helen also went to all the best house parties in the tony end of town, served as secretary of the students' council, and danced on Saturday nights to the music of the Downtowners at the Brighton Club, on the west end of Euston Street.[36]

The Brighton Club wasn't exclusive to townies, but the country mice had grown up with jigs and reels and square dances in the local hall, and felt awkward if they couldn't dance to the orchestra's modern tunes. It was a rather big issue for Don Anderson of St. Peter's Bay. "No question, if you couldn't dance, you felt you had a bit of hayseed between the ears." He learned to dance — a skill he would enjoy for decades to come — from some of the town girls. They conducted lessons in the waltz, the fox trot and the jitterbug in the auditorium before the first socials.[37] That education was helpful, but couldn't fix the essential problem: there were more girls than boys at Prince of Wales. That gender imbalance had existed through the war years, partly because enlistment in the service was thinning out the ranks of both faculty and students. To make matters worse, not all the farm boys were as brave as Don Anderson. "The minority of male students (usually urban) who are given to dancing monopolize the floor, the orchestra and the girls," a contributor to *The College Times* complained. "Other male and female students (usually rural) either because they can't or won't dance merely watch, and watch and watch."[38]

Dancing actually became an issue in the 1944 elections for students' council. The previous year, a two-party system had been set up for the first time. The Red Party theoretically represented urban interests, and the Blue Party, rural ones. One of the election promises of the Blue party, in response to demands from country students, was to provide some old-time dancing at the socials. The hottest band in the region was Don Messer and His Islanders, heard coast-to-coast on radio station CFCY. When the band went on tour in the Maritimes, *The College Times* reported, "thousands of people willingly pay over a dollar a ticket" to get into a Messer dance. One of the band members, drummer Warnie MacRae, was a student at Prince of Wales. Possibly this helped the college secure the band for socials in the auditorium. The first Messer dance was held in the fall of 1944. For once, the post-mortems indicated general satisfaction with the event, although there was still the knotty problem of prying the male flowers off the wall. "There are three girls to every boy at Prince of Wales," *The Times* scolded, "and it is the duty of every boy to dance."[39]

Organized sports presented, like dancing, one more set of skills for rural students to learn. When the call went out in the fall for recruits for the rugby teams, Lawson Drake of Meadowbank, only thirteen when he left the farm, decided to try out. He quickly decided, however, that he was so small and light, he'd be mangled in a rugby match. Track and field sounded more promising. "I did a lot of running around the farm, chasing cows and things, and I thought, 'I'll show these town kids my heels around the half-mile track.' As it turned out, some of those guys were a lot faster than I was."[40]

Once the country boys learned the basics, they more than held their own on the sports teams. And once the college acquired its own rink, the St.

Dunstan's University boys lost some of their former competitive edge. For many years, Prince of Wales hockey and football players had complained of being at a disadvantage in competition with St. Dunstan's. The Catholic school had better practice facilities and, because it offered more years of study, a more experienced pool of athletes. Prince of Wales hockey teams, with no rink of their own, had to beg for ice time elsewhere. That problem was finally addressed with the construction of an open-air rink behind the college for intra-mural hockey and college skates. In 1938–39, under the direction of Professor W. J. Macdonald, a site behind the college was surveyed, leveled, and rolled, and a board enclosure was built to hold the water. Over the Christmas holidays, city students shovelled snow off the rink and flooded it. Students donated 50 cents each toward the costs, then about $125. Steel, not noted for his enthusiastic endorsement of play, gave the rink qualified approval: "The health of those who participate, provided they do not devote too much time to this activity, should be improved," he observed. "Nor should their intellectual development be endangered, if they observe the proviso already noted."[41] The first social of the year in 1939 started with a skating party on the new rink. That winter, perhaps coincidentally, Prince of Wales won the first hockey game of the season: 3-0 over the Montague Primroses.

In the next few years, the rink was plagued with problems, most of them beyond the control of students who were working hard to keep it going. The first was the Island's volatile climate; in a season of frequent thaws and snowstorms it was almost impossible to maintain a good ice surface. Then there was trouble with the neighbours. City vandals repeatedly broke down sections of the fence, smashed locks in the dressing rooms, tore doors from their hinges, burned insulating material, broke light bulbs. After being pressured by students to take action, the city police captured eighteen delinquents, hauled them off to the police station, and then released them, apparently without further punishment. The old "college spirit" issue also raised its head. After a snowfall, the rink had to be shovelled by hand. Not everybody was eager to do this. Female students weren't expected to shovel, but they were expected to cheer. "They could at least show some interest by coming out to see how the work is progressing," a writer to *The College Times* grumbled, "and also by seeing that the boys do their duty." When the girls appeared one afternoon, "the rink was cleaned off in an amazingly short time."[42]

During the 1943–44 season, the student rink committee put considerable effort into the rink, buying a new sound system, renovating the dressing room. The next summer, the federal and provincial governments decided to build a vocational school behind Prince of Wales, on the corner of Grafton and Cumberland streets. It was planned that the school would provide training for ex-servicemen when they returned from the war. The government ordered the rink torn down. Noel MacNevin, a member of the rink committee since its inception, and editor of *The College Times* in 1944–45, argued that this had been unnecessary. In the first place, he said, the rink was located on the Kent Street end of the lot. And the province owned land and a suitable building near the college that could be used for a technical school. "If our College Rink had been abolished so that the final two years of University Training might be given at Prince of Wales, then our hosannas would have drowned any regrets for the passing of the rink. But as things stand now, we can see no good reason for the destruction of our rink."[43]

If the war had indirectly led to that disappointment, it also contributed to a memorable achievement. In the war years, the city hockey league — consisting of three teams from military bases in Summerside and Charlottetown, and one civilian team — was an exceptionally strong one, stocked with some of the best hockey players in Canada, including men with National Hockey League experience. Because of all the former students in military service, neither Prince of Wales nor St. Dunstan's could field enough good players to compete in the league. In the winter of 1944–45, the two schools took the unusual step of merging their two top teams to form "the Collegians." Most of the Collegians were relatively light and inexperienced, and so young they were still eligible for juvenile play. But the college boys also had speed and stamina on their side, and their team combined a formidable forward line from Prince of Wales — Clayton Nicolle, Willie Robertson, and Elmer Blanchard — with an equally strong defensive line from St. Dunstan's — A. J. MacAdam, Mike Hennessey, and Angus MacDonald. With coaching from Johnny Squarebriggs, Rev. Fred Cass of St. Dunstan's, and Gordon Bennett of Prince of Wales, the former rivals melded into a powerful team. At the end of the season, they came second in the league championships and led the league in scoring: Nicolle finished first with the most points, Blanchard second with the most goals, and Robertson third with the most assists. "It was no mean achievement to lead this league in scoring," recalled Noel MacNevin. "For two juvenile-aged players and one junior-aged player it was an amazing performance."[44]

The idea of combining the two teams had met with some skepticism at first. One Charlottetown sports writer had dismissed the college boys as "pond hockey" players. They soon proved otherwise. As *The Times* observed, it was not the ability of individual players that made the Collegians great, but the teamwork. "On the ice, they were all Collegians regardless of whether they were PWC or SDU students. The boys out on the ice were playing for the team and for nothing else."[45]

The success of the merger was noteworthy not only as a sports victory but also as a hopeful sign of accommodation between the two schools. There had been limited co-operation in the past. Before Professor Blanchard joined the Prince of Wales faculty full-time in 1911, he had taught briefly at both schools. Since 1933, St. Dunstan's and Prince of Wales had shared a professor of sociology and economics. The war had brought students together for military training at St. Dunstan's. A number of St. Dunstan's graduates were teaching at Prince of Wales. There had been Roman Catholic students at Prince of Wales at least since 1879, partly because of the teacher-training program. And some graduates of the secular college transferred to St. Dunstan's for their degrees. In 1942, they included four of the first five laywomen ever to enrol at St. Dunstan's — Gertrude Butler, Mary Hennessey, Eileen MacPhee, and Kathleen MacNeely. (In 1938, after years of lobbying by the Congregation of St. Martha, two nuns from the order were allowed to attend classes at St. Dunstan's. In 1941, the year that the University first exercised its degree-granting charter, Sister Bernice Cullen, another alumna of Prince of Wales, became the first person to receive a St. Dunstan's degree.)[46]

There had been failed attempts at co-operation, too. The Carnegie Corporation's attempts to persuade the two schools to share science facilities in the 1930s was one example. The failure of those negotiations had been blamed on the distance between the two colleges, or on the fact that Prince of Wales was coeducational and St. Dunstan's was not. They may have been valid reasons, but it was also true that the two institutions were incompatible in other ways. St. Dunstan's was unmistakably sectarian, with a faculty dominated by clergy and a program of religious studies; Prince of Wales had been run for decades by principals with ties to Protestant churches, but the college was secular by law as well as in practice, and had no religious teaching or observances and no clergy on staff. In fact, for many years it was one of the few Island institutions where Protestants and

Catholics rubbed shoulders to any extent — others being the Legislature and the mental hospital. Aside from the religious issue, the philosophies of education of the two colleges were different, a fact that became abundantly clear to professors like John Croteau, who commuted between the two colleges.

The Collegians proved that co-operation was possible — for a season, at least. The next year, the team disbanded and things were back to normal. "WELSHMEN WHITEWASH SAINTS," screamed a banner headline in *The College Times* (by then back to a newspaper format) after Prince of Wales won a hockey game 6 to 1. "WELSHMEN SMASH SAINTS," another front-page headline announced over an account of a basketball game in which Prince of Wales had "mercilessly beat the Saints into submission." The reporting was more subdued when Prince of Wales lost a football game 14-0 at the opening of another season. The story was relegated to an inside sports page, under the heading, "Football Season Opens."[47]

When the war ended, and servicemen began returning to college, sports at Prince of Wales took on a new life. The newly founded college yearbook for 1945–46 promised that the year would long be remembered as a time when veterans helped create "some of the best athletic teams this venerable institution has ever produced." Even the cheering section was satisfactory. Students had turned out in force to furnish "a supplement and tonic to the fighting spirit of our athletes." Presumably St. Dunstan's teams were also bolstered by veterans, but in the fall of 1945, the Prince of Wales football team, the Flying Welshmen, defeated St. Dunstan's, Acadia, and Mount Allison in exhibition games, and won the Island Intermediate Championship. The hockey team won both the Island intercollegiate championship and the city hockey league championship.[48]

The veterans started trickling back to college in the fall of 1944. The federal government was paying tuition fees and a subsistence allowance to ex-servicemen, and when the war ended, they flocked to colleges and universities everywhere. (At Mount Allison, for instance, almost a third of the students in 1946 were veterans.[49]) Their presence changed the size, shape, and atmosphere of the college. Throughout the war years, enrolment at Prince of Wales had stayed below 500, except for 1942–43, when 506 students were registered. In 1945–46, 63 ex-servicemen registered for various classes, making a total of 602 students, the largest enrolment in the college's history. A few were waiting to be discharged and were still in uniform. Ewen Campbell of Charlottetown showed up in Don Anderson's second-year class wearing his flight-lieutenant's uniform. "And didn't he look nice!" Anderson recalled. "These boys had been through the war, and they'd been literally to hell and back." So many veterans were applying late in the term, it became apparent that an extra teacher would have to be hired. A new special matriculation class began work after the Christmas holidays and continued until the last of July. Although women students still slightly outnumbered men (322 to 280), there were more men than women in all classes except teacher training and commerce. In the 1946–47 year, 117 veterans swelled the student ranks to 650, another record. The next year, 629 students registered, including 77 veterans.[50]

Some of the ex-servicemen had not even completed Grade 10 before the war; some were returning to college. Arnold Hiltz of Seaview had graduated from fourth year before he enlisted. His first year at Prince of Wales was in 1940, when he entered a special matriculation class. Known as the "two in one," it allowed high achievers to take first- and second-year courses in one year. After graduating in 1943, Hiltz enlisted in the Royal Canadian Air Force, trained as a navigator, and served for two years, one of them in England. By the time he was discharged in late August of 1945, it was becoming too late to apply to Acadia University, where he planned to take his degree. Instead, he arranged to take university-level courses at Prince of Wales, which would be accepted as third-year courses at Acadia. He was only twenty-one when he returned — not much older than his classmates — but he had been overseas, worked beside mature men, walked the streets of bombed-out London in the blackouts. "The other students seemed like children," he said. The interruption in his studies didn't hurt his career. After Acadia, he obtained a doctorate in chemistry from McGill and eventually joined the space program in the United States.[51] Another veteran, Robert Forsythe of Charlottetown, returned to Prince of Wales in the fall of 1946. He had joined the Air Force in the spring of 1941, at the end of his second-year course and just after his eighteenth birthday. He was bored with school, loved airplanes, wanted to fly. When the war was over, he got a job offer as a commercial pilot, but he had other plans for his life. He went back to second year, fearing that he had been away too long to jump immediately into university-level courses. He was twenty-three years old and a much-changed individual. "I wasn't fed up with school any more," he said. "We were all there for a purpose — not because we had to be there. And we had all learned what it was like to be out on the loose, too. There wasn't the adolescent horsing around like before." Eventually, he went on to medical school and a career as a psychiatrist.[52]

These were not the only success stories of the postwar years. The veterans adapted to college life surprisingly well. Almost all of them, Steel reported in 1946, "were able to resume or to acquire habits of study in a most satisfactory manner, and almost without exception they have proved that the Government of Canada acted wisely in making possible the broadening of mental horizons and … new ways of making a livelihood by its policy of Education Benefits."[53]

As Steel pointed out, the veterans also injected new life into extracurricular activities. By 1947, in addition to the usual sports and social teams, there was a film club, a choral club, a music-appreciation club, and an art club. An attempt to revive the college glee club failed because of lack of interest, much to Steel's disappointment, but the college acquired a new song, written by Les Alexander of the Downtowners. The Girls' Quartet performed it for the first time at the Christmas social:

College pals haunt my dreams tonight, dear
Recalling the joys we knew.
There were college gals so charming
But none quite as lovely as you.
Social nights when the lights were low, dear
Your eyes seemed to tell me love tales.
Though nights may be blue, I'll always have you
And my memories of old Prince of Wales.

The new song, *The College Times* pointed out, was not meant for sports rallies, but for waltzing when the lights were low. With all those veterans around, the girls now had a wider choice of dancing partners. That year, men outnumbered women at Prince of Wales— 334 to 316.[54] This was one of the rare times this had happened since the turn of the century.

Some of the veterans took part in all aspects of college life. In the fall of 1946, half the football team consisted of ex-servicemen. Veteran Leith Tierney edited both *The College Times* and the newly founded college yearbook, and gave the valedictory address when he graduated in 1948. Keith MacKinnon, who had served overseas in the Air Force, came second in his special matriculation class in 1947, was elected president of the student council, was chairman of the International Student Service appeal, and belonged to the college music club. Phonse Keefe, who had spent almost three-and-a-half years on the North Atlantic with the Navy, rejoined the college hockey team.[55] "The leadership given in the Student Council and the stimulus to other students to make the most of their opportunities has been most excellent," Steel wrote in his 1949 annual report. The veterans seemed to appreciate the efforts of faculty more than the younger students did, and in general set "a wholesome example" to the rest of the college. "What the effect of the presence of these older men among our students will mean in future years can be estimated only in those future years," Steel observed. "That life in the College will never be quite the same as it was I feel is a certainty."[56]

Indeed, the college had changed, and not always in ways that made Dr. Steel happy. The ex-servicemen accepted most of the regulations of college life — they were, after all, used to following orders — but not the one on smoking. For the first time ever, Prince of Wales students were smoking openly in the washrooms and locker rooms. Steel tolerated this practice, but he hated it. "Cursed weed!" he would mutter, kicking at cigarette butts that had rolled underneath a washroom door. "This place is looking more like a barroom every day!"[57] Robert Forsythe recalled an incident in the men's washroom. "Dr. Steel came in and there was a smouldering cigarette on the floor. Dr. Steel said to one of the fellows, 'Is that your cigarette?' He said, 'No sir, you saw it first, it's yours.'"[58] The principal was not amused, but that's the sort of attitude he had to put up with in those days. Once, when liquor was discovered at a college dance, Steel called an emergency assembly. "Look what I found in the gymnasium," he announced, holding up an empty liquor bottle. He was laughed off the stage.[59] The veterans weren't rebellious — just disdainful of what they considered silly rules. Soon, boys and girls were even mingling on the stairs.

The war and postwar years brought changes in the faculty as well. French teacher Robert LeClair, who had joined the armed forces in 1944, came back to Prince of Wales, as did W. J. MacDonald and J. F. MacMillan. E. E. Doucette, another veteran, replaced a well-loved Prince of Wales institution — vice-principal Professor "Peggy" Blanchard. He retired in July 1948, after fifty years as a teacher, including thirty-seven at Prince of Wales. During that time, he had seen two world wars take the lives of many of his students — thirty-eight in the Second World War alone — including his own son, Alfred. James Brow, a man with an entirely different personality from Blanchard's, became acting vice-principal. Garfield Bennett, who had joined the faculty at about the same time as Blanchard, died in 1942 after a short illness. His son, Gordon, replaced him as head of the chemistry department. John Croteau resigned in 1945 to run the PEI Co-operative Union. Clarence Murphy replaced him, carrying on the practice of teaching at both Prince of Wales and St. Dunstan's. Edith Hugh, on the faculty since 1928, died in 1944. Miss Passmore, the librarian, resigned two years later.

The war and postwar years coincided with a decline in the importance of the Normal School. Once considered mainly a teacher-training college, Prince of Wales gradually became an institution where university preparation far outweighed teacher education in size and status. The provincial government had raised the standards somewhat in 1940: a second-class teacher's licence would require two years of study after Grade 10, one academic and one partly professional. But Island teachers still had the lowest salaries in Canada (in 1943, an average of $954 a year for male teachers with a first-class licence, and $720 for female teachers). Enrolment in the Normal School continued to decline, despite a continent-wide shortage of teachers. In 1937–38, when there was a surplus of licensed teachers on the Island, 286 of the 449 students enrolled at Prince of Wales were taking teacher training. By 1945–46, there were only 60 teacher-training students — three men and 57 women — of a total of 602. Willard Brehaut took the education course in 1943. "Normal School students were considered second-rate," he said. "They were looked down upon by the staff and fellow students. The focus was on people who were going on to university on the mainland."[60] The continuing decline in Normal School classes troubled Steel, who blamed low teacher salaries. Certainly wartime prosperity, and the shortage of labour, had opened up better-paying jobs in other fields. The war had also stripped the profession of many male teachers. In an attempt to keep open as many schools as possible, the Department of Education began promoting summer schools at Prince of Wales for former teachers who needed to renew their licences, or high school students who had not completed the prescribed professional course. By the end of the 1940s, the regular Normal School course consisted of a full year devoted to professional training.[61]

In 1948, that training included a course in home economics. This came about almost by accident. In the late 1940s, the provincial government began exploring the idea of building high schools in various Island communities. Premier Walter Jones, whose wife happened to be a home economist, wanted to include home economics courses in these yet-to-be-built institutions. When he discovered that Doris Anderson of St. Peter's Bay, a graduate of Prince of Wales and Acadia, had taught home economics in Hudson, Quebec, for two years, he hired her to design a curriculum and supervise the high school home economics program. In the fall of 1948, Anderson moved into a basement office at Prince of Wales. As yet, she had nobody to supervise, but she did have another role to fill. Dr. Steel was also interested in home economics. Prince of Wales had once offered domestic science courses, but they had been discontinued in 1920. Steel hoped the college could soon begin offering university-level courses leading to a degree. For a start, he asked Anderson to teach a home economics course to the teacher-training students.[62]

That year, another decision by the government created a change in the teaching of Latin at Prince of Wales. For the first time, Latin was no longer a prerequisite for entrance to the college, and was therefore dropped by the public schools. For students who wished to study Latin, the college began offering a course for beginners, and added German in second year as an alternative to Latin. In contemplating the prospect of further changes to the curriculum, Steel thought that Prince of Wales should strike out in new directions, adding counselling and vocational-guiding, as well as university-level courses in geology, geography, and commerce. [63]

As it turned out, Prince of Wales did head off in new directions, in ways that Steel may never have anticipated. He was not around for the new era. On July 1, 1949, he resigned, after forty years on the faculty. Like Alexander Anderson and Samuel Robertson, Steel had held the fort through many a tumult. He was less charismatic than Anderson, more active in the community than Robertson. During his twelve years as principal, Steel served on the board of governors of the Canadian Broadcasting Corporation and as clerk of the session at Trinity United Church, and helped found the local music festival. But, like his two long-serving predecessors, Steel was devoted to high ideals — maintaining academic excellence at the college and building character among its students. If he had any grand plans for Prince of Wales, he didn't share them for posterity. He apparently saw his role as maintaining the status quo. He didn't quite succeed; as he observed, the war and postwar events meant that Prince of Wales would never be the same again.

But the most dramatic changes were still to come. The new principal had a big vision and, for a time at least, the ability to manifest it. His name was Frank MacKinnon.

Chapter Eight

Confronting "The Island Way"

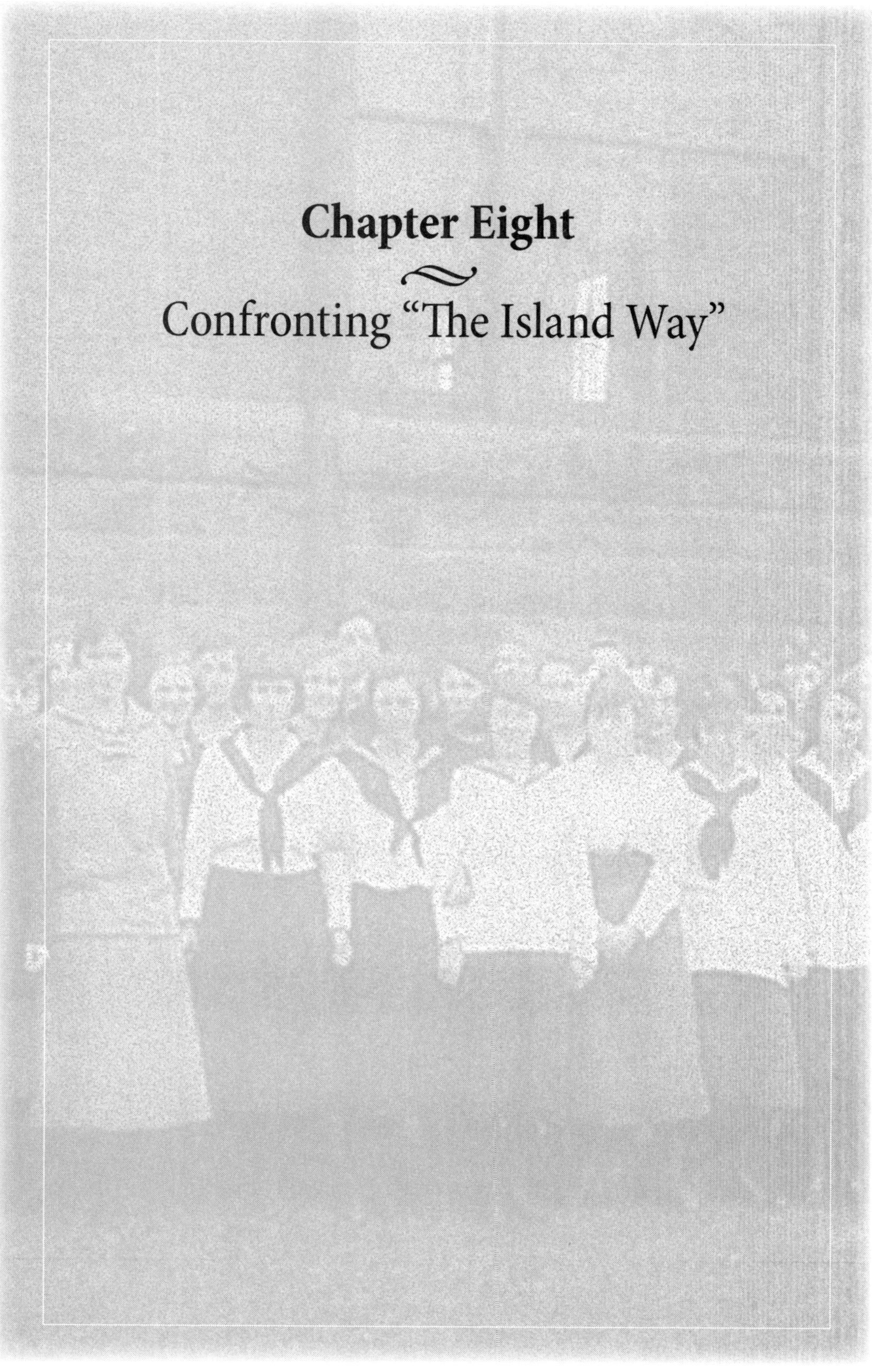

8

"I was personally attacked for so daring a departure from what is so often called 'the Island way of life.'"
—Frank MacKinnon

Now right here in College
We're having lots of fun
The tests and examinations
Have got us on the run
Our teachers and professors
Are busy night and day
They're figuring all the ways and means
To cut our marks away
But why should we get excited
And try to raise a row
For we'll have a "University"
In fifty years from now.

— College Times, April 1932

In 1949, Dr. Frank MacKinnon, then head of the political science department at Carleton University in Ottawa, received a letter from Premier Walter Jones of Prince Edward Island. The premier, who also happened to be an enthusiastic breeder of prize Holstein cows, asked MacKinnon to meet him at a cattle show and auction in Oakville, Ontario, to discuss some business. MacKinnon hardly knew Jones, and couldn't imagine what they'd have to talk about. MacKinnon was a city boy, more at home in a three-piece suit than overalls. "For a day and a half I wandered around the barns and the arena," he recalled, "meeting cattlemen, watching the bidding, and listening to Mr. Jones explain what was going on — and all the while wondering why I was there." Finally, the premier popped the question: G. Douglas Steel, the principal at Prince of Wales College, was retiring on July 1. Would MacKinnon be interested in the job?[1]

MacKinnon was happy in his work at Carleton, enjoyed life in Ottawa, and had had little contact with the Island since he left Prince of Wales as a student in 1937. However, he had fond memories of the college and the Island's pastoral charms, and he took a liking to the premier. After a trip back home, where he looked over the college and the cabinet looked him over, he accepted the job offer.

That unconventional hiring ushered in the most tumultuous two decades in the history of Prince of Wales College. The MacKinnon years would prove to be a roller-coaster ride: on the upside, creativity, optimism, and pride; on the descent, conflict, bitterness, and loss. Under MacKinnon, the college, like a long-dormant plant, would blossom. Then it would become trapped in the dangerous old web of religion, politics, education, and money.

From the time Frank MacKinnon arrived in a cloud of cigar smoke, it was obvious that the new principal was a man who could make things hum. MacKinnon was only thirty years old, about the same age as Alexander Anderson and Samuel Robertson when they took over the position. But his outlook was broader, his vision grander, and his credentials more impressive than any of his predecessors. After his high school years at Prince of Wales, he had studied economics and political science at McGill and obtained a master of arts degree in public administration, and later a doctorate, from the University of Toronto. By the time he arrived back at Prince of Wales, he had also worked as an industrial-relations officer for the federal department of labour, had published numerous academic articles, and was in the final stages of an important and elegantly written reference work, *The Government of Prince Edward Island,* which won the Governor-General's Award for Non-Fiction in 1951. Like his predecessors, he was devoted to the ideal of the small liberal arts college, although his field was political science, a newfangled subject that had never been taught at Prince of Wales. Robertson loved Latin; MacKinnon didn't. He had failed it once as a student and struggled all one summer to study for a mere pass mark. Like his predecessors, he was immensely proud of Prince of Wales College, but he didn't concern himself unduly about the minute details of its life. Anderson and Robertson may have wished their college was a university; MacKinnon acted as though it already was. He would not have dreamed of patrolling the corridors with pocket watch in hand, like a mere high school principal. To a suggestion from a critical legislative committee that he should reinstitute Steel's patrols, he replied, "We trust our students and they have responded admirably to that trust."[2] MacKinnon believed in giving his staff and students as much freedom as possible to teach and learn.[3] Anyway, he had other important things to attend to. Unlike Alexander Inglis, whose life-long motto was to mind his own business, Frank MacKinnon was the kind of person who got his name in the papers.

The attention was not always positive. MacKinnon had the kind of personality that elicited great loyalty and great animosity. *The College Times* immediately gave him its stamp of approval: "It is interesting to note that Principal MacKinnon, when a student at Prince of Wales, was instrumental in acquiring permission to have social evenings and dancing for the students," a *Times* writer observed in the fall of 1949. "Needless to say, he has already proved popular with the students and we feel that the Provincial Government is to be congratulated on this excellent choice."[3] This was not a unanimous opinion, especially outside the college.[4] Some people disliked him on sight. Possibly it had something to do with his somewhat pompous air and odd, plummy accent. Possibly, in an era when hiring a teacher from Nova Scotia was considered alarming enough to be debated in the Legislature, it had something to do with a perception about his Island credentials. His roots on the Island went back for generations, and he was Island-born-and-bred, but he had left at age eighteen and had spent almost half his life in the city. That, alone — plus the fact that he was already gaining national recognition — could have been grounds for suspicion among the big frogs in the little Island pond. When his first, landmark book was published in 1951, he recalled, "Such temerity was greeted by some ... with the question, 'Who does this fellow think he is?'"[5]

His childhood was unconventional for the times. His Scotch-Presbyterian father, Murdoch MacKinnon, was a farmer from Brooklyn in King's County. Elected as a Conservative member of the Legislature in the late 1890s, he had served as commissioner of agriculture and, in the early 1920s, as lieutenant-governor. Apparently a bit on the stubborn side, he made constitutional history in 1924 by withholding Royal Assent from a bill on church union; he objected on the grounds that it would force Presbyterians to join the United Church of Canada.[6] His only child, Frank, was born when Murdoch was fifty-four years old. When his term as lieutenant-governor expired, he left for the West and stayed there. Frank, still a small child when his father left, was raised by his mother and grandmother.

Apparently eager to escape that matriarchal nest and fly on his own,[7] Frank left Charlottetown after his second year at Prince of Wales to get his bachelor of arts degree at McGill. In Montreal, he met and married an Irish-born city girl, the daughter of a McGill professor. By the time he returned to the Island, he either had forgotten, or ignored, the Island custom of keeping one's opinion to oneself on controversial matters. Most Islanders, forever conscious of delicate political and religious balances, knew how to avoid trouble when sailing through those dangerous waters. MacKinnon questioned, and was openly critical of, certain aspects of the Island way of life: the careful consideration of religious and political affiliation in job appointments; the practice of favouring Islanders as teachers; and the lack of "culture" — by which he meant an appreciation for serious music, art, literature, and history. He had barely arrived when he began implementing changes in the way the college was run, and suggesting changes in the way the Island was run. Instead of sticking to college business, as Samuel Robertson had, he became deeply involved in community activities, giving lectures, serving on the Atlantic Provinces Economic Council, the Canada Council, the Canadian Club, the Rotary Club, and a long list of other community and academic associations. His public performances were so impressive, both the Liberals and the Conservatives pressured him, at various times, to run in federal and provincial elections.[8] He resisted, but he remained as high-profile as any politician, and he had many friends in high places. To Islanders like Keir Clark of Montague, a former education minister, he was "a big shot." He was "important," Clark observed. He did not mean this as a compliment.[9]

MacKinnon's most vocal and persistent critic in the 1950s was Dr. W. J. P. MacMillan, a physician, a former Conservative premier, a staunch Roman Catholic (he had been appointed a Papal Knight), and a harsh and sometimes cruel orator. According to MacKinnon, the conflict began before he was even hired. MacMillan, seeking to extend the tradition of alternating religious affiliations in government jobs, thought it was time for a Catholic principal at the government-run college. He was promoting a former army officer (presumably W. J. MacDonald). "I knew 'the turn' in appointments to office had been a nasty and inefficient element in local affairs to both Catholic and non-Catholic appointees and candidates," MacKinnon wrote later. "I said so, and the premier agreed. He had suffered from the results of the practice for years, and he undertook to back me on abolishing it at Prince of Wales, and to fend off the persistent doctor."[10]

It was not the only time Walter Jones backed MacKinnon. In a way, it was an odd alliance. MacKinnon's political biases weren't obvious, but his background was Conservative. His personal style was distinctly urban. Portly, formal, always dressed in a three-piece suit and brandishing a cigar, he looked like a successful banker. Moreover, he had a passion for "culture," which didn't necessarily mean Don Messer and Winston Scotty Fitzgerald. His musical tastes ran to the light operettas of Gilbert and Sullivan, although he also appreciated more serious music; in his student days, he once spent his last six dollars on a ticket to a performance at the Metropolitan Opera in New York.[11] At some point in his life, he took up painting. He once did a portrait of Queen Elizabeth II; his friends claimed his queen was cross-eyed, but he displayed her prominently and proudly anyway.[12] When the Royal Commission on the Arts, Letters and Sciences (the Massey Commission) came to the Island in 1950, he presented a proposal for a multipurpose cultural centre in Charlottetown. Jones told members of the commission he didn't see why it should bother with Prince Edward Island at all: "It doesn't need any culture."[13] Like his predecessors, MacKinnon sympathized with the district school teachers, and believed that education on the Island wouldn't improve until their pay did. Jones was no hayseed — he had once served as principal of the very successful Macdonald Consolidated School, and studied and taught agriculture in the United States — but he identified with farmers. He once told a delegation of Island teachers, "Until farmers' incomes go up, yours won't."[14] Still, MacKinnon considered Jones one of the best leaders the Island had ever had. For one thing, he greatly admired Jones's courage in ending Prohibition and reviving the Island's divorce court. And he was forever grateful for the fact that Jones supported him "generously and continuously" until Jones' appointment to the Senate in 1953.[15]

MacKinnon, never one to leave a hornet's nest unstirred, needed all the support he could get. Trouble arose as early as 1951, when two educational issues set off, in MacKinnon's words, "a tremendous explosion."

One occurred when he set out to fill four vacancies on the teaching staff. He felt the time had come to appoint staff without examining either their credentials as bona fide Islanders or their political and religious affiliation. Three of the prospective professors were "from away" (one was from Pictou County, Nova Scotia). The appointments had to be approved by cabinet, and "It took some forceful coaxing by the premier to get its agreement, because of the obstructions of one or two ministers, despite the feeling in the rest that it was time for a change." When MacMillan heard about the appointments, MacKinnon said, "I was personally attacked for so daring a departure from what is so often called 'the Island way of life.'"[16]

The "Island way" required paying attention to the samurai warning that the tallest chrysanthemum gets its head lopped off first. MacKinnon ignored this sensible advice. He was known as a man with big ideas. Surprisingly, in the early years, they did not entail elevating the status of Prince of Wales College. MacKinnon is widely regarded as the driving force behind the move to obtain degree-granting powers for Prince of Wales. But that did not necessarily fit his philosophy of education: he believed that small is often better. Although he was only too well aware of the deficiencies of many district schools, he thought that a one-room school with a good teacher provided as good an education as a large city school. And he never wanted to lose the intimacy that had characterized Prince of Wales from its inception. In 1954, appearing before a committee of the Legislature, he responded to suggestions that he wanted to turn the college into a university. "If every citizen in PEI agreed that it should be changed into a university," he told the committee, "I'd be the last to agree.... I think the junior college arrangement with two years of high school and the first two years of university, with the normal school and commerce, is very difficult to beat. It's one of the cheapest things you can arrange, and it's very convenient for the students. No attempt has been made whatsoever to change Prince of Wales into a university, and I hope none ever will."[17] MacKinnon eventually would change his mind — but the times were changing, too.

Change, in fact, was the defining characteristic of the postwar years — a period that historian David Weale has termed "the Break" in Island cultural history. In the 1950s, modernization was transforming the Island through paved roads, rural electrification, television, larger and fewer farms, more cars and tractors, fewer horses. The provincial government was spending huge sums on highway construction and maintenance — $38.2 million on construction between 1947 and 1959, and millions more on repairing what historian Edward MacDonald has described as "bumpy grey roads, patched and repatched like an old farmer's overalls." As MacDonald has pointed out, the paved roads were more than a convenience. They transformed a way of life that had not changed much since the 19th century: they made school consolidation practical, allowed farmers to travel to distant fields and rural residents to travel to town to work and shop, contributed to the decline of small towns and villages, and broke down barriers between communities. "Pavement made life larger," MacDonald concluded.[18]

In decades to come, those broadened horizons would erode some of the old religious prejudices on the Island. In the 1950s, the "larger life" had a more negative effect, hastening the gradual decay of rural communities. Of course, that was starting to happen anyway, as a result of the high cost of living and the low rewards from farming. More and more young people were leaving the farms for jobs in stores, offices, and the expanding provincial bureaucracy. Fewer young people wanted to teach school for a living, especially in a rural community where the responsibilities were great, the pay small, the prestige minimal, and the social life unexciting. Consequently, there was an alarming turnover in the public school system. At the end of the 1949–50 school year, 116 licensed teachers left the system, presumably for other jobs or other provinces.[19] The teacher shortage was a continent-wide problem. On the Island, it was exacerbated by the maintenance of hundreds of one-room schools. Every year, a few rural schools remained closed, and many had to make do with poorly qualified teachers. Of 707 teachers in the system in 1950, 63 possessed only a "permit" — that is, they had been given permission to teach without having attended Normal School. Four years later, six schools were without teachers and close to 90 teachers were teaching on permits. Despite incentives from the province to teacher-training students — $100 grants and $200 loans — enrolments in the Normal School classes could not begin to compensate for the shortage. While between 100 and 150 teachers were leaving the profession every year, the Normal School was turning out as few as 42 graduates a year.

It was partly the teacher shortages that prompted the Legislature to appoint a select standing committee on education in 1954. The committee, headed by Education Minister Keir Clark, included Liberals Dr. Lorne Bonnell, Lorne MacFarlane, and J. Wilfred Arsenault (a former Prince of Wales teacher), and Conservatives Dr. W. J. P. MacMillan, John A. Macdonald and J. W. D. Campbell. In the spring of 1954, when the committee began holding public hearings, it became apparent that its major preoccupation was Prince of Wales College and its principal.[20] For three days, members interrogated MacKinnon in a manner rarely seen outside a courtroom. "I then learned," MacKinnon wrote later, "how the Christian felt in the Roman arena with the angry lion."[21] By this time, Walter Jones was gone; a new, less sympathetic Liberal government, headed by Alex Matheson, was in office. And MacKinnon had started off on the wrong foot with the new education minister, Keir Clark. "I wasn't too strong on Frank," Clark recalled decades later. "When I first got appointed, I made a tour of all the [educational] institutions. I couldn't find Frank at Prince of Wales. The first day, I went to his office and asked to see him. The girl said, no, he wasn't there. Two days later, I went back. He still wasn't there. So then I find out he was home. Writing a book."[22]

Fuelled by such impressions, the education committee members, led by MacMillan, grilled MacKinnon on the most minute details of his work. They asked the same questions, over and over, and often in a confrontational way. What time did he arrive for work in the morning? How much had he been paid for a summer course he had taught in Nova Scotia? How many periods a day did he teach? How many staff meetings did he hold? Shouldn't there be more? Who attended? What was discussed? A typical exchange occurred when MacKinnon observed that he preferred to deal directly with the minister of education on college matters, as his predecessors did, rather than with the civil servants.

MacKinnon: That's not unusual procedure.

MacMillan: It is unusual procedure, definitely. I know as much about parliamentary procedure as you do. What's political science?

MacKinnon: Political science is a study of government and politics.

MacMillan: Is it taught at Prince of Wales College?

MacKinnon replied that political science was taught in fourth year at Prince of Wales and in second year at universities. MacMillan then asked whether MacKinnon regarded Prince of Wales as a university.

MacKinnon: No, that doesn't follow from that statement.

MacMillan: It does, exactly. Because political science is taught in the universities of Canada, it must be taught in the Prince of Wales College, and it's a junior college.

MacMillan: Would it make any harm if it wasn't taught at all?

MacKinnon: No, not any more than if Spanish wasn't taught.

MacMillan: Well, I would advise you to drop it and turn your attention to the essentials.[23]

The politicians had a lot more advice. The principal's salary arrangements — made with Walter Jones — were too generous, some members concluded: MacKinnon had started at $4,000 a year, plus living accommodations, and had been promised a $100 raise a year. Members also criticized the failure rate at Prince of Wales, the practice of renting out the auditorium at night (the college, MacMillan said, was "degenerating into a social centre"), the state of student discipline. The committee had inspected the college building and had discovered lockers with doors bent and locks broken; ink stains in the locker room; broken soap dishes in the washrooms. Why was nobody patrolling the halls to ensure that students were behaving themselves? MacKinnon replied that the college was not a prison; too much control would simply make teenagers resentful and encourage them to create trouble. "I have never seen students move from class to class in any institution in a more orderly fashion than at Prince of Wales."

Not all the committee members were happy with the tone or content of the interrogation. MacFarlane, referring to the proceedings as "an inquisition," called it "a damn waste of time." Campbell said he hadn't seen anything at the college to be alarmed about.[24] Other members had.

One of those alarming issues involved religion — perhaps not surprising, given the history of education in the province and MacKinnon's reputation. MacKinnon was nominally Protestant and affiliated with the United Church, although his son Peter remembers him in those years as a skeptic — "perhaps an agnostic."[25] Nevertheless, he had acquired an anti-Catholic label soon after arriving back on the Island. It was a charge, he later wrote, that "not one of my Catholic friends would support,"[26] but it was an albatross that perched on his shoulder for the rest of his years at Prince of Wales. Prince of Wales was and always had been a secular college. The act establishing it in 1860 spelled that out and specifically ruled out the presence of clergy on the faculty (although, in fact, two Catholic priests, Rev. Edmund Roche and Rev. Jim Kelly, taught at Prince of Wales during the MacKinnon era). The almuni included many Catholic students — including future nuns, priests, bishops, at least one archibishop, John T. McNally, and one cardinal, James Cardinal McGuigan. The Catholic Women's League and the St. Thomas Aquinas Society (founded by a Prince of Wales professor, J.-H. Blanchard) offered prizes to promising students at convocation. There were Catholic student clubs as well as Protestant ones. But, for its entire existence, there were Islanders — Protestant and Catholic — who insisted on viewing it as a "Protestant" college, and its interests as Protestant ones. Considering the disparate theological viewpoints in non-Catholic churches, protecting Protestant interests would be quite a feat, but that view fit conveniently into the traditional religious split in the Island's political, educational, and social life. From that perspective, defending Prince of Wales was tantamount to defending an amorphous "Protestantism." And MacKinnon did defend the college, publicly, privately, and vigorously. One notable example was his determination to obtain a share of federal government grants to universities. In 1951, Ottawa began subsidizing universities and colleges at the rate of 50 cents for each citizen. Prince of Wales had applied for inclusion in the program on the basis of its two university-level years. When the president of the University of New Brunswick phoned MacKinnon that year to warn him that St. Dunstan's University was lobbying for the entire Island share (about $50,000), he rushed to Ontario to do some lobbying of his own. He was successful; by the mid-1950s Prince of Wales was receiving roughly $21,000 to $33,600 a year in federal grants[27] — and there was, he reported, "fury in high denominational places in Charlottetown," notably on the part of Dr. MacMillan.[28] The incident — and MacKinnon's interpretation of it — speaks volumes about the relationship between the two Island institutions, and about MacKinnon's attitude toward his rivals. He was openly contemptuous of academic standards at St. Dunstan's and most other Catholic universities in the Maritimes; he considered them little more than glorified high schools. And, in later years, he saw almost every obstruction in the path of Prince of Wales — from the removal of its board of governors in 1879 to opposition to its expansion plans in the 1960s — as the work of what he called church politicians. He had a good personal relationship with Bishop Malcolm MacEachern, a Cape Bretoner who had taught at St. Francis Xavier and apparently shared MacKinnon's appreciation of good food and fine wine:

"I liked Bishop MacEachern very much, but I always felt his office was too powerful a position, and he too overwhelming a potentate, for so tiny a province."[29] His perception was that the Church — especially in the person of the Bishop — was so powerful on the Island that nobody, including the government, and especially including the fractured Protestant churches, would or could stand up to it. The reality was that the two institutions, coexisting in a sometimes-friendly, sometimes-hostile fashion since the 1830s, were often in competition for money to stay alive in a province that was chronically poor. Sometimes Catholics saw the government-run college as a threat — and vice-versa. But conflicts between the two institutions had been repressed — or perhaps simply hidden — for decades. When MacKinnon arrived, they surfaced again.

During the 1954 education committee hearings, MacKinnon was accused of religious bias in both hiring and salary increases. At the time, about 23 per cent of students at Prince of Wales, 30 per cent of the faculty, and half the Model School teachers were Catholic. John A. Macdonald observed that, in a government-supported institution, Catholics should be better represented on the faculty. MacKinnon replied that teaching shortages affected the college as well as the public schools, and that he tried to acquire the best-qualified staff from a very competitive field. "I'm not a Catholic or a Protestant or a Jew or anything else when it comes to the administration of the college, and I would hope that students and staff members all feel that every denomination get fair play and nothing but fair play. I have never asked a teacher what his religion is. We've brought in new Catholic staff members and new Protestant ones, and we've had good and bad on both sides." Later in the proceedings, MacMillan complained that MacKinnon had recommended a salary increase for one teacher "greater than you recommended for all the Catholic teachers put together." MacKinnon denied this; he pointed out that the government was in charge of raises and often ignored his recommendations.[30]

In fact, as the badgering that went on at those committee hearings illustrated, the government was very much in charge of affairs at the college — and of its principal. At the end of the second day of hearings, the committee thanked and dismissed him, and announced that the next witness, scheduled for March 30, would be a high school principal from Summerside. Unfortunately, there was a storm that day, and the principal phoned to say the roads were too bad to travel. Somebody on the committee came up with the idea to recall MacKinnon. "One or two of the committee suggested that we recall Dr. MacKinnon for the purposes of clarification of one or two points brought out in his evidence here the other day," Clark told the hearing. The first question raised that day: how many periods a week did the principal teach?[31]

The politicians, it seemed, could be as overbearing and meddlesome as they wished. They were the bosses. As was the case throughout much of the college's long history, the politicians hired, fired, gave or withheld raises, and at times felt obliged to meddle in curriculum, discipline, and such administrative details as the frequency of faculty meetings. MacKinnon thought the Prince of Wales share of the federal grant — amounting to $33,650 in 1954[32] — should be placed in a special fund, the practice under Premier Jones. Clark decided that, since Ottawa had not imposed conditions on the grant, it was time for a change: he had directed the provincial treasurer to transfer the entire sum to the consolidated revenue fund, and "we shall use this money so granted in the best interests of the university portion of the college."[33]

MacKinnon had always considered this direct government control to be the college's greatest weakness. Unique among colleges and universities across Canada, Prince of Wales had not had the protection of a board of governors since 1879, and was therefore vulnerable to whatever way the political winds happened to be blowing. In 1954, the college was placed under a board of trustees, which was some improvement, although government members still dominated the board. The first trustees were Premier Alex Matheson and cabinet ministers Eugene Cullen, Keir Clark, J. W. Arsenault (succeeded shortly afterward by E. P. Foley) and W. E. Darby, as well as the college principal and the deputy minister of education. In keeping with the usual stab at a religion-based balance, two of the five politicians were Roman Catholic; Cullen, in fact, later served as chair of the St. Dunstan's board.[34]

Despite the earth tremors over damaged lockers and unguarded students at Prince of Wales, even a very conservative board should not have been unduly alarmed at innovations at the college during the 1950s. There were physical renovations at the college in the summers of 1949 and 1950 — new administration and staff offices to replace the office previously shared by principal and faculty, as well as new music, art, and locker rooms. And two big changes had taken place in the academic focus of the college, because of forces beyond anyone's control. MacKinnon was not happy about either. One was the decline in interest in arts courses. Of 115 students in third and fourth year in 1949–50, only 15 were in the arts program; 10 were taking commerce, and 90 were concentrating on science classes. MacKinnon worried that the Island was training too few young people in literature, art, music, and other cultural pursuits, "and, perhaps more important, the province does not appear to encourage the study of economic, historical, and political subjects so necessary to the commercial, political and professional pursuits in modern society." MacKinnon's observations on the place of science in the curriculum echoed those of Samuel Robertson almost half a century earlier. Science had its place, MacKinnon wrote, but was "impractical and indeed dangerous in modern life unless accompanied by the study of the history and culture of man provided by the social sciences and humanities."[35] The other change in emphasis at the college, of course, was in teacher training. Few students seemed to want to take the program, and many of those who did arrived with weak academic credentials: of the 42 students in the Normal School in 1954–55, for instance, only 12 had not failed subjects in the Entrance exams or in previous high school work.[36]

Unlike Robertson, MacKinnon hoped the college would branch into extension work, a field that had always been left to St. Dunstan's — adult education lectures, refresher courses for teachers, commercial courses for young businessmen, agricultural lectures for young farmers. Nothing came of that idea for more than a decade. The most notable innovations in the 1950s were related to the arts. During his second year, MacKinnon instituted an annual concert series at the college, in co-operation with the Toronto Conservatory of Music. The concerts included performances by the college chorus and visiting artists. In 1956, he launched a student production of a Gilbert and Sullivan musical, *The Mikado,* thus reviving a type of live performance that hadn't been seen in Charlottetown since 1912. He did this, he recalled, in spite of opposition from faculty, students not in the cast, and the community, and the show turned out to be a financial and public-relations success. Gilbert and Sullivan operettas became a new Prince of Wales tradition.[37]

One reason for the student opposition that year was that practices for *The Mikado* monopolized students' time and the auditorium, and therefore prevented the staging of a show with a longer tradition, the *Red and Blue Revue.*[38] Students at Prince of Wales weren't allowed to spread themselves too thin. The rule at the college was that you had to perform well in the classroom if you wanted to play hockey or direct a variety show. MacKinnon, unlike Robertson, was not suspicious of levity, but he scorned watered-down courses and lowered standards, and firmly believed that getting an education required self-discipline and, sometimes, hard, unpleasant slogging. At the beginning of every year, he always called an assembly and issued a caution. The speech, fodder for imitations by former students for decades to come, never varied much. He would exhort students to work hard, but not too hard. To have a well-rounded college experience, they should sample a few extracurricular offerings, but not too many. "Don't be a social butterfly [or, on alternate years, hummingbird]," he would warn, "flitting about from limb to limb."

By the time MacKinnon took over, the social life for Prince of Wales butterflies was still pretty tame. Country students still lived in boarding houses; there were still no student union quarters and no gathering place aside from the Old Spain (Catholic) and Rendezvous (Protestant) restaurants. A girls' chorus, formed in 1951, won prizes in the provincial music festival and continued to do "splendid work," according to MacKinnon. A boys' curling team was performing equally well, according to *The College Times*: in 1954, the college won the Island Schoolboy Curling Championship. For entertainment, many students still went to church and joined church youth groups and either Protestant or Catholic clubs at the college. Breaking the Sabbath was considered sinful enough to warrant a letter to *The College Times*. At issue was the fact that some students had decorated the auditorium for the Valentine formal on a Sunday afternoon. "Any College that permits such acts in defiance of God on His day," Interested Student wrote, "should see that such practices are halted before they become customary in the minds of the students...."[39] Liquor was rarely in evidence at college socials. Probably the most serious offence took place in the early 1950s, when members of the football team decided to punish a student who allegedly had his eye on the girlfriend of one of the athletes. Dressed in white sheets, they invaded a college dance, grabbed the unfortunate wretch, dragged him to the basement, and shaved off his lovely ducktail hairdo.[40] MacKinnon suspended the athletes for two weeks, but he said afterwards that they were not bad boys; he didn't hold the offence against them, and did not believe that they held a grudge against the administration.[41]

Generally, misdemeanours were more along the lines of skipping classes or talking too much in the classroom. The rules of segregation by gender had long since disappeared, although they were still part of the Prince of Wales tradition; as a student in the 1950s, Anne Love occasionally took a shortcut by way of the boys' stairs when in a hurry, and felt guilty about it. Mathematics professor Harry Love, who also was a student in the 1950s, recalled that students sometimes disciplined each other. Every year, there was a short-lived water-pistol craze at the college. One day in chemistry lab, a farm boy lost his patience with a classmate who was squirting people in the face. "He walked over, and with one hand grabbed the fellow by the shirt collar and just lifted him right off the floor. He held the other hand up to the fellow's nose, and said, 'Now, I've had enough.' Then he dropped him down, gently."[42]

Except under extraordinary circumstances, MacKinnon was not the college disciplinarian. Troublesome students would either be asked to leave the room or sent to Gordon Bennett, who would banish them to the library to repent under the steely gaze of Miss Mary Donahoe. Through the years, Bennett had become the college's unofficial counsellor and dispenser of justice. Approachable, avuncular and popular, he knew almost everybody by name. In a way, he was Mr. Prince of Wales. His father, Garfield, had taught chemistry there for thirty years; Gordon was an alumnus and had begun teaching chemistry in 1939. He also had coached hockey and football teams at the college for years, and, when Lily Seaman retired in 1954, he was asked to fill in as registrar. His relationship with MacKinnon did not always run smoothly. After more than a year of doing the registrar's job in addition to his many other duties, he wrote to Keir Clark, complaining that he was working too hard for too little pay. In addition to his full-time teaching load, he complained, "Countless other matters, in and about the building, which should have been handled by others, have been left for me to do."[43] He did not specify what these "other matters" were, but Clark could read between the lines. "Gordon Bennett ran the college," he observed.[44]

As Clark observed, MacKinnon was frequently absent from the college, and — presumably to make up for lost time — he would teach high school history by assembling several classes at once in the auditorium. Some of his critics — including some politicians and members of the faculty — were not impressed with this method. However, he was an entertaining instructor, if somewhat bombastic in his delivery. And he treated his students as if they were adults. To Barbara Johnston Macnutt, that attitude epitomized the spirit of Prince of Wales in the 1960s. "One thing we all liked so much was that when he was in class with us, he talked as if we knew exactly what he was talking about. He didn't treat us as if we were little uneducated beings and he was there to open our minds. He accepted that we were intelligent, and that we would understand what he was talking about."[45]

At Prince of Wales, professors were not told what to teach, how to teach, how to treat students, how to mark exams. "Never once when I came there did anybody in administration lecture me on the need for high standards," history professor Ian Brown said. "Never. And never did I lecture my students on the historical high standard demanded at PWC. I just sort of absorbed it. And I think the students did, too." For Doug Boylan, who also taught history in the early 1960s, the lack of structure had its benefits and its drawbacks. There was nobody looking over your shoulder; there were no faculty committees, no Senate, no faculty meetings except for an annual complaint session about salaries. There was also no counselling system, although individual teachers were always willing to help individual students. "In a way, it was kind of a brutal place," Boylan said. "Even in my time, they used to fail 30 per cent or so of the Grade 11 class, and another 20 per cent of the Grade 12 class. The people who were left were very much the cream of the crop. They did well, and they damn well should have. A lot of people simply disappeared at the end of Grade 11 and 12. Today, a public education system simply wouldn't tolerate those rates of failure. And there wasn't that much opportunity in trade schools, vocational schools, alternatives to the classic streams in education. It was a very elitist place in a way."[46]

MacKinnon's philosophy was that students should not be controlled too rigidly; that teachers performed with more creativity and enthusiasm when they could design courses and teach without interference or inspection. In his ideal universe, politicians would take that hands-off approach with school administrators. Such a system, proposed in his second book, *The Politics of Education*, would eliminate politicians altogether from the educational pyramid, except as collectors of tax dollars to run it. That vision never became manifest, although MacKinnon came close in the 1960s. But in the late 1950s, Providence at least gave him the gift of a new, sympathetic minister of education.

In September 1958, the provincial Conservatives, out of office since 1935, decided they needed a new leader to replace lawyer R.R. Bell. Dr. George

Dewar, a Conservative member of the Legislature, had been a classmate of MacKinnon at Prince of Wales, and remembered him as a forceful speaker in the debates in Professor Blanchard's classroom. By this time, too, MacKinnon had made quite a name for himself, and had acquired some influential friends. The previous year, he been appointed to the newly formed Canada Council; in 1958, he was named president of the Atlantic Provinces Economic Council and as a delegate to a NATO conference in Paris.[47] Dewar thought MacKinnon would make a dynamic party leader. "He was interested but had severe financial restraints," Dewar wrote in his memoir, *Prescription for a Full Life.* MacKinnon had a young family to support, and he wanted the party to supply a small salary. The party had no funds. "I wrote to him and suggested that he should cast his bread upon the waters and it would return before many days. If he had taken my advice he would probably have had a distinguished political career...."[48] As it turned out, Dewar himself ran for the leadership, but lost to Walter Shaw, a genial former civil servant similar in style to Walter Jones. A year later, the Conservatives won the provincial election. Fortunately for MacKinnon, George Dewar was named minister of education.

In the meantime, MacKinnon was in the process of making his mark through two construction projects. In a sense, both were designed to complement Prince of Wales College. The smaller project was a women's residence on Kent Street, near the college. The lack of a college residence had been a source of worry and complaint at Prince of Wales for decades. In the 1890s, Lucy Maud Montgomery's boarding house was the single dark cloud in her otherwise happy college year. In the 1930s, Samuel Robertson worried about students who had to endure crowded, noisy housing that prevented them from doing their best work. In the postwar years, the housing shortage made construction of a student residence even more urgent. "The day of the boarding house is over," MacKinnon wrote in his annual report in 1960. "Large houses are being turned into apartments; older people have old-age pensions; help is scarce; a room without meals is useless to most students, and prices for boarding one or two students in a household are going beyond the ability of students to pay."[49]

According to MacKinnon, the Carnegie Corporation had offered to pay for construction of a residence in 1930, but the project had been postponed repeatedly because of opposition from "church laymen."[50] If there was opposition, there was also strong support, from an organization that had been a formidable force in rural education: the Prince Edward Island Women's Institute. By the time they achieved their goal, Women's Institute branches had presented resolutions on the women's residence to the government on fourteen occasions.[51] Two provincial presidents had connections in government: Florence Matheson of Oyster Bed Bridge was the wife of Phillip Matheson, minister of public works, and Lois Dewar of New Perth was a sister-in-law of the minister of education. In 1959, the government announced that it planned to go ahead with a women's residence. Architect Charles Fowler of Halifax was hired to design the building, and when construction was about to begin in 1960, MacKinnon called on one of his influential friends to ensure that the project would go ahead as planned. "When the plans were ready and we were about to proceed," he wrote, "it looked as if a showdown might wreck the project — even at that late date. We had to take some decisive step." He asked a former Canada Council colleague, Governor General Georges Vanier, to lay the cornerstone. "The maximum publicity brought about much public support and gave government a reason to say, 'too late now' to the angry obstructionists," MacKinnon reported.[52] In the fall of 1961, Montgomery Hall, named after the famous alumna who had loathed her boarding house, opened for the first crop of students. It had cost $400,000, of which $106,531 came from the Canada Council's University Capital Grants Fund.[53]

Montgomery Hall consisted of a four-storey residence with rooms for 104 students, connected to a two-storey section containing a dining room, common room, and library. *The Guardian* reported on the opening of the complex with a riot of superlatives. The bedrooms were "almost fantastic in their modernity and convenience." The library had a copper-sheet flue and a "fireplace to end all fireplaces." Several visitors from other provinces had pronounced the residence "the finest building they ever saw on an educational campus."[54]

Montgomery Hall was indeed a fine complex, and Lucy Maud probably would have loved it. It made a huge difference in the life of the college. In addition to its function as a dormitory, it provided, for the first time ever, a place for rural and urban students to eat together, play bridge in the common room, hold dances, conduct meetings and flirtations, and smoke. The residence had a written list of strict rules, giving rural parents the comforting thought that their daughters were behaving most of the time. Residents were allowed out two week nights until 10 p.m., and one weekend night until midnight, but had to sign out, sign in, and indicate their destination. Bedrooms were inspected for neatness every morning. In the residence, boys were not allowed past the ground-floor reception area, and were barred entirely at night. Residents were supposed to be in their rooms, studying, after 7 P.M. In the dining room, with its rows of gleaming oak tables, the girls had to dress respectably for meals and take turns sitting at the "high table," at the right hand of the dean of women. The first dean, Helen Hurst, a dignified, formal, middle-aged woman, gave regular lectures on etiquette, and objected strenuously to signs of moral decay, such as any exchange of good-night kisses at the front-door checkpoint.

Sometimes the rules were broken. Mass escapes, under the cover of darkness, became an annual tradition. It started in the 1962–63 year, when Katherine Dewar, a third-year student from Summerside (and, coincidentally, a niece of Dr. Dewar), devised a plan whereby a few daring residents would slip through a basement window after dark to take in a late-night movie. By the time of the scheduled residence break, word had spread like village gossip, and 80 or 90 young ladies lined up to join the escape. The operation had been planned with military precision, with one resident leaving every three minutes, and was quite successful for a time. Unfortunately, when it was time to go back home, the fugitives found that the basement window had been locked. They spent the next few hours clambering up the face of the building one by one, to reach the second-storey windows. "It was eight in the morning before we got everybody in," Dewar recalled.[55]

The next fall, Montgomery Hall was the setting for an even more outrageous incident, again with Dewar as instigator. It was prom night at St. Dunstan's University, and a campus queen and princesses were about to be crowned. Dewar and her accomplices, under the guise of taking photographs for the Prince of Wales newspaper, drove the formally dressed — and unsuspecting — queen and princesses to Montgomery Hall, and promptly locked them in a kitchenette. Then Dewar phoned St. Dunstan's to demand a $100 ransom, which was to go toward the college yearbook. "It was probably half an hour later when total bedlam broke loose on the lawn in front of Montgomery Hall," Dewar said. "All the guys from St. Dunstan's had landed there. I think a lot of them had been drinking. It was probably 9 or 10 at night, and they were yelling and screaming and throwing things at the building, and we were throwing water bombs at them out the window. Mrs. Hurst phoned the police. And the order came up to let these women go immediately. We were getting scared because these guys were really getting unruly. So we had to let them go. I think the St. Dunstan's girls thought it was a bit of a lark."[56]

Such events were memorable partly because they were such an aberration in an otherwise orderly college and residence life. Professor Ian Brown recalled raising his voice in class only once in eight years, and feeling bad about it for a week. "I never saw rowdiness in the halls of Prince of Wales. The students were mischievous but never mean-spirited. I've never seen a student body so healthy-minded in the sense of a good self-image, good self-confidence and no hang-ups. They were not in awe of faculty. If you came from away and you tried your pompous Ontario attitude on the students they'd kill you."[57]

In the early 1960s, student rebellion had not yet spread across North American campuses, and student preoccupations at Prince of Wales weren't much different from those of the 1940s. One of the most contentious issues in the student council in 1962 appeared to be a dispute over the planned purchase of graduating gowns. Joe Ghiz, a second-year student who was chairman of the Amateur Athletic Association, wanted the money spent on football uniforms. Showing early promise as an orator, he gave a ringing speech at a council meeting: "I openly opposed buying the gowns, and promised to my class that if I was elected, the football team would have new uniforms. Now, seeing as this was the platform that my class elected me upon, I must, I will, and I shall thwart any and all opposition in order to protect the interests of my voters…. "[58] The student council that year was considered fairly radical because it started a campaign for fewer restrictions on students at the college. In the November 1961 issue of *The College Times,* the council listed a number of grievances against the college administration: it had imposed prohibitions on money-raising schemes at the college, discouraged the holding of assemblies, shut down Montgomery Hall on weekends. The registrar had too much power. "The administration has repeatedly and unnecessarily interfered in student affairs," the council complained. It was not specified who the council meant by "the administration," but presumably it was Bennett. He was from the old school, and had studied or worked under two law-and-order principals. It was no wonder Bennett and MacKinnon did not see eye to eye. MacKinnon was the lenient parent, the one who would be more likely to say yes to a request, and less likely to become overly troubled over minor student highjinks.

In any case, MacKinnon was busy working on the big picture. The early 1960s saw a sharp increase in enrolment at the college: 589 in 1960–61, 658 the next year, and 688 the year after that.[59] The facilities hadn't changed much in three decades, he pointed out; the college needed more space and more instructors. By the fall of 1961, three English classes were being conducted in classrooms at the Vocational School building next door.[60] The average teaching load across Canada was 9 to 12 hours a week, while Prince of Wales teachers were in the classroom 16 to 28 hours a week. What was needed — in both the public schools and the college — was an infusion of off-Island teachers to counteract the "educational in-breeding" that had been going on for more than a century. Perhaps even more urgent was an expansion of cultural programs to broaden young horizons. It was all very well to talk about the need for more vocational training, MacKinnon felt, but not without recognizing that even students with little aptitude for academic work needed a solid grounding in the essentials: English, mathematics, and history. In a passage in an annual report that could have been written by Samuel Robertson, MacKinnon wrote, "The good life is more important than the good job, and students need training for life as well as for jobs."[61]

For MacKinnon, cultural opportunities were an essential element of the good life. The reasons for the exodus of young people from the Island were only partly economic, he said; they were at least 50 per cent cultural. "Museums, art galleries, historic sites and the like are immensely valuable in the emphasis on tradition and community spirit which makes young people want to stay.... The Island has no provincial museum or archives, no art gallery, no historic sites, and is now the only province without them. Drama, music and other arts have minor, if any, places in Island education. May this not be one of the main reasons why Island young people know so little of their history and why, when they reach the teenage years, their sights are set on opportunities elsewhere and on places where things happen?"[62]

The theatre and music programs at Prince of Wales were only a minor part of the grand design. The cornerstone was the cultural complex in downtown Charlottetown that MacKinnon had envisioned in the early 1950s. "I worked at it alone for several years," he recalled, "with the government's knowledge and consent, and with public skepticism. 'It won't work but you can try it,' said Premier Matheson."[63] That was all the encouragement he needed. He set up a public trust, recruited a national board, and, with the board, managed to extract promises from the provincial and federal governments to finance the $5.6-million construction costs. Prince Edward Island's contributions were the site and a commitment to maintain the centre. By 1964, the year the Island was celebrating the centenary of the visit of the Fathers of Confederation, the state-of-the-art stone complex, incorporating an art gallery and museum, a 1,000-seat theatre, a library, and a memorial hall, was completed. Some people considered it a magnificent monument to the founders of Canada — and to Frank MacKinnon. Some thought it would make a good potato warehouse. "Frank's Folly," they called it. In the beginning, it looked a little too grand for its surroundings in downtown Charlottetown, and the kind of culture it was bringing to the Island generally had very little to do with the Island's own traditions. Many rural Islanders declined to darken its doors. Nevertheless, it was a moment of triumph for MacKinnon when, in October 1964, Queen Elizabeth II officially opened the Confederation Centre of the Arts. During the formal ball that evening in Memorial Hall, he danced with the Queen. As he was whirling Her Majesty around the hall, Ian Brown happened to be on the dance floor with his wife, Joan. Suddenly Brown realized, to his horror, that his boss was about to suggest changing partners. Brown abruptly changed course; he was more comfortable teaching history than waltzing with royalty. Not MacKinnon. "Frank was totally in his element," Brown said. "He looked totally at ease."[64]

The new cultural centre, for MacKinnon, was almost an adjunct to a new, expanded Prince of Wales. The Centre was only three blocks from the College, and he had plans to move the campus even closer — as far west as Prince Street. First, though, the matter of changing the status of the college had to be taken care of. In his early years at Prince of Wales, he had pronounced himself totally opposed to elevating Prince of Wales to university status; a decade later, he declared degree-granting powers to be a fulfillment of Prince of Wales' destiny. Certainly, it was not a new idea. As early as the mid-1800s, there had been expectations that Prince of Wales would develop into a full-fledged university. In Alexander Anderson's final years as principal, he expressed the hope that Island students would soon be able to take their degrees at the government-run school. And, in

1907, when the government was negotiating affiliation plans with McGill, hopes rose again. Those hopes were finally resurrected in the 1960s.

In the late 1950s and 1960s, enrolment in high schools and universities across Canada increased dramatically. This was due partly to the postwar baby boom and partly to rising unemployment rates. The university-age population almost doubled in those two decades, and the percentage of students attending university rose as well. At McGill, the student population more than doubled; at Dalhousie, the numbers almost quadrupled. Dalhousie had 1,496 students in 1957–58 and 2,613 six years later.[65] After a dip in enrolment at Prince of Wales in the 1950s, apparently as a result of high wages and plentiful jobs, the student population rose in the early 1960s.[66] At the same time, the regional high school system was expanding across the Island. By September 1960, regional high schools had begun operating in Abram's Village, O'Leary, Montague, Alberton, Tignish, Hunter River, and North Rustico. The government had also approved construction of high schools in Crapaud, Kensington, Morell, Souris, Kinkora, and Miscouche.

The high school network produced a huge increase in the number of young people eligible for university programs, and a shortage of teachers with degrees. It also diminished the need for high school courses at Prince of Wales and could even eliminate them altogether, leaving the college in the awkward position of offering only the first two undergraduate university years. By 1962, 175 Island students were enrolled in undergraduate degree programs in overcrowded mainland universities, which meant that a considerable sum of money was leaving the province every year. At Prince of Wales, more than 250 students were enrolled in the first two university years, about the same number as at other small Maritime universities.[67]

Meanwhile, the college had also lost its monopoly on teacher training. In 1957, Education Minister Clark introduced in the Legislature a proposal to certify teachers trained at a normal school at St. Dunstan's. Fred Large, a Liberal member of the Legislature, gave voice to Protestant fears that this represented a first step on the road to separate schools and an invasion of the public school system by sectarian-trained teachers. The measure went into effect, despite bitter debates in the House, within both parties, and in the press.[68] And three years later, the Catholic university's full-fledged bachelor of education program further diminished the importance of the Normal School at Prince of Wales.

With all these circumstances in mind, some Islanders thought it was time to brush off the old degree-granting idea. Once again, the Women's Institutes took up the cause, in the form of resolutions at their annual meetings in 1961 and 1962. In 1961, a number of Charlottetown business and professional men lent their considerable weight to the idea. That fall, Charlottetown psychiatrist Malcolm Beck happened to meet Gordon Bennett on the *Abegweit*, the car-ferry between New Brunswick and Prince Edward Island. Beck had attended Prince of Wales in the 1940s, and Bennett had been his hockey and rugby coach and favourite professor. In the course of their conversation, Bennett suggested that it might be time for Prince of Wales to add two university years. Beck, who still had five children to educate, was personally interested in the idea. By the time the ferry reached Borden, he had decided to form a citizens' group to promote it. A few months later, he phoned Dr. Paul Cudmore, a family physician who had been talking to Frank MacKinnon about the college. "Paul was hot to trot," Beck recalled, "and suggested I slip over to his place that very same night, and we would talk about it. He agreed that we should get a group together, and it didn't take us long to think of eight to 10 really good names."[69]

Before the committee began meeting, Beck and Cudmore decided to contact faculty members at St. Dunstan's to see whether there was any chance that the two institutions might form a single university. Cudmore talked to Dr. Owen Sharkey, and Beck to Dr. Allan MacDonald. Both were young priests who might be expected to regard such a venture positively. "When we talked with these two men," Beck said, "we were told very firmly, but with no animosity at all, that there was no chance for such a thing. And each of them gave us very good reasons why it could, and/or should, never happen." Cudmore and Beck decided that the older faculty would be even less anxious to co-operate.[70]

Eventually a twenty-member committee was formed with some of the leading lights of the community, including lawyers Alan Scales and John Nicholson, businessmen Alan Holman and Ralph Beck, and physicians Beck, Cudmore, and John Gillis. Acting as consultants to the group were Frank MacKinnon and Gordon Bennett from Prince of Wales; Dr. Kenneth Parker, superintendent of city schools; and Malcolm MacKenzie, deputy minister of education. In July 1962, the committee presented its report, recommending the elevation of Prince of Wales to degree-granting status.[71]

The Evening Patriot editorialized that the plan "could prove the key to the Island's future." To meet the Island's social and economic needs, educated young people needed to stay on the Island, the newspaper argued. When they went to university on the mainland, they didn't come back. And if Frank MacKinnon, the architect of the Confederation Centre complex, was backing the idea "in the same spirit, and with the same sort of energy, there should be interesting days ahead."[72]

Chapter Nine

Pride and Prejudice

9

"We have come to an end. For myself as well as for you, I say with deepest feeling: Prince of Wales! Beloved Prince of Wales! Hail—and Farewell!"

—John Sutherland Bonnell, May 16, 1969

Interesting days, indeed. For a time, the project galloped forward. In his 1964 report, MacKinnon said the need to upgrade Prince of Wales was "obvious and urgent" — for the same reasons that new universities were being established elsewhere. Noting that the government was paving about a hundred miles of Island roads a year, he calculated that the planned Prince of Wales expansion could be achieved at the price of only a few miles of pavement. In the winter of 1963–64, more than fifty Island organizations presented briefs to the government requesting degree-granting status for Prince of Wales. They had a sympathetic hearing in the minister of education, Dr. George Dewar. In the Speech from the Throne in 1964, the government promised to give "careful consideration" to elevating Prince of Wales, and to appoint a royal commission to report on the organization and financing of higher education.[1]

During that session, the government introduced a bill giving Prince of Wales degree-granting powers. In contrast to the bill through which St. Dunstan's obtained degree-granting status in 1917, this one created a huge uproar. The potent brew of religion, politics and education injected a poison into the debates — behind the scenes and in the House — that was reminiscent of the 1860s. It was, Dewar recorded later, "the most contentious piece of legislation with which I had to deal during my term of office."[2] Provincial Secretary David Stewart reported that things were said in caucus that people would remember for the rest of their lives.[3] According to Dewar's account of events, leading the charge on the side of the college were MacKinnon, Dewar, MLA Robert Grindlay, and members of the citizens' committee; on the opposite side were the defenders of St. Dunstan's interests, the Bishop of Charlottetown, Provincial Treasurer Alban Farmer, and Conservative MLA Henry Wedge.[4]

Dewar presented "The Prince of Wales College Act 1964" to his caucus on March 5. Caucus members argued over it for two-and-a-half hours. Four days later, Farmer tried to have the bill amended so as to turn the college into a private institution, presumably to place it and St. Dunstan's on equal footing in terms of government funding. "Mr. Farmer will oppose the Act!" Dewar wrote in his diary that day. On March 11, he wrote in his diary that he had discussed the Act with Premier Shaw. "He is very disturbed about bill. Feels government may be defeated on it. Farmer making threats." Shaw tried to persuade Dewar to bring in the bill with a clause stating that the Act would be proclaimed at an unspecified later date. Dewar refused. Henry Wedge proposed an amendment to that effect. The Roman Catholic members of the caucus agreed to support the bill with Wedge's amendment. Dewar remained opposed. Dewar's March 13 entry in his diary notes that Shaw "does not trust Mr. Matheson, leader of the Opposition, not to divide the House on a religious basis and throw Liberal support with R.C.s to overthrow the government. Most R.C.s I feel are reconciled to the P.W.C. elevation but Farmer apparently threatened to resign or cross the floor of the House. He will win a temporary respite."[5]

On March 19, the bill was carried on second reading, with an amendment by Wedge, seconded by Farmer, stipulating that the Act would not come into effect until the Royal Commission had presented its report. Dewar voted against the amendment. MacKinnon, Dewar observed later, was "quite displeased" by what had transpired.[6]

So were students at Prince of Wales. "STABBED IN THE BACK (By Wedge and Farmer)," the headline on a special edition of the student newspaper read on March 23. A cartoon showed the two politicians stabbing a prostrate body, labelled "Youth of P.E.I." "Because of the lackadaisical nature of Royal Commissions this means in effect that the bill is dead and useless.... At first glance this may not look too serious, but Royal Commissions have been noted for doing precisely nothing, and if this happens in this case, PWC will never become a university." Editor John Vaillancourt argued that only one voice had been heard to oppose the degree-granting idea: a brief from St. Dunstan's to the provincial government. "This leads us to the conclusion that the government has not listened to the people as it should, but has obeyed the orders of an organization whose activities should be more properly confined to its *own* business."[7]

Obviously defenders of St. Dunstan's considered expansion of Prince of Wales to be their business, since it appeared to threaten funding to a university that had suffered through decades of financial drought and was more than ever in need of government aid. Without question, Prince of Wales students recognized that degree-granting status for their college would have a dramatic effect on *their* lives. The day the special edition of *The College Times* came out, hundreds of Prince of Wales students marched to the Legislature, waving placards ("Deserted, Disappointed, Disillusioned and Disgusted" and "Royal Commission Be Damned"). On the invitation of an Opposition member, they filed into the building, still carrying their placards, and sat in the public galleries. For the most part, it was a quiet demonstration, but it outraged Premier Walter Shaw. He warned that the plans to make Prince of Wales degree-granting had "suffered a serious setback," and the organizers "should be dealt with severely."[8]

Despite such threats, the government went ahead with the Royal Commission. The chairman was Dr. John Sutherland Bonnell, a retired Presbyterian minister with a soft spot for Prince of Wales. Island-born, he had dropped out of school in Grade 8, but had resumed his education at the college and eventually acquired some fame as a preacher at a large New York City church and as president of the New York Theological Seminary. Bonnell kept up his Island connections by spending his summers at his handsome estate in Georgetown. The other commissioners were Dr. Norman MacKenzie, a former Nova Scotian who had served for fifteen years as president of the University of British Columbia; and Dr. Joseph McMillan, a respected Charlottetown surgeon. MacKinnon had his suspicions about the attitudes of the commission: Bonnell had received an honorary degree from St. Dunstan's and a medal from the Pope for ecumenical services; MacKenzie, known to dislike small colleges, was "susceptible to control by Catholics in Halifax and Charlottetown."[9] Nevertheless, when the commission submitted its report in January 1965, it recommended that the act granting university status to Prince of Wales be proclaimed at once. At the same time, however, the commission questioned the ability of a province of 110,000 to support two universities. In the short term, Prince of Wales and St. Dunstan's needed to start co-operating by sharing some facilities and staff; and, as a long-term goal, to consider a federation of the two institutions — two campuses under the umbrella of a single university. Elevating Prince of Wales and financing St. Dunstan's on an equal basis would place the two universities on a level footing.[10]

"I am not sure Frank MacKinnon will approve of this," MacKenzie wrote in a letter to Eric Harvie, the multi-millionaire Calgary oilman who had served as board chairman of the Fathers of Confederation Memorial Citizens Foundation. "If he doesn't, he will probably not love me any more. We had to recommend immediate proclamation of his Act .... But we went on to say that we felt the ideal solution for the future was to plan and work toward a University of Prince Edward Island with two colleges.... We also recommended that the University receive aid from the provincial government. I don't believe that Frank loves his competitors and will find it difficult to work with them and feels that they will get some of the public money which he had hoped would be reserved for him. Our proposal, however, does make sense in that it should provide more, for less money, than other arrangements, and much as I love Frank and would like to do everything I can to help him, I don't believe one can allow friendship to stand in the way of decisions that one believes to be right and wise, however painful they may be...."[11]

The recommendations may have been "right and wise," but, in the end, only one was adopted. On June 1, 1965, more than a year after the new Prince of Wales Act was passed in the Legislature, the college became a university. At the first meeting of the board of governors on June 29, MacKinnon suggested that the college keep its original name because of its long history.[12] Before the legislation had been passed, he had also pledged to maintain the good reputation the college had built over 130 years. "Here is the most important factor in the entire matter," he wrote in his 1964 annual report. "Prince of Wales wants to give a first-class degree. Standards vary greatly among degree-granting institutions from high to low, a fact not generally recognized by the public which tends to think, for example, that one BA is the same as another. We would wish that a degree from Prince of Wales would be of the highest standard and reputation which would be accepted anywhere on its merit."[13] He insisted that the province *could* afford two universities: if he could get funding equal to the cost of 25 miles of pavement, "I can produce one of the best universities in the Maritimes."[14]

MacKinnon envisioned a small, undergraduate, liberal arts college, avoiding a proliferation of courses and the addition of professional programs. There would be no need to add expensive equipment; the cost would lie mostly in the acquisition of land, buildings and well-qualified faculty. Enrolment in the university years in 1964–65 was 295. MacKinnon predicted that by 1969–70, enrolment would climb to 1,200. But limits would be kept on the size of the college to maintain its intimate quality. As far as possible, classes would be conducted as tutorials of 10 to 20 students and seminars of 5 to 10 students in the humanities, and small teaching labs of 20 to 30 students in the sciences. The college would drop Grade 11 in 1966 and Grade 12 the next year, and add the third year of university in 1967 and the fourth year in 1968.[15]

The new university started out with a complex of four buildings — the main building on Weymouth Street, the two Montgomery Hall buildings, and the former vocational school, which Prince of Wales took over when the new Provincial Vocational School was built in 1964. Plans for the first phase of expansion, designed by architects John Andrews and Associates of Toronto, were to renovate the two main academic buildings and build a new library, with a target of 250,000 books, on Weymouth Street, connected with the main building by an underground concourse. The heating system was to be replaced and linked with the Maritime Electric power plant. The two main academic buildings were to be connected with a concourse containing a lecture theatre. Cost of the renovations, the new heating system, and the link building was estimated at $1 million, and the library at $750,000. The Alumni Association agreed to begin fund-raising for the library, and the board of governors asked permission from the government to borrow the $1 million.[16]

By April 1967, the board was negotiating to buy two properties on Weymouth Street for the library, and discussing with Central Mortgage and Housing Corporation the possibility of buying houses near the college for student residences. Three months later, final drawings were being drafted for the new heating system and renovations and additions to the vocational wing and main building. By the fall of 1967, the board had decided to buy a Kent Street property for $85,000; by January 1968, it had confirmed the purchase of the Weymouth Street properties and approved the purchase of another property on Kent Street and a 600-acre farm at Strathgartney "for research purposes."[17] That year, the college added a third university year, with 88 students enrolled.

Meanwhile, the college was acquiring new professors, many of them "from away," young and eager to implement innovative teaching ideas. "We have been making very good progress with the College and its change to a full university," MacKinnon wrote to Eric Harvie in July 1967. "The new Board is working well; the two final high school years … have been dropped and the high school staff transferred; two years of academic planning have ended with the all necessary new courses and regulations; and a new and very good faculty have started work. The last is most important: we have been able to get very good people by careful recruiting, and we have a number of distinguished scholars coming as visiting professors.… We have had violent opposition from the Catholics who wanted us amalgamated with their St. Dunstan's,[18] which is a completely different institution from Prince of Wales.… It is unbelievable the skulduggery that went on, but we are on the road now and our enrolment from the Island and other provinces has quadrupled in four years.…"[19]

The future looked rosy, even though some of the ambitious plans sank like a half-baked soufflé. One idea was to set up cross-disciplinary studies — examining issues from the viewpoint of disciplines such as English, history, psychology, science, and mathematics. A seminar on "truth," for instance, would illustrate how different disciplines perceived that abstract concept. "Terrific idea," history professor Ian Brown said. "At first, the students were really enthusiastic. But then they put their thumbs down. They said, 'There's no structure. We don't know where we're going.' It was an absolutely valid point." Some faculty also wanted to dispense with the traditional grading system, replacing marks with "pass," "fail," "pass with honour." The premise was that, in a subject such as history or English, numerical marks made little sense. "The students said, 'No bloody way. How can I get into Dal if I don't have a numerical mark?' They were right."[20]

Other aspects of the new university worked very well. Prince of Wales was still small and compact — like a ship where everybody on board knows everybody else — but suddenly infused with a new energy. The new teachers were passionate about the place, Dianne MacLeod Anderson recalled, and the students absorbed their enthusiasm. The principal, far from being the remote personage of an earlier era, had become a hero. "We would have killed for Dr. Frank," Anderson said. "I think it was perhaps passed on to us that we were part of something very special, that we were part of an almost elite group, and were very fortunate to have this type of education."[21] In a lyrical lecture in Charlottetown in 2002, playwright Kent Stetson described the Prince of Wales of the late 1960s as "a Camelot" (or possibly, he amended, a Brigadoon),[22] ushering in "the first golden age of higher education" on the Island. "Dr. Frank ... brought us — some of us still carrying the odour of our barnyard roots — the means to express ourselves to the highest possible degree." For Stetson, that opportunity came through new programs in music and theatre, and new faculty members such as Tom Hahn, the director of music. A transcendent moment, perhaps symbolic of those heady days, occurred as the college choir was wrapping up its second or third practice of the term. The choir had just learned Beethoven's arrangement of the hymn "The Heavens Are Declaring," and they were so in love with their own four-part harmony, they continued singing as they streamed out of the music room on the ground floor. "We filled the halls of PWC with glorious sound.... Still singing, we passed through the lower corridors, we climbed the stairs to the second floor, past biology, past physics, on down past history, and German and poli-sci. We circled back through the ground-floor corridor, still in harmony, still in tune, and made our way to the heart of the new college, the coffee shop. We re-grouped and gave our startled friends the concert of their lives."[23]

The climax to those golden years came in September 1967, when the college celebrated its new status with a special convocation. Prince of Wales wouldn't have its own graduating class for two more years, but the college conferred honorary degrees on a number of distinguished Canadians, including Prime Minister Lester B. Pearson and former principal G. D. Steel. Students hauled Pearson and his wife, Maryon, through the streets of Charlottetown in a buggy; three hundred guests sat down to a banquet; and a thousand people danced at a ball at Confederation Centre. A separate ball was held for students at the college. As they danced, staff and students might well have been humming a few bars of the *Camelot* theme song. "Things at Prince of Wales were going much too well for her critics," MacKinnon wrote decades later, "and all signs pointed to the college's splendid future."[24]

Actually, not all the signs. While the faculty and administration at Prince of Wales were happily constructing Camelot, the board of governors was in the awkward position of trying to figure out whether the new university should even exist. More than a year after the board was appointed, it hadn't decided whether Prince of Wales should develop on its own, amalgamate with St. Dunstan's, or enter some form of federation. During a meeting in August 1966 at the summer home of board member J. S. Bonnell in Georgetown, chairman Dr. John Gillis said the board could make little progress until it decided this basic issue. According to the minutes of that meeting, Gillis felt that the St. Dunstan's board "was just as confused as we were.... Gillis felt we must make the decision on what form the development of PWC would take, as no decision can be made on pressing matters such as men's residence or a library, until this first decision is made." The board, to put it mildly, had mixed opinions. To Wilbert MacInnis, amalgamation was the only answer. To Leone Ross, amalgamation was out of the question. Senator Orville Phillips thought the two universities should begin by co-operating, and move on from there. MacKinnon opposed any kind of affiliation other than a loose form of co-operation; he thought the two schools were too different, and that a church-backed college would overpower Prince of Wales. "Sleeping with an elephant," he called it. By the end of the meeting, the board members decided to postpone their decision. "Then they all went to dinner, along with wives and husbands."[25]

At its September meeting, the board finally approved a motion from Judge W. E. Darby to proceed with the development of the new university on the downtown site, "but ... during the interim period this would not preclude discussion or negotiation for co-operation between Prince of Wales College, St. Dunstan's University and other universities."[26] The board had held its first joint meeting with the St. Dunstan's board in July. Like red-faced prospects for an arranged marriage, the two boards exchanged polite, non-committal pleasantries. Several members offered up instances of past co-operation (their athletes had met on the playing fields; a few St. Dunstan's professors had taught at Prince of Wales), and MacKinnon and St. Dunstan's rector Right Rev. George MacDonald agreed on their willingness to talk things over, any time.[27]

In the spring of 1967, the government reasserted its role as matchmaker by setting up a co-ordinating committee with five members from Prince of Wales and five from St. Dunstan's. Three meetings were held, but, by April 1968, little had been accomplished. It was at that point that the government decided it was time for drastic action. Conveniently, the winds of public opinion were blowing in the right direction.

Part of the impetus for that shift came from a second activist group. One of the founders was John Eldon Green, a civil servant and dedicated Catholic layman who taught part-time at St. Dunstan's. Green had witnessed too many religious divisions in his lifetime, including his own grandparents' mixed marriage, the unofficial Catholic/Protestant segregation in Charlottetown schools, and the nasty debate over the teacher-training issue. He was watching with alarm efforts to elevate Prince of Wales to university status. "I thought, here we go again. We're going to go backwards. Now we're going to have another Protestant/Catholic fight. If Prince of Wales gets degree-granting status, it will be a non-sectarian school, and it will want more of a share than the sectarian school. St. Dunstan's has been there for 110 years and here comes Johnny-come-lately." If the province gave its own university most of the funds, he thought, St. Dunstan's would be effectively strangled.[28]

In the winter of 1964, Green ran into Mac Beck in downtown Charlottetown. Beck had played a key role on the committee advocating university status for Prince of Wales, but he was in the process of changing his mind. The two men set up a meeting with Dr. John Maloney (later to become a Liberal cabinet minister) and Dr. Gordon Lea, chairman of the Charlottetown school board, to discuss the formation of a single university. Lea soon left the group, as did Dr. John Gillis and Judge St. Clair Trainor, who were appointed to the boards of Prince of Wales and St. Dunstan's, but it picked up other members, including six physicians, one dentist, and seven Catholic and Protestant clergymen.[29]

At first, the ministers and priests mingled self-consciously; before they began working together, they actually had to be introduced. But an ecumenical spirit — for the Catholics, a legacy of Vatican II — was in the air, even on Prince Edward Island. It was becoming not only acceptable, but fashionable, to acquire friends on the other side. In MacKinnon's opinion, the allure of ecumenicism was the only reason some of the Protestant clergymen had been persuaded to join the cause in the first place. "One event described it all," he wrote in his memoir of the Prince of Wales years. "The Bishop and I, sitting alone together on a sofa at a dinner party, were convulsed by three ecumenical parsons behaving among a group of priests like virginal young ladies at a coming-out party."[30]

In May 1965, the committee, by then composed of twenty-three men, issued a report calling for the amalgamation of St. Dunstan's and Prince of

Wales. There weren't enough academic or financial resources to justify two separate institutions, the report said. Federation would not work; it simply would lead by the process of attrition to the ultimate annihilation of the two existing universities. The new university would not be a Catholic one, but not strictly a secular one, either. The study of religion should have a place in "an intellectual environment in which the Christian viewpoint of life can thrive and find meaningful expression. We are satisfied that this can be accomplished in a single university with all Christians working toward this common goal."[31]

For some members of the Study Group, the logical foundation of that single university was St. Dunstan's. In the fall of 1966, Green prepared a document for the Bishop, proposing that St. Dunstan's save itself by secularizing — removing the clergy from all but teaching positions, and appointing Protestants to the board. In return, an institution of Christian studies would be established. "St. Dunstan's must be the foundation on which the structure of higher education and adult education for the future is built," the document said in part. "It is not merely a matter of survival but of it continuing to exercise a dominant role in university work...." The Bishop presented this proposal to his board in December. The board turned it down, thereby, Green felt, signing St. Dunstan's death warrant.[32] But a copy of the letter appeared in Frank MacKinnon's mailbox the next day and cemented suspicions at Prince of Wales that secular education was under siege.

The Study Group spent three years lobbying politicians, speaking at public meetings, trying to get the newspapers to air their cause. Sometimes they felt like giving up; sometimes, they saw signs of progress. One small incident in September 1966 gave Mac Beck hope. He had presented a motion to a meeting in Summerside asking for endorsement of the single-university idea. The new young premier, Alex Campbell, was a guest speaker that evening. Campbell asked for a show of hands on Beck's motion. "I damn near died!" Beck recalled. "This was the first public test of our grand plan, and I was sitting there quaking. Then to my great and good pleasure, it seemed that the whole bloody room stood up, just as one body, and the room was full. I heaved a sigh of relief. This was the first time, after 20 or more months working on this project, that I felt at all sure that the public at large was behind what we had been working for so hard for so long."[33]

The new premier proved to be a key element in Beck's "grand plan."

Campbell, a thirty-two-year-old lawyer from Summerside, was a fresh face on the political scene, with no ties to either university, aside from the fact that his father and sister had attended Prince of Wales, and his father had served as chancellor of St. Dunstan's. Alex had graduated from Summerside High School, Mount Allison University and Dalhousie Law School. In May 1966, he led the Liberals for the first time in a provincial election campaign, which ended in a tie vote. The new members of the Legislature included Gordon Bennett, who was appointed minister of education. The Liberals gained two seats in a by-election in July, but, with the appointment of the Speaker, ended up with a majority of one.

The new government was in a precarious position in the Legislature, and almost bankrupt. A number of government ventures, including investments in a ship-building firm and frozen-food plant, had gone sour in the early 1960s. By 1965, the provincial debt was $364.40 per person, far higher than in any other province. By the time the Campbell government tabled its first budget in 1967, the total debt was $99 million. According to deputy provincial treasurer G. D. Dennis, the high per capita debt made it hard to raise money on the bond market, and many of the liabilities were in short-term notes.[34] During Campbell's first summer as premier, the government could barely meet the civil service payroll. The premier and provincial treasurer tried to borrow money from the banks in Montreal, but were turned down. Campbell then appealed directly to Prime Minister Lester Pearson for interim financing to meet the payroll.[35]

Meanwhile, the two universities were going ahead with their separate expansion plans. In the fall of 1967, Prince of Wales asked the government to guarantee a $1-million loan to finance its building program.[36] By 1968, the Prince of Wales board of governors was estimating that it would need $1,876,826 in operating costs the next academic year, with $700,000 expected to come from Ottawa and $719,076 from the province. At St. Dunstan's, the enrolment, the size of the faculty, the number of degree programs, and the facilities on campus were growing rapidly. A women's residence had opened in 1959, a new library in 1963, and a science centre in 1966. In January 1967, the St. Dunstan's board presented to the provincial cabinet a four-year, $5-million building plan that would include men's and women's residences, a new arts building, and an athletic centre.[37]

By then, the province had a new weapon in its efforts to control its troublesome universities: the federal government had started funnelling funds for higher education through the provinces. Ottawa had also been urging universities to save money by co-operating, and provincial governments to find a way to promote more rational planning in higher education.[38] In March 1968, the Campbell government introduced a bill in the Legislature that would allocate those funds through a university grants commission. Campbell saw the bill as a way of accommodating both universities. Because of a clause that would allow the commission to determine curriculum, many academics, at Prince of Wales and at universities off the Island, saw the bill as a threat to academic freedom. "All hell broke loose," Campbell recalled.[39] A barrage of petitions, letters to the editor, newspaper ads, and demonstrations followed, with demands that the government withdraw the bill. Prince of Wales students staged a "sit-in" on the steps of Confederation Centre, packed the visitors' gallery at the Legislature, and went door-to-door with petitions. "There were no alternatives suggested," Campbell said. "Just get rid of it — withdraw. And we were all there with our backs to the wall and there were no escape routes. It was withdraw or else."[40]

At the time, Campbell was negotiating a deal with Ottawa that was supposed to resuscitate the provincial economy by pumping hundreds of millions of federal and provincial dollars into almost every sphere of Island life. In a sense, this plan chewed up and spit out the university issue. The Comprehensive Development Plan was a sweeping, unprecedented, and controversial scheme, designed to modernize the province by, among other things, reducing the numbers of farmers and fishermen, enlarging tourism and manufacturing, and generally effecting change in the Island way of life.[41] Once the Plan was approved in 1969, an army of off-Island planners started to implement it, much to the chagrin of many Islanders. They included two unlikely allies, Keir Clark, then health minister, and Frank MacKinnon. After denouncing the Plan, Clark eventually crossed the floor of the Legislature to sit as an independent. "We have bargained our provincial autonomy for pieces of silver," he said. MacKinnon said the government was pursuing a "death wish" by inviting federal intervention, and with the Plan had come "a large task force which moved to the Island and literally took over the government."[42]

One of those consultants was Del Gallagher, an economist from New Brunswick who headed a Crown corporation called the Economic Improvement Corporation. The province had set up the agency in 1967 to plan and implement the development programs. In the spring of 1968, as protests against the grants commission bill mounted, Campbell spent a week with officials from the agency to find a way out of the university dilemma. "When we were confronted and told to withdraw our legislation on the grants commission, that's when Del Gallagher's shop got active," Campbell said.[43] What emerged apparently was the brainchild of the development agency:[44] the government would establish a college of applied arts and technology and a single, non-denominational university. "We had been aiming at dividing limited resources between the two institutions, and when that didn't fly, we went for the clean break," Campbell said. "And we really didn't waste a lot of time contemplating the possibilities of mergers and amalgamations and so on. Because that road was so full of ruts and potholes, even the most daunting had floundered on it. This seemed to be a way out for the government and a way for the future." Prince of Wales supporters may have been counting on the government's supporting its own child, the public college, Campbell said. "But how could we as a government ignore the fact that St. Dunstan's was educating as many Island students as Prince of Wales was? We were certainly not prepared to ignore that fact." Campbell presented his decision to the Liberal caucus and obtained unanimous support — apparently even from his education minister, Gordon Bennett.[45]

But it was Campbell, not Bennett, who stood up in the Legislature on the morning of April 2 to present the government's White Paper on higher education. "I could feel my heart resounding in my boots. I speculated on how Opposition members might act. How would the people of Prince Edward Island react? Would my own caucus remain unanimous? Only time would tell." The speech lasted more than an hour. The government had hoped, Campbell said, that the two universities could co-operate. "Recent events have now demonstrated that the hope of co-operative arrangements cannot be realized." Instead, the government would establish a new university. Prince of Wales and St. Dunstan's could continue on their own if they wished. "But let one thing be very clear: The government will support financially, with all the funds at its disposal, only a single public university in Prince Edward Island."[46]

The visitors' gallery was jammed with Prince of Wales students. Among them was Horace Carver, a farm boy from Cross Roads who was editor of the yearbook that year, as well as a member of student council. His immediate reaction was surprise. He hadn't expected that a government with such a razor-thin majority would dare to incur the wrath of people with intense loyalties to two venerable institutions. Besides, he had believed, with the naïve optimism of youth, that students could save their college if they just circulated enough petitions and spent enough hours in the visitors' gallery at the Legislature. Then the hurt set in. "I would say that this was the most traumatic thing I experienced up to the age of 18, and if I was to name half a dozen of the most traumatic things that happened in life, this would be included."[47] In Halifax, a group of Dalhousie students from the Island gathered at the home of Lawson Drake, then on sabbatical, to listen to the report of the premier's announcement on the radio. "Everybody was devastated," Barb Johnston Macnutt said. "I think deep in our hearts we knew it was going to happen. In retrospect, it probably was the best thing to happen, but there was no way anybody could convince anybody of that at the time. There were a lot of hard feelings and hurt people."[48]

The mood of the general public was probably more accurately reflected by the reaction of the Opposition. Conservative Leader Walter Shaw described Campbell's statement as "comprehensive, far-reaching and almost startling."[49] He expressed no opposition, and neither did his caucus. Congratulatory messages starting rolling in to Premier Campbell. "Three hearty British cheers," Lieutenant-Governor W. J. MacDonald wrote. MacDonald, who had taught at Prince of Wales for four decades, said he had been advocating a single university for many years. "I had almost given up hope, and I must say your splendid address came as a very pleasant surprise."[50] Another former professor, Bruce Hodgins, wrote from Trent University in Peterborough, Ontario. He said he and several colleagues at Prince of Wales had advanced the argument for a single university many times in the early 1960s. "It seemed to me and to my colleagues that it was time Prince Edward Island set aside many of the prejudices of the 19th century in favour of educational excellence and economic reality."[51]

Naturally, there were equally strong opinions from the opposite side. John Sutherland Bonnell sent a sympathy note to MacKinnon from New York City: "I want you to know that your stock was never higher on Prince Edward Island than it is today. However, the Prince Edward Islanders seem to have lost their nerve and the will to put up any kind of battle. It looks as if PWC will be wiped out, which will be a first-class disaster for education in the Maritime Provinces. It wouldn't surprise me if most of the students will go over to the mainland for their education and the government will find itself saddled with a sectarian university on its hands.... It's a sad business."[52]

MacKinnon couldn't have agreed more. Calling the proposed alliance "a shotgun wedding," he resigned on September 8. He said the government had abruptly cut off support to its own college with no warning, and without consulting either its principal or its board of governors. Dr. Gillis, the board chairman, publicly chastised the government for its lack of consultation and privately criticized it for making MacKinnon "the victim of a raw deal." He told the board that the government had forced MacKinnon out of the college "and marked him as unacceptable," with the result that certain community groups were conducting a campaign of slander against him. According to the board minutes, Gillis said the pressure on MacKinnon and his family was so severe, "Mrs. MacKinnon telephoned Dr. Gillis and told him to release to the newspapers the fact that Dr. MacKinnon had resigned. She stated that if this wasn't done by the Board, then she would do it herself."[53]

In the midst of all this, Peter MacKinnon, one of the principal's three sons, was twenty years old and in the middle of final exams at Dalhousie, but returned home to discuss the situation with his father. "He had already reached the conclusion that he had no choice but to resign," Peter recalled. "And so I could not help him other than by joining my sister in providing whatever comfort we could to him and my mother as they suddenly faced an uncertain future."[54] The impact of the government's action on the family was dramatic, he recalled. "While there was much speculation about what the government of P.E.I. might do in the spring of 1968, my father did not know. There had been none of the one-on-one discussions between him and the premier that one might have expected on an issue of this scope and magnitude. Nor was there consultation between the government and PWC on other levels. It was a shabby way to do the public's business and my father was the real and, no doubt by some, the intended victim. Given the way things happened he had no choice but to resign and leave the province, and there is sadness in that."[55]

MacKinnon did get moral support from some prominent members of the community. One of them was Frank Storey, a Charlottetown businessman who was chief executive officer of Confederation Centre. "Because

Frank MacKinnon is a man of vision and action," he wrote in a memo to the Fathers of Confederation Memorial Citizens' Foundation, "he has had some serious encounters, has made some bad friends and indeed has made some bitter enemies. However, to Frank the full development of Prince of Wales College was more important than his personal comfort or his physical well-being, and he spared nothing in pressing on to his goal. In the cause of Prince of Wales College, he had many friends and well wishers, but in the end, he together with those who actively supported him could not withstand the continuous and finally overwhelming pressures exerted by some serious minded persons in government, serious or bitter opponents and finally the hostility of some lookers-on who found some initial satisfaction in seeing him 'cut down to size.'"[56]

MacKinnon's own parting remarks to the board of governors bore few traces of the bitterness that he would nurse for many years to come. According to the minutes, "concerning the drastic change in plans, he classed himself as being like the Arctic explorer who was driven back by a storm ten miles from the Pole, as he much preferred to have had the adventure than not go at all."[57]

The 1968–69 academic year was to have been a celebratory one for Prince of Wales — the year that the first graduates of the four-year university program would be receiving degrees. But the year began on an unsettling note. After MacKinnon resigned, sixteen faculty members[58] did as well. They included Ian Brown, chairman of the social science division, and Robert Carter, chairman of the humanities division. Brown, an extremely popular teacher who happened to be the son of a Presbyterian Church clergyman, was being pressured by Protestant clergymen to stay to teach at the new university; otherwise, they said, "there will be more of 'them' than 'us.'" Brown had come to the Island to teach at a secular institution; nobody, including him, could foresee how the new one would turn out, but the "one-university" activist group was pushing a distinctly "Christian" presence, and he had no interest in mixing religion and education.

For students, it was a confusing, distressing time. Many left for universities on the mainland. Some feared that a Prince of Wales degree had become meaningless. Some didn't want a degree from the as-yet-unborn university. Horace Carver, about to enter his third university year, decided to transfer to Dalhousie. "I decided that, having been a student leader extremely proactive for Prince of Wales and against the position the government had taken, I would resign from the council, give up a modest $200 bursary and go off to a foreign university where I knew next to nobody. I just said, in my opinion the fight is over, the cause is lost and I do not intend to be an irritant to the new university — and I also don't want the new university to irritate me in the next several years." Dianne MacLeod Anderson, due to graduate in the spring of 1969, decided to stay. "We wondered whether the degree would be any good. But most of us stayed because we were Islanders, I guess, and didn't have enough vision or money to go anywhere else. A lot of people with maybe loftier ambitions left for the mainland."[59]

As it turned out, 62 of the 83 students in the third year graduated with degrees from Prince of Wales. The total enrolment that year was 623 full-time students, an increase of more than 100 over the previous year, plus 251 in part-time and extension programs.[60] The government assured the board of governors the college would be able to carry on for another academic year. And, like a terminally ill patient determined to present a smiling face, the board, faculty, and students did their best to act as though the death sentence didn't exist. Some of the faculty received promotions and were no doubt preparing for the next life. Twenty-two new professors were hired to replace those who had left. New furnishings were bought. The board of governors was even obliged to go ahead with the purchase of at least one neighbouring property; it had already been appropriated, and it was too late to turn back.[61] The 1968 summer session, with courses in music, theatre, and teacher education, was described as the most comprehensive ever. In the fall, a university Senate was formed. In February 1969, a new lecture theatre was opened and named after Frank MacKinnon.[62]

For the students, it was mostly business as usual. "At that time in your life, you're going on, you're moving," Dianne MacLeod Anderson said. "We were still having fun, and it was still cosy and comfortable at the college. We still had everything. We had the proms, the concerts, the dances. You're thinking, 'What am I going to wear to the prom, who am I going to go with?' Not 'this is the last one.' You're buying the ring, you're caught up in all that. But the convocation itself was like the funeral."[63]

The convocation-cum-funeral took place on May 16. The eulogist was John Sutherland Bonnell, the former Royal Commission chairman. He remarked on the proud history of the college and reminisced about his own happy years there. Just when Prince of Wales had attained its highest development, he lamented, its separate, distinct life was drawing to a close. "At times during my address today we have laughed together, but it is only, as Lord Byron says, that we may not weep. We have come to an end. For myself as well as for you, I say with deepest feeling: Prince of Wales! Beloved Prince of Wales! Hail — and Farewell!"[64]

It was the valedictory address — surely the only angry one in the history of the college — that prevented the convocation from wallowing in bathos. The graduating class had chosen Edward Boates as their spokesman. They knew he felt strongly about the death of the college, and that he would not be afraid to say so. Perhaps they didn't realize how savage his remarks would be. With the premier, the education minister, the lieutenant-governor, and various other dignitaries behind him on the stage at Confederation Centre, Boates called the government's single-university decision "the rape of Prince of Wales College and the crucifixion of its principal." The convocation ceremony was "a memorial service for Prince of Wales College, and the paradoxical irony of it all is that the perpetrators of the travesty are here today as honorary pallbearers." The graduating class, he said, had worked for their degrees under the most trying circumstances imaginable. "We have endured industrial jack-hammers and political jackasses.... We have prepared hastily written term papers and listened to hastily prepared white papers. We have attended seminars in political science, only to go down to the P.E.I. Legislature and learn, much to our chagrin, that there really isn't anything scientific about politics...."[65]

Some people in the audience were outraged by such impertinent remarks. For the graduates, Boates's sarcasm made up for disappointment at the absence of MacKinnon. The senior class had asked the Senate to invite MacKinnon to speak at convocation, and to grant honorary degrees to MacKinnon and Ian Brown, "who have made an outstanding contribution to Prince of Wales."[66] (Brown then was acting principal of Algoma University College in Sault Ste. Marie, Ontario.) The response, according to Boates and class president Harley Harper, was that MacKinnon was still technically a faculty member and therefore ineligible for an honorary degree, and "they couldn't give a degree to Brown if they didn't give one to MacKinnon."[67] In April, ten members of the graduating class had written to the board of governors, asking that MacKinnon be given an honorary degree. Tom Lothian, the interim principal, said Senate felt this couldn't be done because MacKinnon was still on full salary. The board had given him a year's sabbatical leave, plus six months' retirement pay.[68] MacKinnon had a different interpretation: "I told the students I would accept the degree and be at the convocation in person. I was later told by students and others that the nomination was rejected because a) the St. Dunstan's authorities were (or would be) annoyed and b) the government, particularly Gordon Bennett, would consider such an action to be a reflection on it."[69] It is hard to imagine why St. Dunstan's — itself a terminal case — would care about honorary degrees at Prince of Wales, although the government might. In any case, Lothian did invite MacKinnon to take part in the academic procession. His daughter replied that her father couldn't attend; he had just left on a six-week vacation and would be out of the country. The honourary degrees went, instead, to Dr. Gillis, a sometime-member of the citizens' group promoting a single university, and to Lieutenant-Governor MacDonald, a man who had just applauded the decision to liquidate Prince of Wales with "three hearty British cheers."[70]

There were other ironies. When MacKinnon returned home, a $530 salary cheque came in the mail, in a St. Dunstan's University bookstore envelope. The cheque bore the name of St. Dunstan's University, apparently because the bank account for the new university was still under the old name. He was so bemused by this, he sent a photocopy of the cheque stub to Mr. Justice R. R. Bell, a member of the Prince of Wales board of governors. "It will no doubt amuse you in view of the circumstances," MacKinnon wrote "... it must be without precedent in education anywhere in the world. As a symbol, it is a sad culmination of the developments of the past few years. As a practice, sending it to me is the equivalent of paying Gordon Bennett with a cheque from the Progressive Conservative Headquarters or the Bishop with one from the Orange Lodge...."[71]

In the fall, MacKinnon began teaching political science at the University of Calgary. Many of his Prince of Wales colleagues moved to the St. Dunstan's campus and started the delicate task of helping build a new, integrated university. St. Dunstan's continued to exist on paper, but its campus, once the training ground for generations of Catholic priests, was sold for $5.7 million to the new, secular university. In another ironic twist, the building that once was Prince of Wales — a college so proud all its life of its high academic standards, and so long criticized for neglecting students whose aptitudes lay in other directions — became a technical and vocational school.

In public, at least, the two universities went surprisingly quietly. In

April, when the government sprang its surprise in the Legislature, the Charlottetown newspapers predicted great unrest. *The Evening Patriot* forecast that the issue would split both political parties, and create "the bitterest debate the province has witnessed in years."[72] The *Patriot* was only partly right. Bitter debates did continue for years, but they took place in coffee shops and living rooms, not in the Legislature or in the newspapers. Former students went on with their lives. Some thought a single university was the best thing that could have happened to the Island; some mourned the decision for years. Horace Carver eventually became a lawyer and a provincial cabinet minister. For a long time, he and Mac Beck, members of the same church, had many a hot argument over Prince of Wales. Then Carver resolved to stop thinking about his beloved college. He said it hurt too much.[73] Half a century after he graduated from Prince of Wales, Arnold Hiltz, war veteran, PhD, scientist for twenty-seven years in the United States space program, was still somewhat emotional about his first and best-loved college: "When I first heard that Prince of Wales was no more, I was very, very angry. What have they done to us? They have taken away our birthright. Everything is gone. UPEI is wonderful — but I still feel a bit like an orphan, in a sense."[74]

Naturally, there was hurt on the other side of the fence, as well. The same month that Prince of Wales was conferring bachelor's degrees for the first and last time, St. Dunstan's was holding a convocation for its last graduates, the largest class in its history. Somehow it was fitting that the two old rivals would exit in tandem. For almost a century and a half, their paths had taken a parallel course. Beginning as primitive boys' classical schools in the 1830s, they had developed into colleges within five years of each other, had both undertaken major building programs at the turn of the century, and finally had both achieved university status. Like two crotchety, quarrelling old neighbours, they had fought over money, harboured dark suspicions about each other, and even made periodic stabs at helping each other out. In the end, when co-operation was a matter of life and death, the old habits had calcified. Tradition, pride, and prejudice won out.

For many years, MacKinnon, like Tam O'Shanter's wife, nursed his wrath to keep it warm. The year after he left Prince of Wales, he gave a speech to the Charlottetown Rotary Club that some politicians never forgot or forgave. As blunt and forceful as ever, he said people in central Canada were regarding the Island with "disgust and hilarity" because of the way its public figures — "boys sent on men's errands" — did business.[75] Two decades later, when he returned to give another lecture at the University of Prince Edward Island, the chancellor presented him with a book by one of the clerical professors. Somewhat to his amusement, the subject was the feast days and lives of the saints. It was, he remarked, "an action tantamount to giving old Dr. W. J. P. [W. J. P. MacMillan] a life of Martin Luther."[76] Even in his retirement years, he soldiered on for Prince of Wales. In his mid-seventies, he published a bitter, scathing book connecting the death of his college to machinations by the Catholic hierarchy.

For other alumni, time and circumstances did much to heal old wounds. When Ed Boates delivered his unique valedictory in 1969, he predicted as much: "A year from now we may still look back on these events with a feeling of nausea; 10 years from now we will look back on them with nostalgia, and 20 years from now we will undoubtedly view them from the perspective of amnesia." Perhaps the amnesia part wasn't quite right. But many who witnessed the growth of the new university became reassured that it was a worthy successor to the two old institutions. When the Prince of Wales Alumni Society held its 1991 reunion, Barbara Macnutt was among the 1,500 delegates to attend an event on the campus. Listening to an address by the UPEI president, Willie Eliot, she suddenly decided that the university was properly honouring the traditions and values of Prince of Wales. "I finally had the feeling that the baby had been passed to the right people."[77]

For the MacKinnon family, however, shadows lingered for decades in memories of the life and death of the college. "My father loved and loves P.E.I.," Peter MacKinnon, president of the University of Saskatchewan, wrote in the fall of 2004. "He returned to the Island despite opportunities elsewhere. He was once its Citizen of the Year. He chaired its Centennial celebrations. He was an Islander who achieved national stature. And he was indisputably the founder and builder of the Confederation Centre of the Arts. He made magnificent contributions to the Island. My mother, brothers, sister and myself felt that he was treated very badly — entirely apart from whatever views one might have about the university question.

"My father and mother made new lives for themselves in Calgary, and in many respects those new lives were fulfilling. But I do not think the wounds were ever closed. And for that, the sadness lingers."

By the end of the 1990s, Frank MacKinnon had published his eighth book, at the age of eighty. It was a charming collection of anecdotes about assorted events in his life — many of them told with self-deprecating humour, all of them written in his inimitable, crisp, clear style. In his preface, he wrote: "I hope these stories encourage what Canadians need most these days — less complaint, more gladness, less lethargy, more spirit, fewer black sheep, more live wires."[78] None of the stories mentions Roman Catholic bishops, the death of Prince of Wales College, or the perfidy of Prince Edward Island politicians.

Chapter Ten

Postscript

10

"Education at Prince of Wales was a pearl of great price. You were terribly proud to be there."
—Rev. Bryer Jones

"College closed today," Lucy Maud Montgomery wrote in her diary on June 7, 1894. "I feel so sorry. My pleasant PWC days are all over. Very sadly I gathered up my books and passed out as hundreds have done and hundreds more will do. But no one ever left or will ever leave that old college with deeper and more genuine regret in her heart than did I."[1]

"I can't tell you the joy Dr. Frank [MacKinnon] unleashed in those brief years when Prince of Wales was Camelot," playwright Kent Stetson declared on October 17, 2002. "Or, perhaps more accurately, Brigadoon— for Brigadoon, like the enlightened human spirit, is known to vanish and reappear when most needed. Those of us who knew it hold the hope that Prince of Wales will emerge again."[2]

Two accomplished Island writers, more than a century apart, recorded their thoughts about an institution that inspired extraordinary loyalty and affection during its 109-year history, changed young lives, and lived on in memory long after its days were over: Montgomery considered her year at Prince of Wales "the happiest of my life."[3] Three decades after his graduation, Stetson maintained that the college had forged "the richest memories of my young adulthood."[4]

Montgomery's college was a crowded, ill-ventilated, smoke-blackened, rickety wooden building, with 5 professors and 164 students. Over the years, it evolved into a well-maintained and equipped brick building with 40 professors and more than 600 students. Yet, had Montgomery reappeared at the college in the 1930s, or even the early 1960s, she might not have felt too out of place. One of the hallmarks of Prince of Wales was its extraordinary stability, due, in part, to the fact that in 108 years, it had only five principals. Until the 1960s, most of the faculty were Islanders, educated at Prince of Wales and St. Dunstan's, and some spent their entire working lives at Prince of Wales.

The relationship between students and teachers probably didn't change appreciably from Montgomery's day. Into the 1960s, teenage boys and girls were still "Miss" and "Mister," and knew enough to address male teachers as "Sir." There was a great air of civility about the place. It was, in the best sense of the word, Victorian. If the character-building virtues of punctuality, integrity, service, temperance, and industry were not preached as vigorously as they had been in Anderson's time or Robertson's time, they still informed the spirit of the place. With few exceptions, teenagers— like their Victorian ancestors— were expected to behave like adults, and usually did. Among alumni of the college asked to describe the Prince of Wales experience, the one word most often heard is "respect." That relates to a tradition that went as far back as the Central Academy in the 1800s, when headmaster E. R. Humphreys advised a staff member that complaints about students were to be made only in writing, and that "quiet determination" was a better deterrent to bad behaviour than anger. When Alexander Anderson took over the Prince of Wales principal's job in 1868, he set the tone for years to come— not just in terms of academics, but also of ambience. According to Sir Andrew Macphail, he never uttered so much as a rebuke to his students; he treated boys just off the farm with respect, as if they were destined for greatness.

Some of them were. As early as the 1870s, when the public school system was still in a dismal state, graduates of Prince of Wales were enrolling in the second year of Dalhousie, Queen's, McGill, and Harvard universities, and winning scholarships and prizes to boot. Some became writers, doctors, lawyers, scientists, judges, university professors, ministers, priests. Among the long lists of eminent academics were Fulton Anderson, chair of the philosophy department at the University of Toronto from the 1940s to the 1960s; Millar MacLure, a former member of the Prince of Wales faculty, who was chair of the English department at the University of Toronto in the 1970s; Cyrus Macmillan, another former Prince of Wales professor, who became dean of arts at McGill; William Scott Ferguson, an historian and specialist in ancient Greece, who was appointed dean of arts and science at Harvard.[5] In the ecclesiastical world, John Sutherland Bonnell, a public school dropout who eventually graduated from Prince of Wales in 1915, rose to prominence as the preacher at a large Presbyterian church in New York City and president of the New York Theological Seminary. James McGuigan, who graduated from Prince of Wales in 1911, became Canada's first English-speaking Roman Catholic cardinal. J.-H. Blanchard, who taught full-time at Prince of Wales for thirty-seven years, was also a leading historian and promoter of higher education in the Acadian community. Gordon Bennett and W. J. MacDonald, both long-time faculty members at the college, were eventually appointed to the post of lieutenant-governor.

Thousands of normal school graduates, Catholics and Protestants, taught countless Island children. Many of them wound up in the best universities in Canada. Despite some deficiencies in the college program— arts courses taught mainly as lectures-and-notes, no language laboratories, and French courses you could pass without actually having to pronounce a word *en français*— they tended to do well. Rev. Bryer Jones, a graduate in the 1940s, went on to the University of Toronto. "When I got to Victoria College at the University of Toronto, I was surprisingly at home," Jones said. "We had to speak and act correctly and have papers marked for small matters. I was well pleased that I was fairly well up on English and history, things like that. Prince of Wales was quite a preparation." Jones, a retired United Church minister, described his college experience in Biblical terms. "Education at Prince of Wales was a pearl of great price. You were terribly proud to be there. Nothing pleased the P.E.I. parent more than when people came from away, and asked what you were doing, they could say, 'He (or she) is going to Prince of Wales College"— as though that were the highest thing unto which you would aspire." Rev. Francis Bolger, a Catholic priest and history professor who also studied at St. Dunstan's and the University of Toronto, enrolled at Prince of Wales in the 1940s, when he was barely 15. "I was tremendously impressed by the faculty," he said. "You were so enthralled. You were young, and it was the beginning of your formal education. The teachers were very much your mentors. You felt a certain awe just to be in their presence."[6] Ian Ross Robertson, history professor at the University of Toronto, attended Prince of Wales in the early 1960s, and remained grateful to the college ever after. It probably was his history teachers there— Basil Phillips, Ian Brown and Bruce Hodgins— that determined he would become an historian, he said. "The really important part about the PWC experience, it seems to me, was the exemplary way in which it prepared us for further study elsewhere. It was commonly said and believed that if one could do well at PWC, one could do well anywhere else one might go, and I— and my peers— found this to be so, as did generations before us." Among them, Robertson noted, was Sir Andrew Macphail. In his memoir, *The Master's Wife*, Macphail told about his train trip to Montreal and McGill. Worried about entering the big city university and "oppressed by a sense of inexperience and ignorance," he was reading. "A senior student also on his way discovered me at the task. 'Put that book away,' he said, 'and tell them you come from the Prince of Wales College.'"[7]

Many bright boys and girls, coming from communities where intellectual ability received scant praise, received the first validation of their worth at Prince of Wales. At the college, book-learning was valued for its own sake, as was academic excellence. Able students learned they had potential, and were encouraged to live up to it. Lucy Maud Montgomery might have become a famous author if she had never gone to college, but it was there, at age twenty, that she received her first real encouragement as a writer: Principal Anderson, whose opinion she regarded highly, told her she had great talent, and that she should develop it. Jacob Gould Schurman, who became president of Cornell University, and later an American diplomat, once described Anderson as his greatest teacher and benefactor: "Calmly reflecting on the matter, I believe there is none to whom, all considered, I personally owe so much as to him."

In later years, other alumni, some famous, some not, acknowledged the influence of their college years on their lives. In a teacher-training class in the 1940s, Zelda MacNevin was mildly surprised to learn that she had the potential to go on to university, which she did, eventually earning an arts degree from Queen's, and a certificate in special education from McGill.[8] A generation after that, Barb Macnutt, the first in her family to go to university, discovered at Prince of Wales that she had the ability to do so. "Every piece of my life, I felt, was being fed through that college. We were given lots of opportunity to think for ourselves. If we didn't make it to class, it was not anybody's fault but ours, and it would show up at the end of the course. We weren't being spoon-fed. But it was still a very supportive and caring learning environment."[9]

The college didn't just nurture academic ability. It was at Prince of

The Historian's Historians

Among the many Prince of Wales graduates who have made their mark are an extraordinary number of fine historians, some of them experts in Maritime history. Ian Ross Robertson, a Prince of Wales alumnus and history professor at Scarborough College, University of Toronto, discovered this in the fall of 1973, when he began teaching the first course in Maritime history ever offered at the university. "That required a lot of reading on my part, because I had never, at any educational level, been systematically taught the history of the region," Robertson said. "I found in my reading that the leading authority on the history of each of the three provinces —that is, the writer who had provided the most comprehensive and most reliable scholarly account — was a Prince of Wales graduate."

In Robertson's opinion, the leading authority on the history of Nova Scotia was Daniel Cobb Harvey, a native of Cape Traverse, a Prince of Wales graduate, a Rhodes Scholar, and long-time provincial archivist of Nova Scotia. "Harvey established his reputation on Nova Scotia history through several authoritative scholarly articles, especially in the 1930s and 1940s," Robertson observed. "Some of these were also pioneering within Canadian history as a whole, because of their focus on such previously neglected areas of inquiry as intellectual history." Harvey also wrote on Island history. In 1926, he published, with Yale University Press, The French Regime in Prince Edward Island, a book that is still highly regarded.

The leading authority on New Brunswick history was W. Stewart MacNutt, who died in 1976. MacNutt, a native of Charlottetown, and a graduate of Prince of Wales and the University of London, was for many years dean of the faculty of arts at the University of New Brunswick. "His great work on his adopted province was New Brunswick, A History: 1784–1867. Among Canadian historians generally, he was probably best-known for The Atlantic Provinces: The Emergence of Colonial Society, 1712–1857. Both books, clearly the product of many years' work, were published in the 1960s. MacNutt's general survey of the region prior to Confederation was not surpassed until the 1990s. He also wrote a couple of articles on the history of Prince Edward Island."

The leading authority on Prince Edward Island history, in Robertson's opinion, was the last principal of Prince of Wales, Frank MacKinnon, who was a graduate of Prince of Wales, McGill University, and the University of Toronto. While still a young man, he published The Government of Prince Edward Island, which won the Governor-General's Award for Non-Fiction in 1951, and is still is regarded as a classic.

"I think it is a source of legitimate pride for PWC alumni that these three pioneers, in writing the history of the Maritime region to a high professional standard, passed through PWC," Robertson observed. "It is also worth noting in this regard that these writers made their mark — a lasting mark —writing on the history of the Maritime region before 'regional history' became fashionable. The scholarly periodical Acadiensis: Journal of the History of the Atlantic Region, published twice a year, only commenced in late 1971.

"The professional choices these PWC graduates made are revealing. Among other things, the focus of their research and publication speaks to their sense of 'place.' This impression is deepened by the fact that both Harvey and MacNutt published work on Island history as well as the history of the mainland. One might also speculate that if Prince Edward Island had had a full-fledged public university throughout the 20th century, perhaps Harvey and MacNutt might, like MacKinnon, have returned to the Island to teach and to do their research."

Wales where many students perfected debating skills, learned to play team sports, developed friendships with people from other religious traditions, discovered leadership talents. A great sense of camaraderie developed, partly because— until enrolment outstripped space— all the classes were held in one building, making it easy for students and staff to get to know each other, at least by sight. True, one of the recurring themes in the Prince of Wales history was the incessant breast-beating in *The College Times* over the perceived lack of college spirit. "It has been truly stated by former pupils," one anonymous writer sagely noted in the 1940s, "that the college spirit never gets into a person until he has left PWC, then if somebody says something against it— wow...." Comments like those were less evident in later years, when Montgomery Hall made it possible for women to board together and for students and faculty to meet in the dining room and common room. By convocation time, many students would leave, like Maud Montgomery, "with deep and genuine regret." If anybody needed a reminder to be grateful for the privilege of the college experience, English teacher J. J. Coyle would bark, "Look! These are the best years of your life, and don't you forget it!" There was certainly no lack of expressions of gratitude to Prince of Wales in the mid-1960s, when the college appeared threatened. When the axe finally fell, it was, for some, like a death in the family.

A cynic might point out that death usually burnishes the departed with a brighter glow than was ever attained in life. And Prince of Wales was not a happy experience for everybody. The failure rate was always high. Marks were kept low, which was something of a shock to those accustomed to getting good grades in public school. In Montgomery's day, Alexander Anderson was known as a hard marker; seventy years later, J. J. Coyle, striding into the classroom with his beagle, Pat, trailing behind him, would mutter, "If God Himself were writing a term paper for me, He wouldn't get 90 per cent." Professors were generally approachable and more than willing to help a floundering student, but the student had to take the initiative. There was no counselling system. Many products of a public school system that, like the curate's egg, was very good only in spots, found themselves unprepared for the Prince of Wales curriculum. Those who majored in bridge often found themselves "graduating" at Christmas. The "Christmas graduate" tradition pretty well ended in Frank MacKinnon's time, when students got a second chance at the end of the year, but politicians and the public continued to complain about the high failure rate, and the lack of opportunities for those with non-academic aptitudes.

The college— and the Central Academy before it— was always open to charges of elitism, complaints about the curriculum, and even threats of abolition. Without endowments, it was entirely dependent on provincial governments, whose level of support varied greatly. The politicians might brag about the success of Prince of Wales graduates— and speak with nostalgic longing about their own college days— but they often treated the college shabbily. Until at least the 1880s, there was loose talk in the Legislature about cutting off government support. The brilliant, charismatic Alexander Anderson, one of the most outstanding teachers of his time, had to beg the government for decades to do something about the crowded, unsafe building he was obliged to work in for forty years. He finally had to figure out a way of replacing it. His successor, the humble and mild-mannered Samuel Robertson, took the drastic step of leading a teachers' strike to pry raises out of one premier, and had to watch helplessly as another caved in to political pressure, thus preventing the college from affiliating with McGill University. The last principal, the not-so-humble Frank MacKinnon, was once interrogated in public by his bosses like a delinquent schoolboy, and had to answer to the politicians on the most minute of matters until the mid-1960s, when the college finally won degree-granting powers and a non-political board of governors.

By then, it was too late. Prince of Wales burst into bloom one last time and then died. Time had passed it by. It was not just (perhaps not at all) that the economy couldn't support two universities that couldn't, or wouldn't, co-operate. In a sense, it wasn't even a religious issue, even though religion had muddied the waters of education since the early 1800s, and maintaining the fiction that there were two sectarian universities no doubt made the destruction of the public one more palatable. By then, though, St. Dunstan's was gradually secularizing itself, and university-age students, in contrast to their elders, were becoming less and less interested in who went to which church.

But in the Swinging Sixties, both institutions were starting to look like anachronisms. It was the onset of a utilitarian age on the Island. Small farms, schools, churches, credit unions— the foundation of the old way of life— were on their last legs. Lucy Maud Montgomery's beloved haunts were being overrun by cash registers and visitors in socks and sandals.

The mindset of the government was one of expansion. The Comprehensive Development Plan was still in the planning stage in 1968, but the concept of one, big university clearly fit the Development Plan model. The buzzwords were "rationalization," "consolidation," and "economy of scale." More than ever, the pressure was on to turn education into job preparation. "The direct needs of the province of Prince Edward Island consist primarily in the acquiring of skilled and educated people for the various sectors of the provincial economy," Premier Alex Campbell told the Legislature in April 1968. They included trained teachers, specialists in resource administration and management, technicians, and management personnel for both government and business. The vocational school was turning out plumbers and carpenters; the economy was demanding workers capable of dealing with the new technology.

If Prince of Wales College had survived, could it have fulfilled those needs? Would it want to? Would it ever have accumulated the space and resources needed for the kind of research expected of a modern university? Would Prince Edward Island have acquired a world-class veterinary college? Would graduate studies be available? Would two universities be fighting endlessly for dollars? Could Prince of Wales have maintained its high standards in a society that abhors the idea of "failure"? Could it have survived as the embodiment of MacKinnon's dream of a small, liberal-arts institution? Or would it have turned into something unrecognizable to generations of graduates? And, if so, would these grey-haired and wrinkled loyalists still flock to college reunions, doing passable parodies of Frank McKinnon's annual social-butterfly speech, singing in revivals of the old Red and Blue Revue and shedding a nostalgic tear to the strains of Les Alexander's "Memories of Old Prince of Wales"?

Kent Stetson might long for a rebirth of Prince of Wales, but in a way its safest fate might be to reside in the hearts of those who loved it. In a symbolic sense, the college is present in the new university— in the plumes in the coat of arms, the Steel Building and the Steel Recital Hall, the Robertson Library, the Dr. Frank MacKinnon Lecture Series. In a real sense, some of its graduates and faculty helped shape the spirit of the university. And recent administrations at the university have taken pains to recognize both Prince of Wales and St. Dunstan's as the cornerstones of the new institution.

And yet... there remains a sense of regret for what might have been, especially if Prince of Wales had been allowed to affiliate with McGill and attain degree-granting powers early in the 20th century. Would scholars who distinguished themselves elsewhere in Canada— Islanders such as D. C. Harvey, W. Stewart MacNutt, and Ian Ross Robertson— have returned to the Island to teach? Would Prince of Wales have continued to set high standards for the public schools? Would many of the thousands of Islanders who left for university education on the mainland have stayed to enrich the Island's social, economic, and cultural life? Would many financially stressed dropouts have completed a university education? One can only speculate. What is not in doubt is the steadfast loyalty of many of the sons and daughters of the old college. Some of them never pass the old college building without a pang. "I think Prince of Wales College was one of the finest educational institutions that one could possibly attend," Father Bolger said. "I pass the college often, and I don't think of it as Holland College. To me, that's Prince of Wales College, and I love it. I just love Prince of Wales." Some alumni long for a physical memorial containing the college name— a reminder to students who have never heard of the place that Prince of Wales was part of their heritage, and that, for more than a century, it gave a great gift to the province, and in many cases, to the outside world. In the meantime, as long as the aging loyalists of Prince of Wales survive, they can cling to an untarnished memory of the place where, like Lucy Maud Montgomery, they spent some of the happiest years of their lives.

Appendices

Appendix A
The Principals of the Central Academy and Prince of Wales College

Charles Lloyd
1835–1836

James Waddell
1836–1843

Edward R. Humphreys
1844–1847

William Cundall
1847–1856

John Kenny
1856–1860

Alexander Inglis
1860–1868

Alexander Anderson
1868–1901

Samuel Napier Robertson
1901–1937

G. Douglas Steel
1937–1949

Frank MacKinnon
1949–1968

Thomas M. Lothian (Interim)
1968–1969

Appendix B
PWC Faculty Listed by Principal with Courses Taught (where known)

Alexander Inglis, Principal, 1860–1868

French, German, Greek, Latin, Mathematics, Natural Science

Alexander Anderson, Greek, Latin, Mathematics

Leander MacNeil, Second Professor

William Monk, Second Master

Samuel Napier Robertson, Fourth Professor, English, Latin

George Robinson

Herbert H. Shaw, Agriculture, Mathematics, Science

Herbert N. Shaw, Second Professor

Arthur E. Shuttleworth, Second Professor

Frederick West

Alexander Anderson, Principal, 1868–1901

Greek, Latin, Mathematics

William John Alexander

Joseph Arsenault, Principal of the Model School, French

John Caven, First Professor, English, French, School Management

Benjamin Darby, Second Professor

Wellington Dixon

J. C. Dunlop

George Harcourt, Agriculture, Science

John Harper, teacher training

Edward E. Jordan, Third Professor, Latin, Mathematics

Thomas Lepage

Rev. F. E. J. Lloyd, Music

Alexander Lowe, Second Master, Ancient and English History, English Literature and Composition, French Grammar and Composition, Geography, German, Bookkeeping, Preparatory English and Grammar

D. J. MacLeod, Third Professor

Leander MacNeil, Second Professor

John MacSwain

Bruno Martin, Fifth Professor

Thomas May, Second Professor

L. B. Miller, Bookkeeping

Anne Montgomry, Model School

Samuel Napier Robertson, Principal, 1901–1937

Greek, Latin, School Management

Percy Barlow, Drawing, Manual Drawing

James G. Bennett, Chemistry, English, Latin, Physics

J. Henri Blanchard, Botany, French, Physiography, Rural Science

James B. Brow, Mathematics, Physics

J. T. Clarkin, Botany, Drawing

J. D. Collier, Director of Manual Training, Drawing, Manual Training

John F. Connolly, Arithmetic, Bookkeeping

Howard H. Court, Supervisor of Teacher Training

John T. Croteau, Economics, Sociology

Wilfred T. Dawson, Chemistry, Physics

Warren, Duchemin, Biology, Science

Grace E. Dutcher, Domestic Science, Household Science

Alvin F. Hansuld, Rural Science

Edith Hugh, Mathematics, Physics

Adelaide Humphrey, Chemistry, History, Penmanship

Edward E. Jordan, Second Professor, Mathematics, Bookkeeping

Roy Leitch, Substituting

Alfred M. Linkletter, Physics, English

Eleanor Lowe, Drawing
J. A. MacDonald, English, French, Latin
John A. MacDonald, Fourth Professor, Third Professor
Williabold J. MacDonald, Physiography, Latin, French
J. E. MacLarty, Rural Science
Cyrus John Macmillan, English, History, Third Professor
J. Frank MacMillan, Mathematics, Botany, History
Martin, Household Science
Bruno Martin, Arithmetic, Assistant in French, Fifth Professor, French, Principal of Model School
Allan F. Matthews, English, Fourth Professor, Latin
S. B. McCready, Rural Science
Annie L. McGrath, Botany, English
Ella M. MacGrath, Stenography, Typewriting
Lemuel J. Miller, English, Penmanship
James A. Murphy, Latin, Mathematics
Letitia M. Passmore, Teacher Training, Librarian
J. G. Paterson, Economics, Mathematics, Sociology
Helen P. Ramsay, Biology, English
William A. Reddin, Agriculture, Botany
Theodore Ross, Agriculture, Botany, Physical Geography
Athol W. Seaman, English, Fourth Professor
Lily H. Seaman, Latin, English, History
Herbert H. Shaw, Chemistry, Physics, Physiology, Vice-Principal
Herbert N. Shaw, First Professor
Lloyd Shaw, Supervisor of Teacher Training
Russell P. Smith, Mathematics
G. Douglas Steel, English, Vice-Principal
H. R. Waugh, Manual Training
R. Hazen Wigmore, Biology, English, History
Helen Yeo, English, Teacher Training

G. Douglas Steel, Principal, 1937—1949

English
Doris M. Anderson, Home Economics, Nutrition
J. Wilfred Arsenault, French, Latin
Dorothy I. Auld, History, Latin, Mathematics
Ferne Bell, Chemistry
Gordon L. Bennett, Mathematics, Physics, Chemistry
James G. Bennett, Chemistry
J. Henri Blanchard, French, Vice-Principal
Ernest M. Bradley, Assistant in Commerce, Bookkeeping, Commercial Arithmetic
James B. Brow, Physics, Vice-Principal
Lorne C. Callbeck, Botany, Chemistry
Marion (Mahar) Chandler, Assistant in Commerce
John F. Connolly, Arithmetic, Bookkeeping, History, Latin, Mathematics
Howard H. Court, Supervisor of Teacher Training
Coyle, M. Catherine (Bethune), English
John T. Croteau, Economics, Sociology
Francis L. Doiron, Assistant in French
Mary Donahoe, Librarian
E. E. Doucette, French, Mathematics
Warren Duchemin, Biology
Ann Duffy, Chemistry
Margaret R. Gould, English, German
Edith Hugh, Mathematics, Physics
Wilfred I. Inman, Physical Education
Olive M. Keeping, Mathematics, Physics
Lambourn, Drafting
Edward Laughlin, Mathematics, Physics
J. Robert LeClair, French, Latin
Alfred M. Linkletter, Chemistry, English, Latin, Physics
Zilpha J. Linkletter, History, Latin
Eleanor Lowe, Drawing
James H. Lynch, French, Mathematics, Science

Williabald J. MacDonald, French, Latin, Mathematics
C. Ralph MacLean, Agriculture, Botany
J. Miller MacLure, English, Latin
William A. MacPhee, Supervisor of Teacher Training
J. Frank MacMillan, Botany, History, Latin, Mathematics
Richard T. Matheson, Biology, Chemistry, Physics
J. Winston Mayne, Mathematics, Physics
Royston E. Mugford, Music
Ella M. McGrath, Stenography, Typing
J. Clarence Murphy, Economics, History, Latin, Sociology
P. Cletus Murphy, English, Latin
Letitia M. Passmore, Teacher Training, Librarian
J. G. Paterson, Mathematics
Helen P. Ramsay, Biology, English
William A. Reddin, Agriculture, Botany
Lily H. Seaman, English, Greek, History, Latin, Registrar
Vera O. Simpson, Chemistry, Mathematics
Theresa G. (Murphy) Sullivan, Commerce, English, History, Mathematics, Physics, Stenography, Typewriting
R. Hazen Wigmore, Biology, English, History, Teacher Training
Earl Wonnacott, Math, Physics
Arthur S. Woolner, Agriculture, Botany, English, History
Helen M. Yeo, English, Teacher Training

Frank MacKinnon, Principal, 1949–1968

History, Political Science
Christiane Aarons, Chemistry
M. Aarons, Psychology
John R. Abbott, History
Keir L. Adams, Chemistry
Harry Aikens, French
Doris M. Anderson, Home Economics, Nutrition
Fulton H. Anderson, Philosophy
George M. Andrew, Physical Education
Ian Ashford, Mathematics, Physics
Dorothy I. Auld, History, Mathematics
Gordon L. Bennett, Chemistry, Registrar
Helen B. Bishop, Physical Education
Roger D. H. Black, Education
Wilmer Blanchard, French, Latin
Alberta Boswall, Mathematics
Douglas Boylan, History
Ernest M. Bradley, Bookkeeping, Commerce, Commercial Arithmetic, Secretarial Studies
James B. Brow, Physics, Vice-Principal
Ian W. Brown, History
Wendall Brown, Chemistry, Education
Lorne C. Callbeck, Agriculture, Botany, Chemistry
D. Roy Campbell, Psychology
Lyall Campbell, English, History
Sheila Campbell, English
Robert E. Carter, Philosophy
Hung-Min Chiang, Psychology
H. Garth Coffin, Agriculture
John F. Connolly, Mathematics
James J. Coyle, English, German
M. Catherine (Bethune) Coyle, English
Bill Craig, Chemistry
A. Byron Cutcliffe, Chemistry
John W. Dalgard, Mathematics
Robert D'amato, English
Wilfred Dindial, English
Mary Donahoe, Librarian
Dorothy Duchemin, English
Warren Duchemin, Biology
E. E. Doucette, French, Mathematics
Ivan Dowling, Mathematics
Lawson Drake, Agriculture, Anatomy and Physiology, Biology
Warren Duchemin, Biology
Ann Duffy, Biology, Chemistry
Russell Ewing, Psychology
Anna (Pratt) Fraser, Commerce
Catherine Fraser, Education
George Friend, English

A. Iain R. Galloway, French
Louise Gay, Registrar
Douglas Gordon, English
Margaret R. Gould, English, German
S. K. Gupta, Mathematics
David Hall, Agriculture
Ernest L. Heighton, Mathematics
John P. Heisler, History
Elizabeth Henderson, Librarian
Jean-Louis Herivault, Economics
Eric S. Hillis, Education
Elise (Love) Hiscott, Commerce
Bruce W. Hodgins, History
A. Charles Holmes, Philosophy
James Ibbott, Chemistry
Wilfred I. Inman, Physical Education
M. Islam, Physics
Frank Johnston, Music
Pamela Keirstead, English
Rev. Jim Kelly, Latin
Harold Kemp, Physics
Harry Kennedy, English, Mathematics
Eric Kipping, French
Sandra Kohler, English
Lambourn, Drafting
Harold Landry, History
Edward Laughlin, Mathematics, Physics
Ninian LeBlanc, Biology
Edmond LeClair, French
J. Robert LeClair, French
Robert Lemon, Biology
Benjamin Leonard, English
Peter Lewis, Greek, Latin
R.E. Lightfoot, French
Thomas M. Lothian, Biology
Anne (Michael) Love, Commerce
Harry R. Love, Mathematics
Eleanor Lowe, Art, Drawing, English
Allister MacDonald, English
Mary MacDonald, Art
Williabald J. MacDonald, Mathematics
Archie A. MacFadyen, Chemistry
Barrie MacGregor, Physical Education
Jean H. MacKay, Home Economics
Wendell MacKay, English, Mathematics
C. Ralph MacLean, Agriculture, Botany
Marjorie MacLeod, Commerce
J. Frank MacMillan, History, Latin, Mathematics
Barb (Worth) MacNevin, English
Heather MacNevin, History
William A. MacPhee, Supervisor of Teacher Training, Teacher Training
Joyce (Wigginton) MacPherson, Mathematics
John Mainwaring, Mathematics
Richard T. Matheson, Biology, Chemistry, Physics
Ella M. McGrath, Stenography, Typing
Mary McIlwraith, Mathematics, Physics
Lorne Moase, Education
Geoffrey Moore, Mathematics, Physics
Royston E. Mugford, Music
Jamie Muir, Education
Barbara Mullaly, Physical Education
Charles Munroe, Mathematics
James Murdock, Mathematics
J. Clarence Murphy, Economics, Latin, Sociology
P. Cletus Murphy, Mathematics
H. Blair Neatby, History
Earl Nicholson, Physical Training, Director of Athletics
Errol Nicholson, Physics
S. T. Pai, Physics
Glenn Palmer, Physics
J. G. Paterson, Mathematics
Barbara Pepperdene, Sociology
Basil Phillips, History
Francis E. Piercey, Chemistry, Math
Jack Proude, Physical Education
Donalda Putnam, Librarian
John H. Quincy, Classics
Helen P. Ramsay, Biology, English
William A. Reddin, Botany, Physics
Michael Roach, Mathematics
George Robbins, Political Science
Rev. Edmund Roche, Mathematics
Ruth I. Ross, Health, College Nurse
Valerie Ross, History
Louise Samson, English
George Scantlebury, Physical Education

Robert Scott, English
Lily H. Seaman, English, Greek, History, Latin, Registrar
Saul Silverman, Political Science
Vera O. Simpson, Biology, Chemistry, Mathematics
John Smith, English
Norman E. Smith, Mathematics
Miroslav Spacek, Chemistry, German
Robert Stead, Biology
Hugh A. Stevenson, History
Harold P. Stewart, Anatomy, Physiology
Norman Stewart, English
Ronald G. Storey, Business Administration
Theresa G. (Murphy) Sullivan, Commerce, Stenography, Typewriting
John C. Sutherland, Mathematics
Lowell Sweet, Mathematics
W. E. Swinton, Geology, Zoology
Frederick Thompson, History
Yvette Thompson, French
Linda Tweel, German
M.A. Viswanathan, Biology
Don Waugh, Biology
Gail Wellner, Education, Librarian
Moncrieff Williamson, Fine Arts
G. Alan Wilson, History
Earl Wonnacott, Mathematics, Physics
Helen M. Yeo, Education, English, Supervisor of Teacher Training, Teacher Training
Lothar Zimmerman, German

Thomas M. Lothian, Interim Principal, 1968–69

Biology
Keir L. Adams, Chemistry
Doris M. Anderson, Home Economics, Nutrition
David S. Aurandt, English
P. N. Bali, Biology
Roger D. H. Black, Education
Maryvonne Boucher, History
Ernest M. Bradley, Secretarial Studies
D. Roy Campbell, Psychology
Ivan Carey, Education
Hung-Min Chiang, Psychology
Bill Craig, Chemistry
M. Graham DeCarie, History
Lawson Drake, Biology
Frank Falvo, French
Stephen Ferris, Economics
Brian Fitzgerald, English
Catherine Fraser, Education
George Friend, English
A. Iain R. Galloway, French
Louise Gay, Registrar
Donald Gillis, Engineering
Leonard Good, Economics
Thomas Hahn, Music
Elizabeth Henderson, Librarian
Jean-Louis Herivault, Economics
Eric S. Hillis, Education
A. Charles Holmes, Philosophy
Edward M. Holmes, English
M. Islam, Physics
Ute Islam, English
C. Edward Johnston, Biology
Christopher A. Kent, History
Ninian LeBlanc, Biology
J. Robert LeClair, French
Hsey-Er Lin, Physics
Wei Ching Lin, Physics
Leon F. Loucks, Chemistry
Harry R. Love, Mathematics
Walter Lutz, Music
Barrie MacGregor, Physical Education
Jean H. MacKay, Home Economics
Marjorie MacLeod, Secretarial Studies
Robert Mahen, Education
John Mainwaring, Mathematics
Richard T. Matheson, Chemistry
Shirley (MacDonald) Moase, Home Economics
Robert Morris, Psychology
Jamie Muir, Education
Barbara Mullaly, Physical Education
J. Clarence Murphy, Sociology
Earl Nicholson, Director of Athletics
S. T. Pai, Physics

Glenn Palmer, Physics
Donalda Putnam, Librarian
John H. Quincy, Classics
Michael Roach, Mathematics
Tiparat Schumrum, Psychology
Adele M. (MacLeod) Seaman, Home Economics
George Semsel, English
Saul Silverman, Political Science
John Smith, English
Robert Stead, Biology
Harold P. Stewart, Anatomy, Physiology
Lowell Sweet, Mathematics
W. E. Swinton, Geology, Zoology
Moncrieff Williamson, Fine Arts
Earl Wonnacott, Mathematics, Physics
Cornelius Zaat, Music
Lothar Zimmermann, German

The faculty listing was compiled by Harry Love, with research by Ryan O'Connor and Carolyn Roberts.

The editors apologize for any errors or omissions in this listing. For example, what individuals actually taught in a given year was subject to the needs of the time. Individual faculty, as needed, would teach a course in a subject quite different from what shows on the official record for their employment. Two known cases of this kind are:

— Lawson Drake teaching a course in Agriculture and also a course in Anatomy and Physiology;
— Eleanor Lowe teaching a course in English.

Appendix C
Courses Taught at Prince of Wales College

There is little surviving documentation that provides much detail on the PWC curriculum in the latter part of the 19th century, but Dr. Anderson did present a complete course list in his 1875 Principal's report: Latin, Greek, Mathematics, English, French, German, History (Ancient), History (English), Geography, Arithmetic, and Book-keeping.

To give some sense of the evolution of the PWC curriculum in the 20th century, course listings are presented below at 20-year intervals, from 1904–05 through to 1964–65. Also, to help illustrate the dramatic expansion of the curriculum following PWC's elevation to university status in 1965, a PWC course list for the 1968–69 academic year is included.

1904–05

First Year: English, History, Latin, French, Arithmetic, Algebra, Geometry, Book-keeping, Agriculture, Botany, Household Science, Physics, Scientific Temperance, Geography, School Management and School Laws, Teaching, Manual Training, Drawing, Nature Study

Second Year: *Continued studies in the above courses (except Drawing), plus*: English Literature, Greek (optional with French), Trigonometry

Third Year: *Continued studies in English, Latin, Greek, History, French, Geometry, Algebra, Botany, Chemistry, Physics, and Manual Training, plus:* Composition

1924–25

First Year: English, History, Latin, French, Arithmetic, Algebra, Geometry, Book-keeping, Physiography, Rural Science [formerly Agriculture], Botany, Elementary Science, Household Science, Scientific Temperance, Phonics, School Management and School Laws, Teaching, Manual Training, Drawing, Physical Exercise

Second Year: *Continued studies in the above courses, plus*: English Literature, Greek (optional with French), Trigonometry, Geometry (women students may substitute a course in Psychology for Geometry), Chemistry, Physics

Third Year: *Continued studies in the above courses, plus*: Composition (two written exercises each week)

1944–45

First Year: English, History, Latin, French, Arithmetic, Algebra, Geometry, Science (Elementary Practical Physics/High School Chemistry), Botany and Agriculture, Drawing, Physical Exercise

Second Year: *Continued studies in English, History, Latin, French, and Geometry, plus*: English Literature, Physics, Chemistry, Greek (optional with French), Trigonometry, Biology

Normal [Teacher] Training Course: Reading, Language, Methods of Teaching, Practice Teaching, Psychology, Botany, Nature Study, Art, Music, Health, Physical Training, Public Speaking

Third and Fourth Years [listed together]:*Continued studies in English, Latin, French, Greek, History, Chemistry, Physics, and Biology, plus*: Economics, Sociology, Mathematics [including Calculus], Draughting

Commerce Course: "A Commerce Course extending over two years is offered to the students of this institution who do not wish to prepare for the teacher's license. In lieu of the professional and certain academic courses, there will be given courses in Stenography, Typewriting, Business Arithmetic, Business Law, Bookkeeping, and Office Practice."

1964–65

First Year: English, History, Latin, French, German, Arithmetic, Algebra, Geometry, Chemistry, Physics, Art, Physical Exercise, Agriculture

Second Year: *Continued studies in English, History, Latin, French, German, Algebra, Geometry, Physics, Chemistry, and Agriculture, plus*: Biology

Teacher Training Course: * First Year: Methods and Practice teaching I, English I, Mathematics I, Psychology I, one elective (French I, Chemistry I, Physics I, Biology I, Home Economics I, Canadian History, Physical Education and Health)

* Second Year: Methods and Practice teaching II, General Principles of Education *or* Child Psychology, Canadian History (if not already taken) *or* another elective, a Science (if not already taken) *and* another elective

University Course (Third and Fourth Years) [listed together]: *Continued studies in Agriculture, Biology, Chemistry, English, French, History, Latin, and Physics, plus:* Business Administration, Draughting, Economics, Greek, Home Economics, Mathematics, Political Science, Psychology, Sociology

Prince of Wales College was elevated to full, degree-granting university status with the proclamation of a new *Prince of Wales College Act* on June 1, 1965. As a consequence, the above curricular model, which had not dramatically altered for at least two decades, needed to be completely overhauled to accommodate four-year Bachelor's degrees and other University programs. Following is a listing of degrees and courses offered by the new University in its final academic year

1968–69

The following degrees and diplomas were offered: Bachelor of Arts, Bachelor of Arts w/ Music Major, Bachelor of Science (majors available in Biology, Chemistry, Mathematics, Physics, and Home. Ec./Nutrition), Bachelor of Education (four-year undergrad. or one-year post-grad.), Diploma in Education, Diploma in Secretarial Studies.

In addition, the following two- or three-year preparatory programmes were offered: Pre-medical and Pre-dental (three-year preparation for Dalhousie admission), Pre-Engineering (three-year preparation; no school specified), Agriculture (two-year preparation for Macdonald College admission), Veterinary Medicine (three-year preparation for Ontario Veterinary College admission), Business Administration (two-year preparation for UNB admission).

Anthropology

Introduction to Anthropology was not offered 1968-69

Biology

100 – General Biology
101 – Anatomy & Physiology
200 – Chordate Anatomy
201 – General Zoology
202 – Botany
300 – Genetics
301 – Microbiology at work
302 – Embryology and Histology
303b – Human Anatomy and Physiology
304 – Introductory Entomology
400 – Cytology
401 – Physiology
402 – Ecology
403 – History of Biological Thought

Business Administration

100 – Introduction to Business
200 – Accounting

Chemistry

100/101 – General Chemistry
200 – Organic Chemistry
201 – Quantitative Analysis
300 – Biochemistry
301 – Physical Chemistry
303 – Advanced Organic Chemistry
401 – Advanced Physical Chemistry
402 – Advanced Inorganic Chemistry
405 – Special Topics

Classics

Greek 100 – Elementary Greek
Greek 200 – Intermediate Greek
Classics 100 – Greek and Roman Civilization
Greek 300 – Advanced Greek

Economics

100 – Introduction to Economics
201 – Money and banking problems
202 – North American economic problems
301 – Economic development
302 – International economic relations
400 – Introduction to Econometrics
401 – Economic development on PEI (seminar)

Education

100 – General Principles of Education
200-500 – Communications Arts
201-301-401-501 – Methodology, Practice Teaching
208 – Elementary methods
209 – Secondary methods
304 – Curriculum development
305-505 – Testing and measurement
406 – Comparative education
407-507 – Supervision and administration
502 – Educational Psychology
503 – History of Education

Pre-Engineering

100 – General Engineering
101 – Surveying
102 – Architectural History
200 – Graphics for Engineers
201 – Mechanics (Statistics)
202a – Thermodynamics
202b – Fluid Mechanics
203 – Graphics for Architects
300 – Electric Circuits
301 – Mechanics (Dynamics)
302 – Computers and Programming
303a – Strength of Materials
303b – Engineering Materials

English

Writing Laboratory
100 – English Composition and Literature
200 – English Literature, a Survey
201 – American Literature
202 – Victorian Literature
203 – Development of the English Novel
204 – Restoration and 18th Century Literature
205 – Literature of the Romantic Period
206 – Introduction to the Western Drama and Theatre
250 – Theatre Production
260 – Appreciation and Techniques of Film
301 – Chaucer and his Contemporaries
302 – Recent Literature in English
303 – Spenser and Milton
304 – English Drama [Middle Ages - 1660]
305 – Modern European, British and American Drama
306 – Modern Poetry
400 – Old English, Language and Literature
401 – Literary Criticism and Critical Writing
402 – Canadian Literature
403 – Creative Writing
460 – Half Courses in Individual Authors/Special Topics

Geology

100 – [Introduction to physical and historical geography]

History

100 – Evolution of Modern Europe
200 – Great Britain, 1485 to present
300 – History of Canada
301 – History of the U.S.
302 – History of British Empire and Commonwealth
303 – History of Western Education
313 – History of Europe, 1870 to present
400 – History of American Foreign Policy
401 – Selected Problems in Canadian History
402 – British Civilization in the 19th Century

Home Economics

100 – Introductory Clothing
200 – Introductory Foods
300 – Normal Nutrition
301 – Management of Family Resources
302 – The Family
303 – Advanced Clothing
400a – Home Economics Education
401a – Advanced Foods
401b – Food Science
402a – Therapeutic Nutrition
402b – Nutrition Seminar
403 – Institution Management and Quantity Cookery
404 – Art and the Home

Interdisciplinary Studies

100 – Interdisciplinary Science
100/101 – Mathematics [Senior matriculation] Sciences/Social Sciences/Humanities]
200 – [Calculus]
201 – Applied Statistics
202 – Pure and Applied Statistics
301 – Algebra
400 – Interdisciplinary Seminar [Natural Mathematics]
400 – Theory of Functions of a Complex Variable
401 – Differential Equations

Modern Languages

French 100 – Style and Composition
French 200 – Literature and Civilization
French 300 – Survey of French Literature 1700-1900
French 301 – Survey of French Literature 1500-1700
French 303 – French Culture and Civilization
French 400 – Contemporary French Literature
French 401 – Theatre in France
French 402 – The Novel in France
French 403 – French Poetry
French 444 – Period study

German 100 – Introduction to German
German 200 – German Composition

Music

100 – Theory
101 – Music History
111 – Applied major
112 – Applied minor
121 – Chorus
122 – Band or orchestra
123 – Piano
200 – Theory
201 – Music history
203 – Music literature
211 – Continuation of 111
212 – Continuation of 112
213 – Instrumental technique
215 – Choral technique

Philosophy

100 – Introduction to Philosophy
201 – Moral Philosophy
304 – Contemporary Philosophy and Existentialism
305 – Survey of Indian Thought

202 – Philosophy of Education
300 – Modern Philosophy
301 – Philosophy of Religion
302 – Introduction to Logic
303 – Social and Political Philosophy
495 – Tutorial
400 – European Philosophy
401 – Philosophy in Literature
402 – Metaphysics and Epistemology
404 – Philosophy of History
405 – Philosophy of Science

Physical Education
200 – Physical Education Methods and Materials for the Classroom Teacher

Physics
100 – General Physics
200 – Mechanics
202 – Electricity and Magnetism
300 – Thermodynamics and Statistical Physics
400 – Electromagnetism
401 – Modern Physics
402 – Mathematical Methods
301 – Optics Vibration and Sound

Political Science
100 – Introduction to Political Analysis
300 – Political Theory
200 – Comparative Political Systems
400 – International Relations

Seminars
305a/b – Canadian Government and Politics/ Canadian Foreign Policy
310a/b – Political Theory/ Contemporary Ideologies and Political Movements
315a – Political Parties and Pressure Groups
320a – British Government and Politics
330a/b – U.S. Government and Politics/ U.S. Foreign Policy
340a – Communist Political Systems
350a/b – International Relations/ International Organization
355a – Problems of Defense Policy and Arms Control
410a/b – Science and Public Policy/ Public Administration
450a/b – Research Seminar in Political Behaviour
475a/b – Directed Reading/Individual Research

Psychology
100 – General Introduction to Psychology
200 – Educational Psychology
201 – Developmental Psychology
202a/b – Theories of Personality/ Motivation and Emotion
203a/b – Abnormal Psychology/ Experimental and Health Psychology
204 – Social Psychology
205a/b – Learning Theory/Cognition
206a/b – Physiological Psychology/ Ethological and Comparative Psychology
207 – Experimental Psychology
301a/b – Holistic Psychology East and West/ Psychology of Symbols and Myths
302a/b – Conciousness and Perception/ Phenomenological and Existential Psychology
303a/b – Enquiry into Creativity/ Psychology of Aesthetics
304 – Parapsychology
305 – Statistics
401a/b – Systematic Psychology/ Philosophical Psychology
495 – Tutorial, Special Research, Special Problems

Sociology
100 – Introductory Sociology
200 – Social Problems
201-301 – Social Class and Stratification
203-303 – Sociology of Work
300 – Social Thought
302 – The Family
305-405 – The Individual and Society
400 – Social Theory
401 – Seminar

Appendix D
Enrolment at Prince of Wales College

1860	ca. 36
1864–65	37
1874–75	70
1884–85	66
1894–95	171
1904–05	197
1914–15	299
1924–25	338
1934–35	461
1944–45	435
1954–55	493
1964–64	792
1968–69	774

Source [unless otherwise noted]:
PWC Principals = Reports, *Journal of the Prince Edward Island House of Assembly.*
1860 enrolment is the author's estimate, drawn from various sources.
1968–69 enrolment was reported in *The Evening Patriot*, October 15, 1968.

Appendix E: The Entrance Exam (1893)

III. A boy is engaged for 28 days at 60 cents a day, with the condition that for every day he is idle, instead of receiving anything he is to pay 24 cents for his board; he receives altogether $12.48. How many days was he idle?

IV. My agent in Montreal sold a shipment of flour at $8.00 a barrel on a commission of 3%; I then instructed him to purchase certain goods for me on a commission of 2%; his whole commission was $5.00; find how many barrels of flour were shipped.

V. A Room whose height is 10 ft., and length $1\frac{1}{3}$ times its breadth, takes 140 yards of paper 2 feet wide to cover its four walls. What will it cost to carpet the floor with carpet 27 inches wide and costing $1.50 a yard?

VI. A person sold a horse gaining $11\frac{1}{9}$% of the proceeds. Had he received $35.00 less he would have lost $9\frac{3}{8}$% of what the horse cost him. Find the cost and selling price of the horse.

VII. I can obtatn $6.00 more per annum by investing a certain sum in 5 per cents. at $128\frac{1}{4}$ than in the 3 per cents at 81; What is the sum?

SCHOOL MANAGEMENT.

CLASS I and II.

TIME, TWO HOURS. June, 1893.

I. What are the chief means by which a teacher can prevent the necessity of punishments in the government of a school?

II. "Do not make any threats in advance of offences."—*Swett.* Why?

III. Compare the advantages of *oral* and *written* examinations.

IV. Sum up the *uses* of the object-lesson as a department of school work.

V. How and by whose authority can *special* meetings of ratepayers be called?

VI. How can vacancies in Boards of School Trustees be filled.

VII. What returns must Trustees make to the Education Department?

APPENDIX F.—*Continued.*

PRINCE OF WALES COLLEGE AND NORMAL SCHOOL

ENTRANCE EXAMINATION.

ARITHMETIC.

TIME THREE HOURS. July, 1893.

I. What is the difference between bank discount and true discount? What is Insurance? Policy? Premium? Negotiable Note? Draft? Exchange? Currency? What is a prime number? When are numbers prime to each other? What is a vulgar fraction? A decimal fraction?

II. Reduce $\dfrac{\frac{1}{6} \text{ of } 1\frac{1}{5} - \frac{1}{5} \text{ of } \frac{2}{3}}{\frac{1}{2} - \frac{2}{3} + \frac{4}{9} - \frac{1}{18}} \div \frac{3}{4}$ of $\frac{4}{5}$ of $\frac{6}{8}$ of a rod to the fraction of 2 furlongs.

III. Express the value of $.8\dot{3}$ of 8s. + $.\dot{0}\dot{5}$ of 2 guineas + 1.8 of 5s.

IV. Bought a number of cattle for $2,000; had I bought 20 head more at a cost of ten dollars per head less, my entire outlay would have been $2,800. How many cattle were purchased?

V. A farmer has 500 bushels of wheat; he can sell it at once for $1.20 a bushel; by storing it for six months at a cost of $20.00 paid in advance, he can realize $1.30 a bushel, he adopts the former course; money being worth 8% per annum, determine how much he has gained or lost by so doing.

VI. A box, with cover made of board an inch thick, measures on the outside, 20 inches long, 14 inches wide, and 8 inches deep; find the cubic contents of the interior, and the cost of painting the outside at 18 cents per square foot.

VII. A person insured a house for $\frac{4}{5}$ its value at $1\frac{1}{4}\%$ annually; after paying 6 premiums the house was destroyed, the entire loss being $1,945. Find value of the house.

VIII. What price must I pay for Montreal Bank Stock, three mouths before the dividend is due, in order to make 9% on my money, the bank paying half-yearly dividends of 8%.

IX. A B and C met, A had 5 loaves, B had 3 loaves, and C had 40 cents; they divided the loaves fairly; and C divided the money fairly between A and B, how much did each receive?

BRITISH HISTORY.

TIME, TWO AND A HALF HOURS. July, 1893.

I. Write notes on (*a*) The rise of the Heptarchy (*b*) The Danish Invasion. (*c*) Feudelism in England.

II. What occasioned the war with France in Edward III's Reign? When and on what terms was it *nominally* concluded in same reign?

III. Write a short account of Henry IV's Reign.

IV. Cause of the Civil Wars of Henry VI's time? When were they finally terminated? Their effect on the social condition of the people?

CANADIAN HISTORY.

I. Sketch briefly the history of Port Royal to 1710.

II. When did France and England commence hostilities in America? When and on what conditions were the wars terminated?

III. What led to the agitation for responsible government.

IV. Assign events (Canadian History) 1627, 1667, 1689, 1713, 1748, 1755, 1763, 1774, 1783, 1784.

GEOGRAPHY.

TIME, TWO AND A HALF HOURS. July, 1893.

I. Draw a map of the Province of Quebec and locate its five largest towns and rivers and also its mountain chains.

II. Name the counties of Ontario bordering on Lake Ontario with the county town of each.

III. Give the four leading industries of the several Provinces of the Dominion.

IV. Name the several bodies of water passed through in going by water from Charlottetown to Chicago.

AGRICULTURE.

I. What constitutes a good soil? How do you determine the value of a soil?

II. Discuss briefly the care and application of farmyard manure.

III. How should lime be applied to the land? Enumerate the advantages resulting from its use.

FRENCH.

II. Give singular of *feux*, *des travaux*, *les yeux*, and the masculine plural of *belle sèche*, *folle*, *fraîche la leur*, *and celle-ci.*

II. Write out pres. indicative interrogatively of *teuir* and prêter.

III. Translate into French:—

(*a*) We have no horses.

(*b*) No, I am not afraid. I am sleepy.

(*c*) Do I come too soon?

(*d*) Have you seen my sisters and your friends?

(*e*) I am going away to-morrow morning.

ENGLISH.

TIME THREE HOURS. July, 1893.

I. Give the general analysis of :—

"O blest *retirement*, *friend* to life's decline,
Retreats from care, *that* never must be mine,
How blest is he who crowns, in shades like these,
A *youth* of labour with an age of ease ;
Who quits a world *where* strong temptations *try*,
And, since 'tis hard to combat, learns to fly !
For him no *wretches*, *born* to work and weep,
Explore the mine, or tempt the dangerous deep."

II. Parse the italicized words.

III. Quote four lines of each of the following, beginning with :—

(*a*) Ill fares the land, etc.

(*b*) Thus to relieve the wretched was his pride.

(*d*) As some tall cliff, etc.

(*c*) O luxury ! thou curst by Heaven's decree.

IV. Give the meaning and derivations of the following words :—

Feat, usurp, copse, ballad, brocade, impotence, vistas, profusion, baneful, covert.

V. What name is usually associated with the Deserted Village ? And what persons are supposed to be described in the poem ?

VI. Write a short sketch of the life of Burns or Byron, and quote not fewer than two stanzas from either. Give the names of the authors of the selections in the Sixth Reader from page 200 to the end.

VII. (*a*) What is the office of the perfect tense ?

(*b*) Give the rule for the correct use of shall and will, and illustrate by example.

(*c*) What do you understand by the absolute case in English ? Give an example of its use.

VIII. Correct the following sentences, giving reasons :—

(*a*) This step is not only as bad but worse than the former.

(*b*) She walked with the lamp across the room still burning.

(*c*) I have never been at France. (*d*) When will we meet again?

LATIN.

The Beginners' Latin Book, "Collar and Daniell."

TIME TWO AND A HALF HOURS. July, 1893.

I. Decline together *summus deus, pulchra filia, meus frater, bonus filius, ingens corpus, alia respublica*.

II. Write down the comparatives and superlatives of *prudens, acer pulcher;* and the adverbs (positive, comparative and superlative) derived from *miser, multus, acer, malus.*

III. When are the pronouns *is, hic, ille, iste* used? Decline *idem.*

IV. Write out the future indicative and present subjunctive active of *augeo, scio, pono, muto.*

V. Write out the infinitives active and passive of the verbs in (4) and give the English equivalent of each.

VI. Write out the present indicative of *volo*, and mark the quantity of the penultimate syllable of the first person plural. Also write out the imperative of *fero* and the present subjunctive of *eo.*

VII. Translate :

"Cæsar, exposito *exercitu* et loco castris idoneo capto, ubi ex captivis cognovit quo in loco hostium copiæ *consedissent,* de tertia vigilia ad hostes contendit. Noctu progressus *milia* passuum circiter duodecim hostium copias conspicatus est. Illi *equitatu* atque essedis ad flumen progressi ex loco superiore nostros prohibere et proclium committere coeperunt. Repulsi ab equitatu *se* in silvas abdiderunt, locum nancti egregie et natura et opere *munitum.*"

VIII. Parse the italicilized words, giving the reason for case or mood.

IX. Translate the following sentences into Latin :—

(*a*) No one doubted that he had gone to see and praise his friends.

(*b*) One consul with a few horsemen had fled to Venusia.

(*c*) The Lieutenant General said that he was occupying the mountain.

(*d*) The soldiers by hurling their javelins broke the enemy's line.

(*e*) We ought to cultivate virtue.

(*f*) See that you take care of your health.

ALGEBRA AND GEOMETRY.

TIME, TWO AND A HALF HOURS. July, 1893.

I. Simplify $5(3a-5b)^2-3(2a-3b)(2a+3b)-5(2a-3b)(2a-5b)$.

II. Divide $6a^4-a^3b+2a^2b^2+13ab^3+4b^4$ by $2a^2-3ab+4b^2$.

III. Divide $a^2(b+c)-b^2(a+c)+c^2(a+b)+abc$ by $(a-b+c)$.

IV. Resolve into elementary factors :—

$$5x^2-15x-20$$
$$a^2-x^2-ab-bx$$
$$5x^2-8xy+3y^2+7x-5y+2$$

V. Simplify the following fractions :—

$$\left(\frac{1}{m}+\frac{1}{n}\right)(a+b)-\left(\frac{a+b}{m}-\frac{a-b}{n}\right)$$

$$\frac{1}{a(a-b)(a-c)}+\frac{1}{b(b-c)(b-a)}+\frac{1}{c(c-a)(c-b)} \qquad \frac{a^3+3a^2x+3ax^2+x^3}{x^3-y^3} \div \frac{(a+x^2)}{x^2+xy+y^2}$$

VI. A and B play together for a stake of $5.00. If A win he will have thrice as much as B ; but if he lose he will have only twice as much. What has each at first ?

GEOMETRY.

VII. Prove that the sum of the three angles of every triangle is equal to two right angles.

VIII. Prove that if the straight line which bisects the vertical angle of a triangle also bisects the base, the triangle is isosceles.

IX. If the square described upon one side of a triangle be greater than the sum of the squares described upon the other sides, the triangle is obtuse angled.

X. Define circle, rectangle, parallelogram, alternate angles, acute angled triangle, adjacent angles.

Endnotes

Chapter One
Bibles, Bigotry, and Beardless Youths

1 J. L. Lewellin, "Emigration, Prince Edward Island," in *Journeys to the Island of St. John or Prince Edward Island, 1775-1832*, pp. 182, 205.
2 Sr. Mary Olga McKenna, *History of Higher Education in the Province of Prince Edward Island,* Canadian Catholic Historical Association, Memorial University, 1971, p. 22.
3 Frank MacKinnon, *The Government of Prince Edward Island*, University of Toronto Press, Toronto, 1951, p. 51.
4 Ibid., pp. 68-74.
5 G. Edward MacDonald, *The History of St. Dunstan's University 1855-1956,* Board of Governors of SDU and PEI Museum and Heritage Foundation, 1989, p.
6 Robert Irving Blake (reporter), *Normal School Soiré: Report of the Speeches and Procedings of the Inauguration of the Normal School*, Charlottetown, 1856.
7 *Prince Edward Island Magazine,* January 1903.
8 MacDonald, *History of SDU,* p. 13.
9 McKenna, *History,* p. 22.
10 Robin Harris, *A History of Higher Education in Canada 1663-1960,* University of Toronto Press, Toronto, Buffalo, London, 1976, pp. 32, 33.
11 D. A. MacKinnon and A. B. Warburton, *Past and Present of Prince Edward Island*, Bowen and Co., Charlottetown, p. 365a.
12 A. B. Warburton, *A History of Prince Edward Island*, Saint John, NB, 1923, p. 379.
13 *Prince of Wales College Observer*, April 1900.
14 F. W. P. Bolger, "The demise of Quit Rents and Escheat, 1824-1842," *Canada's Smallest Province*, F. W. P. Bolger (Ed.), The Prince Edward Island Centennial Commission 1973, pp. 97, 98.
15 House of Assembly *Journal* 1835, p. 57.
16 *Observer,* May 1900.
17 *Royal Gazette,* April 14, 1835.
18 Frank W. Jelks, *The Parish of Charlotte and the Church of St. Paul's*, Charlottetown, 1990.
19. Book of Minutes of the Board of Trustees, Central Academy, June 7, 1834.
20 House of Assembly *Journal* 1837.
21 *Prince of Wales College Observer,* June 1900.
22 *Royal Gazette,* Oct. 6, 1835.
23 *Royal Gazette,* Sept. 29, 1835.
24 "Academicus," in *Royal Gazette*, Oct. 13, 1835.
25 House of Assembly *Journal* 1838.
26 That attitude probably reflected the composition of the Assembly. In 1838, the Escheat Party, radical land reformers with a marked anti-elitist attitude, had won control of the House.
27 House of Assembly *Journal* 1839.
28 Sir William Macdonald changed the spelling of his name.
29 Central Academy Notebook., August 1844.
30 Central Academy Notebook, Dec. 22, 1835.
31 Minutes of Board of Trustees, Central Academy.
32 Ian Ross Robertson, *Religion, Politics and Education in Prince Edward Island, 1856-1877,* MA thesis 1968, p. 36.
33 Central Academy Notebook.
34 Central Academy Notebook, 1845, minutes of trustees, Feb. 20, 1845.
35 Minutes of trustees, December 1836.
36 Minutes of trustees, March 1842, Central Academy Records.
37 Letter to Lieutenant-Governor Vere Huntley, minutes of trustees, Jan. 21, 1846.
38 House of Assembly *Journal* 1846, p.61
39 Harris, *History of Higher Education,* pp. 34, 35.
40 House of Assembly *Journal* 1847, p. 38.
41 E. R. Humphreys, letter to Board of Trustees, Minutes, Aug. 29, 1847.
42 *Appleton's Cyclopaedia of American Biography,* Vol. 3, p. 313.
43 John Thomas Mellish, "Reminiscences of My School Days," Prince of Wales College *Observer,* April 1907.
44 House of Assembly *Journal* 1851.
45 House of Assembly *Journal* 1852.
46 House of Assembly *Journal* 1846.
47 Robertson, *Religion, Politics and Education,* pp. 31, 32.
48 W. S. MacNutt, "Political Advance and Social Reform," in *Canada's Smallest Province,* pp. 125-6.
49 Ibid., p. 128, 129.
50 MacDonald, *History of SDU,* p. 53.

51 Irving, *Normal School Soirée.*
52 House of Assembly *Journal* 1857, Appendix I.
53 House of Assembly *Journal* 1855, Appendix M.
54 Ibid.
55 House of Assembly *Journal* 1856.
56 Irving, *Normal School Soirée.* The last mention of the National School in the Assembly *Journals* was in 1855, when John Stark reported that the 45 boys enrolled were not doing well in reading, writing, or arithmetic. The next year, the Assembly voted to give W. H. Nelis, who had taught at the school for many years, a grant of eight pounds to help him move to the United States.
57 Gail Hopkirk, *Prince Edward Island's First Normal School — A History 1856-1969.* Unpublished thesis p. 13.
58 Irving, "Report."
59 Ibid.
60 Ibid.
61 Robertson, *Religion, Politics and Education* , p. 3.
62 Irving, "Report."
63 Robertson, *Religion, Politics and Education,* pp. 3-7.
64 Ibid., pp. 4, 5.
65 Ibid., p. 5.
66 Ibid., pp. 6-8; McKenna, *History,* pp. 15-17.
67 Robertson, *Religion, Politics and Education,* p. 6.
68 William Hamilton, "Society and Education in New Brunswick and Prince Edward Island," in *Canadian Education: a History,* J. Donald Wilson, Robert M. Stamp, Louis-Philippe Audet (Eds.), Prentice-Hall of Canada Ltd., Scarborough, ON, 1970.
69 Robertson, *Religion, Politics and Education,* pp. 13, 14.
70 McKenna, *History,* p. 16
71 Hopkirk, *First Normal School,* pp. 16, 17.
72 Ibid., p. 19.
73 *Royal Gazette,* Jan. 3, 1859.
74 MacDonald, *History of SDU,* p. 22.
75 Ibid., p. 50.
76 Ibid., p. 61; House of Assembly *Journal,* 1858, p. 35.
77 *The Islander,* March 17, 1843.
78 Irving, "Report."
79 House of Assembly *Journal* 1860.
80 Ibid.
81 "An Act to Establish a College in Prince Edward Island under the Name and Style of the Prince of Wales College," Laws of PEI, 1860.
82 *Parliamentary Reporter* abstract of Debates and Proceedings of the Legislative Council and House of Assembly of PEI, Feb. 20, 1860.
83 McKenna, *History,* p. 32.
84 House of Assembly *Journal* 1860.
85 Robertson, *Religion, Politics and Education,* p. 76.
86 Irving, *Normal School Soirée.*
87 "An Act to Establish a College."
88 Report of School Visitor, House of Assembly *Journal* 1861, App. W.

Chapter Two
The Prince and "The Princely College"

1 Benjamin Bremner, *Memories of Long Ago,* Irwin, Charlottetown, 1930, pp. 13, 14.
2 Kinley Roby, *The King, The Press and the People,* Barrie and Jenkins, London, 1975, p. 47.
3 Ibid., pp. 56-57.
4 *The Islander,* reprinted in *The Royal Gazette,* August 21, 1861.
5 *Royal Gazette,* Aug. 21, 1861.
6 Robert C. Tuck, ed., *The Island Family Harris, Letters of an Immigrant Family in British North America, 1856-1866,* Ragweed Press, Charlottetown, 1983, p. 94.
7 There were, of course, others who borrowed the Prince's name, undoubtedly without permission. A few months after his visit, for example, *The Examiner* advertised the Prince of Wales potato digger, which had "proved to be the best invention of the kind ever seen on the Island."
8 Peter McCourt, *A Biographical Sketch and Speeches of Edward Whelan,* pp. 178-183.
9 Robertson, *Religion, Politics and Education,* p. 75. The myth of Prince of Wales as a sectarian institution lived on for another century and a half.
10 Letter to *The Examiner,* Dec. 17, 1860.
11 *Monitor,* May 16, 1860.
12 G. Edward MacDonald, *History of SDU,* pp. 75-6.

13 *The Examiner*, Nov. 19, 1860.
14 Ibid.
15 Ibid.
16 *Royal Gazette*, Dec. 4, 1860.
17 *The Examiner*, Dec. 10, 1860.
18 Ian Ross Robertson, "The Bible Question in Prince Edward Island from 1856 to 1860," *Acadiensis* Vol. 2 (Spring 1976), p. 21.
19 House of Assembly *Journal* 1862, pp. 96-97.
20 Historian Robin Harris observes that the Scottish curriculum was introduced to Canada by Rev. Thomas McCulloch, founder of Pictou Academy in 1815, and later president of Dalhousie. His view that higher education should include mathematics and science as well as the classics was shared by other men trained in Scotland who helped found Dalhousie, McGill, and the University of Toronto.
21 *Protestant and Evangelical Witness*, Jan. 5, 1861.
22 *The Protestant*, Jan. 12, 1861.
23 "Conservative" in *The Examiner*, Jan. 28, 1861.
24 "A Lover of Justice," in *The Examiner*, Jan. 14, 1861.
25 James Scotland, *The History of Scottish Education*, University of London Press Ltd., 1970, p 223.
26 Ibid., pp. 221-225.
27 *Royal Gazette*, March 26, 1861.
28 Inglis, letter to *The Examiner*, Dec., 15, 1862, cited in Robertson, *Religion, Politics and Education*.
29 MacDonald, *History of SDU*, p. 84.
30 Ibid., pp. 91, 92.
31 Ibid., p. 65.
32 Harris, *History of Higher Education*, p. 9.
33 House of Assembly *Journal* 1863, 1864.
34 John Blanchard, "A Historical Development of the Educational System of Charlottetown," Unpublished thesis, 1966-67.
35 House of Assembly *Journal* 1866.
36 Harris, *A History of Higher Education*, p. 622.
37 House of Assembly *Journal* 1868.
38 *Bathgate Gazette*, April 14, 1894.
39 Robertson, *Religion, Politics and Education*, p. 145.
40 *Islander*, Dec. 5, 1862.
41 Alexander Anderson letter to Sir Andrew Macphail, Dec. 4, 1908, Andrew Macphail Papers (in private possession when used), notes taken by Ian Ross Robertson.

Chapter Three
The Lion of Prince of Wales

1 Sir Andrew Macphail, *The Master's Wife*, Institute of Island Studies, Charlottetown, 1994 (facsimile of 1939 edition), pp. 177-8.
2 *A Cyclopedia of Canadian Biography*, edited by Geo. MacLean Rose, Toronto, Rose Publishing Co., 1888, p. 54.
3 MacKinnon and Warburton, *Past and Present*, p. 331.
4 "Dr. Schurman," *The Daily Examiner*, Jan. 31, 1899.
5 Maurice Pope (Ed.), *Public Servant, The Memoirs of Sir Joseph Pope*, Toronto/Oxford University Press, 1960, p. 18.
6 MacKinnon and Warburton, *Past and Present*, pp. 390, 555, 621.
7 J. Wilmer Blanchard, *Islanders Away*, Charlottetown, 1992.
8 *The Examiner*, July 17, 1871.
9 Probably mathematics professor Charles Macdonald, who had taught high school in Anderson's home town, Aberdeen.
10 *The Examiner*, Nov. 8, 1875.
11 MacKinnon and Warburton, *Past and Present*, pp. 380a- 388a.
12 Ibid., p. 382a.
13 Alexander Anderson to Andrew Macphail, Nov. 19, 1908, Andrew Macphail Papers.
14 House of Assembly *Journal* 1875, Appendix BB.
15 *The Examiner*, July 10, 1871.
16 *Island Argus*, August 22, 1873.
17 "Delta," letter to *The Patriot* , June 20, 1873.
18 *The Patriot*, May 10, 1873.
19 Weeks, an engineering student at McGill, eventually surveyed the PEI railway, studied law, and became a law partner of Sir Louis Davies. He was appointed prothonotary, but died in 1886, at the age of thirty-two. He was succeeded as prothonotary by his younger brother William, another

PWC alumnus, who graduated from McGill with honours in mathematics and studied law in Charlottetown.

20 *The Patriot*, May 15, 1873.

21 Edward Manning, Board of Education report, House of Assembly *Journal* 1878, Appendix K.

22 Ian Ross Robertson, "Sir Andrew Macphail and Orwell," in *The Island Magazine*, Number One, Fall-Winter 1976.

23 Ibid.

24 Macphail, *Master's Wife*, p. 179.

25 Macphail, "Old PWC Days Described by Noted Islander," from *The Guardian*, Jan. 6, 1938, reprinted in the PEI Genealogical Society *Newsletter*.

26 Macphail, "Old PWC Days."

27 As an adult, Andrew Macphail spelled his family name "Macphail"; his father retained the original spelling.

28 Macphail, *Master's Wife*, p. 177.

29 Book list dated Nov. 25, 1880, Macphail Papers.

30 House of Assembly *Journal* 1882.

31 Harris, *History of Higher Education*, p. 54.

32 Macphail, "Old PWC Days."

33 Ibid.

34 Macphail, *Master's Wife*, p. 179.

35 Macphail, "Old PWC Days."

36 Macphail, Ibid.

37 Macphail, *Master's Wife*, p. 179.

38 Macphail, "Old PWC Days."

39 Macphail, *Master's Wife*, p. 177.

40 Ibid., p. 178.

41 Pope, ed., *Public Servant*, p. 17.

42 MacDonald, *History of SDU*, p. 110.

43 Ibid., p. 116.

44 F. W. P. Bolger, "Long Courted, Won at Last," in *Canada's Smallest Province*, F. W. P. Bolger (Ed.), The Prince Edward Island Centennial Commission 1973, pp. 207-231.

45 *Parliamentary Reporter*, 1874, p. 464.

46 Ibid., p. 471.

47 Ian Ross Robertson, "Joseph Harding Webster," *Dictionary of Canadian Biography*, 1861-1870, Vol. 9, p. 824; *The Examiner*, Nov. 26, 1860.

48 House of Assembly *Journal* 1875.

49 *Parliamentary Reporter*, 1879.

50 Nancy MacNeill MacBeath, "Sir William Wilfred Sullivan," *Dictionary of Canadian Biography 1911-1920*, Vol 14, pp. 981-983.

51 Report of Board of Education, House of Assembly *Journal* 1879.

52 House of Assembly *Journal* 1842.

53 Harris, *History of Higher Education*, p. 116.

54 MacKinnon and Warburton, *Past and Present*, p. 383a.

55 Convent schools remained, however.

56 House of Assembly *Journal* 1879.

57 *Parliamentary Reporter* 1879, pp. 223-225.

58 House of Assembly *Journal* 1890, Appendix C.

59 House of Assembly *Journal* 1879.

60 Ibid.

61 House of Assembly *Journal* 1880.

62 Harper moved to Quebec in 1880, obtained a doctorate, wrote a number of books, and held several influential positions in the Quebec education system.

63 Macphail, *Master's Wife*, p. 180.

64 J. H. Fletcher, "Newspaper Life and Newspaper Men," *The Island Magazine*, Vol. 2, No. 5, July 1900, p 149.

65 Macphail, "Old PWC Days."

66 "William John Alexander (1855-1944), Co-Editor 1912-26," *Representative Poetry On-line*, I. Lancashire (Ed.), Web Development Group, Information Technology Services, University of Toronto Library 2000.

67 MacKinnon and Warburton, *Past and Present*, pp. 379a, 388a.

68 Ibid., pp. 330-332.

69 House of Assembly *Journal* 1882, App. D.

70 House of Assembly *Journal* 1885, pp. 41, 42. Historian P. B. Waite (*The Lives of Dalhousie*, Vol. 1) observes that there were "three good high schools" in the Maritimes in the 1880s: Pictou Academy, Halifax High School, and Prince of Wales.

71 House of Assembly *Journal* 1888.

72 Probably Alexander Johnson.

73 "Extracts from the Minutes of Corporation of McGill University — Meeting Held October 26th, 1887," Macphail Papers.

74 Janetta (Nettie) Macphail to Andrew Macphail, March 27, 1890, Macphail Papers.

75 MacLeod eventually was appointed Superintendent of Education for PEI.

76 A. D. Fraser to Andrew Macphail,

April 11, 1883, Macphail Papers.

77 Dan MacLeod to Andrew Macphail, Oct. 29, 1885, Macphail Papers.

78 Janetta Macphail to Andrew Macphail, April 26, 1885, Macphail Papers.

79 House of Assembly *Journals.*

80 Macdonald, *History of SDU,* p.153.

81 Ibid., pp. 151-5.

82 Ibid., p. 160.

83 House of Assembly *Journal* 1888, App. E.

84 Harris, *History of Higher Education,* pp. 103-108.

Chapter Four

The Lion in Winter

1 Mary Rubio and Elizabeth Waterston, ed., *The Selected Journals of L.M. Montgomery, Vol. 1,* Oxford University Press, Toronto, 1985, pp. 91-92.

2 Ibid., p. 93.

3 Legislative Assembly *Journal* 1894.

4 Report of Principal of Prince of Wales College, Legislative Assembly *Journal* 1892.

5 Report of Chief Superintendent of Schools, *Journal,* 1891.

6 "Prince of Wales College Commencement," *The Patriot,* June 9, 1894.

7 Report of Principal, PWC, Legislative Assembly *Journal* 1896, App. E.

8 Alexander Anderson to Andrew Macphail, Sept. 17, 1895, Macphail Papers.

9 D. Ferguson to Andrew Macphail, Sept. 20, 1895; Macphail Papers.

10 Andrew Macphail to Alexander Anderson, May 3, 1897, Macphail Papers.

11 Alexander Anderson to Andrew Macphail, May 9, 1897, Macphail Papers.

12 Report of Principal of PWC, House of Assembly *Journal* 1891.

13 Rubio and Waterston, *Selected Journals, Vol.1,* p. 388.

14 Lucy Maud Montgomery, "The Day Before Yesterday," *The College Times,* No. 3, Vol. 3, May 1927.

15 E. H. Ramsay, "Pictures of Old PWC," *The College Times,* No. 3, Vol. 7, March 1931.

16 Kevin McCabe, *The Lucy Maud Montgomery Album,* Fitzhenry and Whiteside Ltd., Toronto, 1999, p. 94.

17 Ramsay, *The College Times*

18 Montgomery, *The College Times.*

19 Ibid.

20 Mary Rubio and Elizabeth Waterston, *The Selected Journals of L.M. Montgomery, Vol. II,* Oxford University Press Toronto, p. 341; Rubio and Waterston, *Selected Journals, Vol. 1,* pp. 103, 104.

21 Lloyd eventually left the Island, moved to the United States, and converted to Catholicism.

22 Ramsay, *The College Times.*

23 Montgomery, *The College Times.*

24 Rubio and Waterston, *Selected Journals,* Vol. 1, p. 104.

25 Ramsay, *The College Times.*

26 Hedley MacKinnon would later write a book about his Boer War experiences.

27 McCabe, *Montgomery Album,* p. 97.

28 *The College Times,* October 1899.

29 *The Observer,* February 1900.

30 *The Daily Patriot,* June 3, 1897.

31 *The Observer,* February 1900.

32 Ibid.

33 MacDonald, *History of SDU,* pp. 191, 192.

34 Ibid., pp. 169-171.

35 "Prince of Wales College Commencement," *The Patriot,* June 9, 1894.

36 *The Daily Examiner,* Oct. 15, 1895.

37 *The Daily Patriot,* May 13, 1899.

38 Report of the Principal of PWC, Legislative Assembly *Journal* 1896.

39 Montgomery, *The College Times.*

40 Report of the Principal, Legislative Assembly *Journal* 1898.

41 Report of the Principal, Legislative Assembly *Journal* 1896.

42 Report of the Chief Superintendent of Schools, Legislative Assembly *Journal* 1900.

43 Legislative Assembly *Journal,* various years.

44 Report of Chief Superintendent of Schools, Legislative Assembly *Journal* 1897.

45 "Closing Exercises," *The Daily Patriot,* June 1, 1899, and May 11, 1899.

46 *The Daily Patriot,* June 1, 1899.

47 Alan A. Brookes, "Islanders in the Boston States," *The Island Magazine,* No. 2, Spring/Summer 1977, p. 11.

48 Report of the Principal, Legislative Assembly *Journal* 1896.

49 "Prince of Wales Commencement," *The Daily Patriot*, May 28, 1896.
50 *The Daily Patriot*, Feb. 24, 1898,
51 "Malpeque," *The Daily Examiner*, Feb. 23, 1898.
52 *The Daily Examiner*, Feb. 23, 1898.
53 *The Daily Patriot*, May 11, 1899
54 *The Daily Patriot*, Feb. 5, 1900.
55 Ibid.
56 Rubio and Waterston, *Selected Journals, Vol. 1*, p. 248.
57 *The Daily Patriot*, *The Daily Examiner*, March 1, 1900.
58 "New Prince of Wales," *The Daily Examiner*, March 10, 1900.
59 *Diaries of Henry Cundall*, March 9, 1900 (PARO).
60 Presumably one of the talented children of Charlottetown musician S. N. Earle.
61 *The DailyPatriot*, March 10, 1900.
62 G. Edward MacDonald, *History of SDU*, p. 168.
63 *The Daily Patriot*, March 10, 1900.
64 MacDonald, *History of SDU*, pp. 224-227.
65 Report of the Principal of Prince of Wales College, House of Assembly *Journal* 1900, App. E.
66 Alexander Anderson to Premier Farquharson, March 1, 1899. PARO RG 5.8.1/788.
67 Rubio and Waterston, *Selected Journals, Vol. 1*, p. 112.
68 Adele Bremner, May 1899, letter in "Communications to Executive Council," PARO.
69 J.-H. Blanchard, interview with Ian Ross Robertson, Jan. 13, 1967.
70 Anderson to Farquharson, March 1, 1899.
71 William Caven to Farquharson, Oct. 29, 1901. PARO RG 5.8.1/1358.
72 Bishop J. C. McDonald to Executive Council, Dec. 11, 1901. PARO RG 5.8.1/1357.
73 Executive Council Minutes, Dec. 12, 1901.
74 S. N. Robertson, Report of Principal, Prince of Wales College, Legislative Assembly *Journal* 1902.
75 *The Daily Patriot*, March 1, 1901.
76 The new principal, S. N. Robertson, seemed to think Anderson was making $1,500 a year. He mentions this in a letter to the Executive Council in 1904; however, Anderson's salary is listed in the Legislative Assembly *Journal* as $1,200 plus $300 travelling expenses.
77 Anderson letter to Executive Council, April 16, 1900. PARO RG 5.8.1/1123.
78 Macmillan, a native of Wood Islands, who later received a PhD in English from Harvard, was appointed professor and then dean of arts and science at McGill, and served as federal fisheries minister for several years.
79 Alexander Anderson to Andrew Macphail, April 22, 1901, Macphail Papers.
80 School districts generally paid about 25 per cent of a teacher's wages, raised from local taxes.
81 Legislative Assembly *Journal* 1909.
82 Ibid.
83 Ibid.
84 Legislative Assembly *Journal* 1912.
85 P. B. Waite, *The Lives of Dalhousie University*, Montreal: McGill/Queen's University Press, 1994, pp. 204-206.
86 William Peterson Letterbooks, vol. 12, MacGill University Archives: 1908, notes taken by Ian Ross Robertson.
87 W. S. Stewart, "An Appreciation," *The Guardian*, January 15, 1925.
88 Ibid.
89 Warburton, *Past and Present*, pp. 330-332.
90 Report of the Chief Superintendent, Legislative Assembly Journal, 1902.
91 Alexander Anderson to Andrew Macphail, Nov. 19, 1908. Macphail Papers.
92 Rubio and Waterston, *Selected Journals, Vol. 1*, pp. 390-391.
93 Warburton, *Past and Present*, p. 332.
94 Report of Principal of Prince of Wales College, Legislative Assembly *Journal* 1900

Chapter Five
Working for the Government

1 Lester B. Sellick, *Some Island Men I Remember*, Hantsport, NS: Lancelot Press 1980, p. 47.
2 S. N. Robertson, letter to Premier Farquharson, June 8, 1900. PARO RG 5..8.1/1008.

3 Petition to Premier Farquharson, Feb. 15, 1901. PARO RG 5.8.1.2/40.
4 Horace MacEwen, "Samuel Napier Robertson, Educator" (unpublished memoir); *The Patriot*, Oct. 4, 1937.
5 He obtained his Master of Arts degree from Dalhousie in 1901 by examination in modern languages. By 1906, he was signing his annual reports as "S. N. Robertson, LLD."
6 Report of Principal of Prince of Wales College, Legislative Assembly *Journal* 1896, App. E.
7 Joseph Devereux, "Looking Backward," unpublished memoir, Robertson Library.
8 Ibid., pp. 128-132. In his *History of SDU*, Edward MacDonald describes an expulsion in the 1920s of two senior students who broke a curfew. The memory of the event lingered long afterwards.
9 MacEwen, "Samuel Napier Robertson."
10 Devereux, "Looking Backward," p. 130.
11 Report of principal of PWC, Legislative Assembly *Journal* 1902.
12 Report of commissioner of Agriculture, Legislative Assembly *Journal* 1908.
13 S. E. Reid, commissioner of agriculture, speaking to Farmers' Institutes, reprinted in Legislative Assembly *Journal* 1907. Reid, of course, was not obliged to shovel manure every day, as he happened to own the Tryon woolen mills.
14 G. Edward MacDonald, *If You're Stronghearted, Prince Edward Island in the Twentieth Century*, PEI Museum and Heritage Foundation, 2000, Charlottetown, p. 67
15 Alexander Anderson, General Report of the Chief Superintendent of Education, Legislative Assembly *Journal* 1902.
16 Stanley Brice Frost and Robert H. Michel, *Dictionary of Canadian Biography, Vol. XIV, 1911-20*, pp. 689-693.
17 Report of principal of Prince of Wales College, Legislative Assembly *Journal* 1903.
18 D. C. McLeod, S. N. Robertson, and F. J. Buote, *Report of the Commission on Education in Prince Edward Island*, Charlottetown, 1910. The provincial government did not act on findings of the report.
19 Darin MacKinnon, "The Macdonald Consolidated School, 1905-1912," in *The Island Magazine*, Fall/Winter 1992, No. 32, pp. 3-11.
20 Frost and Michel, *Dictionary of Canadian Biography; John Ferguson Snell, Macdonald College of McGill University*, McGill University Press, Montreal, 1968, pp. 8-34.
21 Snell, *Macdonald College*, p. 33.
22 Cassandra Armsworthy, "An Exceptional Expatriate," quoting from a letter from Cundall to David Laird, Nov. 11, 1899, in *Cundall Letterbooks*, PARO 4159/8.
23 Armsworthy, "An Exceptional Expatriate," quoting a letter to James Robertson, Feb. 3, 1908, in *Cundall Letterbooks.*
24 James Robertson, principal of Macdonald College, address reprinted in Legislative Assembly *Journal* 1908.
25 Stanley Brice Frost, *McGill University Vol. 1 1801-1895*, McGill-Queen's University Press, Montreal, 1980, pp. 193-197.
26 Blanchard, *Islanders Away*, p. 355.
27 Frost, *McGill University*, p. 198.
28 Dr. Bagnall, report to Arthur Peters, Sept. 12, 1906, Frank MacKinnon Fonds, PARO Acc. 4449.
29 Andrew Robb, *Dictionary of Canadian Biography*, Vol. XIII, University of Toronto Press 1998, pp. 834-836.
30 Arthur Peters to J. A. Nicholson, Sept. 13, 1906. PARO RG 25.20.
31 J. A. Nicholson to Arthur Peters, Sept. 21, 1906.
32 Peters to Nicholson, Sept. 24, 1906.
33 Charles Moyse to Arthur Peters, Sept. 17, 1906.
34 William Peterson to Arthur Peters, Nov. 12, 1906.
35 Ibid.
36 Arthur Peters to S. N. Robertson, Nov. 20, 1906, op. cit.
37 Peters to Nicholson Jan. 10, 1908.
38 Nicholson to Peters, Jan. 4, 1907, and Jan. 23, 1907, op. cit.
39 Proceedings of the House of Assembly, Feb. 19, 1907, Legislative Assembly *Journal* 1907.
40 Frank MacKinnon Papers, PARO.
41 Legislative Assembly *Journal* 1907.
42 J. A. Nicholson to Arthur Peters, April 5, 1907, PARO.

43 *The Examiner*, April 11, 1907.
44 Ibid.
45 *The Guardian* April 17, 1907.
46 Arthur Peters to J.A. Nicholson, April 17, 1907, PARO.
47 Peters to Nicholson, April 25, 1907.
48 Nicholson to Peters, April 20, 1907, PARO.
49 *The Observer*, April 1907.
50 Robb, *Dictionary of Canadian Biography.*
51 Tory later was appointed president of Carleton University, where MacKinnon taught political science in the 1940s.
52 MacKinnon identifies the professors in handwritten notes filed with his papers at the PARO.
53 MacKinnon, Frank, *Church, Politics and Education in Canada, The P.E.I. Experience*, Calgary: Detselig Enterprises, 1995, p. 35.
54 Ibid.
55 MacDonald, *History of SDU*, pp. 252-254.
56 Snell, *Macdonald College*, p. 167.
57 Unsigned memo in Arthur Peters's papers, PARO RG 25.20.
58 Stanley Brice Frost, *McGill University, For the Advancement of Learning, Vol. II 1895-1971*, McGill-Queen's University Press, Kingston and Montreal, 1984, pp. 74-76.
59 Dr. Bagnall, Sept. 12, 1906.
60 Robb, *Dictionary of Canadian Biography.*
61 Frost, *McGill University*, p. 76.
62 Snell, *Macdonald College*, p. 25.
63 Haszard's letter is not included with the official Peters correspondence, and, unfortunately, that point is not spelled out.
64 James Robertson to F. L. Haszard, March 11, 1907, PARO.
65 James Robertson, address on "Education for the Improvement of Rural Conditions," July 1907, printed in Legislative Assembly *Journal* 1908.
66 G. D. Steel letter to F. L. Haszard, July 24, 1909, PARO RG 5.2/218.
67 Haszard letter to G. D. Steel, July 28, 1909, PARO.
68 J.G. Bennett letter to John Agnew, May 9, 1910, PARO RG 5.2/225.
69 Bennett letter to Haszard.
70 Devereux, "Looking Backward."
71 MacDonald, *If You're Stronghearted*, p. 78.
72 Prince of Wales Report, Legislative Assembly *Journal* 1916.
73 McInnis twice won the Governor General's Award for Literature, and taught at the University of Toronto and York University.
74 Legislative Assembly *Journal* 1916.
75 Ibid.
76 Legislative Assembly *Journal* 1914.
77 Prince of Wales College Report, *LAJ* 1918. St. Dunstan's College rectors were sending out the same message during this time. See Edward MacDonald, *History of SDU.*
78 Legislative Assembly *Journal* 1918.
79 Helen Yeo, "Teaching the Teachers to Teach," in P.E.I. Teachers' Federation *Newsletter*, October 1980, pp 33, 34.
80 Report of Superintendent of Schools, Legislative Assembly *Journal* 1918 , pp. xviii to xix.
81 *The Guardian*, May 31, 1919.
82 *The Guardian*, May 11, 1918.
83 Boyde Beck and Edward MacDonald, *Everyday and Extraordinary: Almanac of the History of Prince Edward Island*, PEI Museum and Heritage Foundation, 1999, p.91; MacDonald, *If You're Stronghearted*, pp. 107-109.
84 Legislative Assembly *Journal* 1919.
85 Prince of Wales College Report, Legislative Assembly *Journal* 1921.
86 *The Guardian*, Aug. 27, 1914.
87 Frost, *McGill University*, p. 79.
88 MacDonald, *History of SDU*, pp. 267-269.

Chapter Six
"A Great Teacher and a Great Soul"

1 MacDonald, *If You're Stronghearted*, p. 113.
2 Ibid., p. 116.
3 *The Guardian*, Oct. 9, 1920.
4 Ibid.
5 Executive Council Minutes, Oct. 4, 1920.
6 Ibid.
7 *The Guardian*, Oct. 6, 1920.
8 *The Prince Edward Island Patriot*, Oct. 5, 1920.
9 *The Guardian*, Oct. 3, 1920.

10 *The Patriot*, Oct. 8, 1920.
11 *The Patriot*, Oct. 2, 1920
12 *The Guardian*, Oct. 7, 1920.
13 Executive Council Minutes, Oct. 8, 1920.
14 Ibid.
15 Executive Council Minutes, Oct. 22, 1920.
16 "Closing of Prince of Wales College," *The Guardian*, May 29, 1920.
17 *The Patriot*, Oct. 2, 1920.
18 MacDonald, *If You're Stronghearted*, p. 113. Walter Jones later became leader of the Liberal Party and premier of the province.
19 Sellick, *Island Men*, p. 53.
20 Helen MacDonald, "An Affectionate Look Back at Dr. Sammie and PWC," in *Moments and Time and Other Memories, Vol. II*, Extension Department, UPEI, 1990, p. 15.
21 MacDonald, "An Affectionate Look Back," p. 16.
22 *The Patriot*, May 26, 1923.
23 A certain amount of gender segregation existed in larger Maritimes campuses until the Second World War. Both Dalhousie and Mount Allison Universities enforced segregations in their libraries.
24 Neil Matheson, "Across the Island," *The Guardian*, Dec. 2, 1965.
25 Ibid.
26 MacDonald, "An Affectionate Look Back," pp. 15, 16.
27 *The Patriot*, Oct. 6, 1937.
28 John R. McGrath, phone interview with Marian Bruce, April 16, 2004.
29 MacDonald, "An Affectionate Look Back," p. 16.
30 Report of Prince of Wales College, Legislative Assembly *Journal* 1921.
31 MacDonald, *History of SDU*, pp. 181, 182.
32 Blanchard, *Islanders Away*, p. 39.
33 Report of Prince of Wales College, Legislative Assembly *Journal* 1936.
34 MacDonald, *If You're Stronghearted*, p. 156.
35 P. B. Waite, *The Lives of Dalhousie University 1925-1980*, McGill-Queen's University Press, Montreal and Kingston 1998, pp. 408-409; John G. Reid, *Mount Allison University: A History, to 1963, Vol. 2*, University of Toronto Press, Toronto, Buffalo, London, 1984, p. 104.
36 Report of Prince of Wales College, Legislative Assembly *Journal* 1932.
37 *The College Times*, April 1932.
38 *The College Times*, May 1933.
39 MacDonald, *If You're Stronghearted*, pp. 158-9.
40 Department of Public Works Report, Legislative Assembly *Journal* 1933.
41 Jas. E. Harris and E. S. Blanchard, "PWC Plan," letter to *The Guardian*, April 7, 1932.
42 A similar situation occurred at Mount Allison University in 1933, after fire destroyed three buildings on campus. The Stewart company won the rebuilding contract, and an out-of-province firm the architect's contract, somewhat to the distress of the building committee (Reid, *Mount Allison University*, p. 118).
43 *The Patriot*, Jan., 14, 1933.
44 *The Guardian*, Jan. 17, 1933.
45 *The Patriot*, Feb. 17, 1933.
46 *The Patriot*, Jan. 17, 1933; Horace MacEwen, "Memories of Prince of Wales College."
47 In the early 1920s, the corporation had proposed to finance a union of colleges and universities in the Maritimes, a plan that fell through.
48 MacDonald, *History of SDU*, pp. 341-344.
49 John T. Croteau, *Cradled in the Waves*, Ryerson Press, Toronto, 1951, pp. 12-13.
50 MacDonald, *History of SDU*, p. 305.
51 Croteau, *Cradled in the Waves*, p. 14.
52 Report of Prince of Wales College Legislative Assembly *Journal* 1936.
53 Croteau, *Cradled in the Waves*, p. 17
54 MacDonald, *History of SDU*, pp. 350-354.
55 Enrolment was still four times as high as that of St. Dunstan's College.
56 *The College Times*, March 1927.
57 *The College Times*, December 1931.
58 Horace MacEwen, "Memories of Prince of Wales College" (1930-1933), Charlottetown, 1978.
59 *The College Times*, December 1937.
60 The day after the funeral, MacDougall also died unexpectedly, also of a heart attack.
61 *The Patriot*, October 6, 1937.
62 *The College Times*, December 1937.

Chapter Seven
Memories of Old Prince of Wales

1 Helen Killorn, interview with Carolyn Roberts, Aug. 22, 2002.
2 *The College Times*, December 1938.
3 Francis Blanchard, interview with Marian Bruce, April 23, 2004.
4 Roy Campbell, interview with Marian Bruce, May 12, 2004.
5 Lloyd Lockerby, interview with Marian Bruce, July 24, 2003.
6 Don Anderson, interview with Marian Bruce, Sept. 16, 2003.
7 Roy Campbell, interview.
8 Doris Anderson, interview with Marian Bruce, May 21, 2004.
9 Arnold Hiltz, interview with Marian Bruce, Aug. 11, 2003
10 Francis Blanchard, interview.
11 Annual report, Prince of Wales College, Legislative Assembly *Journal* 1940.
12 *The Guardian*, July 8, 1941.
13 *The College Times*, December 1941.
14 Willard Brehaut, interview with Marian Bruce, September 26, 2003.
15 Annual Report of Prince of Wales College, Legislative Assembly *Journal* 1939.
16 Earl Wonnacott, interview with Carolyn Roberts and Ryan O'Connor, July 24, 2002.
17 Lawson Drake, interview with Ryan O'Connor, August 9, 2002.
18 Zelda MacNevin, interview with Marian Bruce, April 27, 2004.
19 Earl Wonnacott, interview.
20 Roy Campbell, interview.
21 Austin Bowman, interview with Ryan O'Connor, August 13, 2002.
22 Clive Stewart, interview with Carolyn Roberts and Ryan O'Connor.
23 Roy Campbell, interview.
24 Catherine Coyle, interview with Carolyn Roberts, August 19, 2002.
25 Bryer Jones, interview with Marian Bruce, Aug. 21, 2003.
26 Willard Brehaut, interview.
27 Ruby Matheson, interview with Carolyn O'Connor.
28 Annual report of Prince of Wales College, Legislative Assembly *Journal* 1943.
29 Annual report 1941; *The College Times*, March 1943.
30 Annual report, Legislative Assembly *Journal* 1943.
31 Annual report, Legislative Assembly *Journal* 1944.
32 *The College Times*, May 1944.
33 *The College Times*, October 1947.
34 *The College Times*, May 1942.
35 Roy Campbell, interview with Carolyn Roberts and Ryan O'Connor, August 1, 2002.
36 Helen Killorn, interview.
37 Don Anderson, interview.
38 *The College Times*, December 1944.
39 Ibid.
40 Lawson Drake, interview.
41 Report of Prince of Wales College, Legislative Assembly *Journal* 1940.
42 *The College Times*, March 1943.
43 *The College Times*, December 1944.
44 *The College Times*, April 1945, October 1945; Noel MacNevin, interview with Marian Bruce, April 27, 2004.
45 *The College Times*, October 1945
46 MacDonald, *History of SDU*, pp. 416-418.
47 *The College Times*, February, April and October 1947.
48 Prince of Wales College *Year Book* 1945-46.
49 Reid, *Mount Allison University*, p. 212.
50 Legislative Assembly *Journals* 1940-1948.
51 Arnold Hiltz, interview.
52 Robert Forsythe, interview with Marian Bruce, May 2, 2004.
53 Report of Prince of Wales College, Legislative Assembly *Journal* 1946.
54 *The College Times*, January 1947; Legislative Assembly *Journal* 1948.
55 *The College Times*, 1946–1947.
56 Report of Prince of Wales College, Legislative Assembly *Journal* 1949.
57 Roy Campbell, interview.
58 Robert Forsythe, interview.
59 Roy Campbell, interview.
60 Willard Brehaut, interview.
61 Legislative Assembly *Journal* 1937–1949.
62 Doris Anderson, interview.
63 Report of Prince of Wales College, Legislative Assembly *Journal* 1949.

Chapter Eight
Confronting "The Island Way"

1 Frank MacKinnon, "Memorandum on the Union of Prince of Wales College and St. Dunstan's University in 1968–69" (undated), MacKinnon Fonds, PARO, Acc. 4449.
2 *The Patriot*, March 24, 1954.
3 *The College Times*, Nov.24, 1949
4 See Frank MacKinnon, *The Politics of Education*, University of Toronto Press, 1960.
5 MacKinnon, "Memorandum."
6 Edward MacDonald, *If You're Stronghearted*, p. 145.
7 Peter MacKinnon, e-mail to Marian Bruce, Nov. 5, 2004. Frank MacKinnon also had relatives in Montreal.
8 MacKinnon, "Memorandum."
9 Keir Clark, interview with Marian Bruce, June 2, 2004.
10 MacKinnon, "Memorandum."
11 MacKinnon, *A Buffet of True Stories, Politics, Live Wires and Black Sheep*, Detselig Enterprises Ltd., Calgary, 1999, pp. 118-120.
12 Ian Brown, interview with Marian Bruce, June 3, 2004.
13 MacKinnon, *Church, Politics and Education*, p. 54
14 Quoted in MacDonald, *If You're Stronghearted*, p. 234.
15 MacKinnon, "Memorandum."
16 Ibid.
17 Transcript of proceedings of a hearing of the Select Standing Committee on Education, March 24–30, 1954 (118 pages), collection of Ian Ross Robertson.
18 MacDonald, *If You're Stronghearted*, pp. 240-242.
19 Report of the Chief Supervisor of Schools, Legislative Assembly *Journal* 1951.
20 Transcript of Selection Standing Committee on Education, March 24, 1954.
21 MacKinnon, "Memorandum."
22 Keir Clark, interview.
23 Transcript of hearings of Select Committee on Education.
24 Ibid.
25 Peter MacKinnon, e-mail to Marian Bruce.
26 MacKinnon, "Memorandum."
27 Report of Prince of Wales College, Public Accounts Reports, Legislative Assembly Journal 1951–1956.
28 MacKinnon, "Memorandum."
29 Ibid.
30 Whether or not the charge against MacKinnon was fair, it stuck; fifty years later, Keir Clark's recollection was that MacKinnon had favoured Protestants in salary increases.
31 Transcript, Select Standing Committee on Education.
32 Legislative Assembly *Journal* 1955.
33 Transcript, Select Standing Committee on Education.
34 MacKinnon, "Memorandum."
35 Prince of Wales College Report, Legislative Assembly *Journal* 1950.
36 Prince of Wales College Report, Legislative Assembly *Journal* 1955.
37 Prince of Wales College reports; McKinnon, "Memorandum."
38 *The College Times*, March 15, 1956.
39 *The College Times*, March 7, 1951.
40 Murray Stevenson, interview with Carolyn Roberts and Ryan O'Connor, Aug. 8, 2002.
41 Transcript of Select Standing Committee on Education.
42 Harry Love, interview with Carolyn Roberts and Ryan O'Connor, Aug. 9, 2002.
43 Gordon Bennett to Keir Clark, MacKinnon Fonds, PARO, Acc. 4449.
44 Keir Clark, interview.
45 Barbara Macnutt, interview with Marian Bruce, Aug. 13, 2003.
46 Doug Boylan, interview with Marian Bruce, June 9, 2004.
47 *The College Times*, February 1958.
48 George Dewar, *Prescription for a Full Life*, Williams and Crue, Summerside, 1993, pp. 140-141.
49 Department of Education Report, 1960.
50 MacKinnon, "Memorandum."
51 *Through the Years, the Women's Institutes of Prince Edward Island, 1913-1963*, p. 112.
52 MacKinnon, "Memorandum."
53 The Canada Council Third Annual Report to March 31, 1960, pp. 8, 9.
54 *The Guardian*, Oct. 3, 1961.
55 Katherine Dewar, interview with Marian Bruce, May 30, 2004.
56 Ibid.

57 Ian Brown, interview.
58 *The College Times*, Feb. 9, 1962.
59 Reports of Prince of Wales College, 1960-63.
60 "PWC Expansion Seen Necessary," *The Guardian*, Sept. 29, 1961.
61 Report of Prince of Wales College, 1961.
62 Report of Prince of Wales College, 1960.
63 MacKinnon, *Church, Politics*, p. 83.
64 Ian Brown, interview.
65 Waite, *The Lives of Dalhousie University, Vol. 2*, p. 249.
66 Report of Prince of Wales College, 1961-2.
67 Report of a Citizens' Committee to Study the Feasibility of PWC Becoming a Degree-Granting Institution, July 1962.
68 David A. Milne, "Politics in the Garden," in *The Garden Transformed, Prince Edward Island 1945-1980*, Ragweed Press, Charlottetown 1982, p. 54.
69 Dr. Malcolm Beck, "PWC Citizens' Committee Report in Retrospect, July 1998," from papers of Dr. Beck, collection of John Eldon Green.
70 Beck, "PWC Citizens' Committee."
71 Ibid.
72 *The Evening Patriot*, Oct. 19, 1963.

Chapter Nine
Pride and Prejudice

1 Dewar, *Prescription*, p. 183.
2 Ibid., p. 179.
3 MacKinnon, *Church, Politics*, p. 96.
4 Dewar, *Prescription*, pp. 179-183.
5 Ibid., pp. 184-5.
6 Ibid., p. 186. As historian Ian Ross Robertson observed in his 1968 MA thesis, a strikingly similar incident occurred in 1860, when an Opposition member of the Assembly, Francis Kelly, proposed postponing third reading of the bill establishing the new college.
7 *The College Times*, March 23, 1964.
8 *The Evening Patriot*, March 24, 1964.
9 MacKinnon, *Church, Politics*, pp. 96-7.
10 Mary Olga McKenna, "Higher Education in Transition," *The Garden Transformed*, p. 211.
11 Norman MacKenzie to Eric Harvie, Jan. 28, 1965, Glenbow Archives, Calgary, Alberta. Notes taken by Edward MacDonald.
12 Minutes of the Board of Governors, Prince of Wales College, Wanda Wyatt Fonds, PARO, Acc. 3151.
13 Annual Report Prince of Wales College, 1964.
14 "Two Colleges Too Much for P.E.I.?" *The Financial Post*, July 24, 1965.
15 Report of Prince of Wales College, 1965.
16 D. N. Bell and J. P. Lantz, Alumni Association Report, Wanda Wyatt Fonds.
17 Minutes of PWC board of governors, April 1967 to January 1968.
18 While some Catholics and some Protestants favoured the single-university idea, this was not the preferred plan of St. Dunstan's.
19 Frank MacKinnon to Eric Harvie, July 3, 1967, Glenbow Archives, Calgary, Alberta.
20 Ian Brown, interview.
21 Dianne Anderson, interview with Marian Bruce, June 4, 2004.
22 Kent Stetson, "Home From Away, Memory and Imagination in P.E.I. Culture," the Inaugural Frank MacKinnon Lecture, Oct. 27, 2002.
23 Ibid.
24 MacKinnon, *Church, Politics*, p. 101.
25 Minutes of the PWC board of governors, August 20, 1966.
26 Minutes of PWC board of governors, September 9, 1966.
27 Minutes of PWC board of governors, July 8, 1966.
28 John Eldon Green, interview with Marian Bruce, April 21, 2003.
29 Mac Beck, "Group Reunion, Proceedings of the 34th and Last Meeting of the University Study Group," November 1993, collection of John Eldon Green.
30 MacKinnon, "Memorandum."
31 Mac Beck, "Retrospective Notes on the Group for a Single University for P.E.I."
32 John Eldon Green, interview; "Thoughts on the Future Role of St. Dunstan's in Higher Education in P.E.I.," Frank MacKinnon Fonds, PARO.
33 Mac Beck, "Group Reunion."
34 Edward MacDonald, *If You're Stronghearted*, pp. 267-296.

35 John Eldon Green, Alex Campbell, interviews.
36 Minutes, PWC board of governors, Oct. 18, 1967.
37 Edward MacDonald, *History of SDU*, p. 439; *Journal-Pioneer* January 19, 1967.
38 Mary Olga McKenna, "Higher Education in Transition," p. 213.
39 Alex Campbell, interview with Marian Bruce, Sept. 2, 2003.
40 Ibid.
41 MacDonald, *If You're Stronghearted*, pp. 296-332.
42 Ibid., pp. 299-300.
43 Alex Campbell, interview.
44 Ibid.
45 Ibid.
46 Alex Campbell, "The Birth of A Great Small University," UPEI Founders' Day Address, Sept. 4, 2003.
47 Horace Carver, interview with Marian Bruce, June 16, 2004.
48 Barb Macnutt, interview.
49 *The Journal-Pioneer*, April 2, 1968.
50 W. J. MacDonald, letter to Alex Campbell, April 10, 1968, Alex Campbell Papers, PARO, RG 25/36.
51 Bruce Hodgins, letter to Alex Campbell, April 15, 1968, Alex Campbell Papers.
52 J. S. Bonnell, letter to MacKinnon, MacKinnon Fonds PARO, Sept. 13, 1968.
53 Minutes of Board of governors meeting April 29, 1968, PARO.
54 Peter MacKinnon, e-mail to Marian Bruce, Feb. 7, 2005.
55 Peter MacKinnon, e-mail to Marian Bruce, Nov. 5, 2004.
56 Frank Storey to directors of Fathers of Confederation Memorial Citizens' Foundation, April 22, 1968, Glenbow Archives, Calgary, Alberta.
57 Minutes of PWC board of governors meeting, April 29, 1968.
58 MacKinnon, *Church, Politics*, p. 117.
59 Horace Carver, Dianne Anderson, interviews.
60 *Evening Patriot*, Oct. 15, 1968.
61 Minutes of PWC board of governors meeting, Dec. 11, 1968.
62 "Theatre is Focal Point," *The Guardian*, Feb. 6, 1969.
63 Dianne Anderson, interview.
64 *The Guardian*, May 17, 1969.
65 Ed Boates, "On the Boundary," Valedictory Address at PWC, May 16, 1969, Frank MacKinnon Fonds, PARO.
66 Minutes of PWC board of governors meeting, April 26, 1969.
67 MacKinnon, "Memorandum."
68 MacKinnon to R. R. Bell, MacKinnon Fonds, PARO.
69 *The Evening Patriot*, April 2, 1968.
70 Horace Carver, interview.
71 Arnold Hiltz, interview.
72 *The Guardian*, Feb. 11, 1969.
73 MacKinnon, "Memorandum."
74 Barb Macnutt, interview.
75 MacKinnon, *Buffet of True Stories*.

Post Script

1 Rubio and Waterston, *Selected Journals, Vol. 1*, p. 111.
2 Kent Stetson, "Home From Away.",
3 Rubio and Waterston, *Selected Journals, Vol 1*, p. 388.
4 Kent Stetson, "Home from Away."
5 Ian Ross Robertson, letter to Marian Bruce, July 13, 2004.
6 F. W. P. Bolger, interview with Ryan O'Connor, Sept. 17, 2002.
7 Ian Robertson, letter to Marian Bruce July 18, 2004; Macphail, *Master's Wife*, p. 184.
8 Zelda MacNevin, interview.
9 Barb Macnutt, interview.

Bibliography

Books

Beck, Boyde, and Edward MacDonald. *Everyday and Extraordinary: Almanac of the History of Prince Edward Island.* Charlottetown: PEI Museum and Heritage Foundation, 1999.

Blanchard, J. Wilmer. *Islanders Away.* Charlottetown: 1992.

Bolger, F. W. P. (Ed). *Canada's Smallest Province.* Charlottetown: The Prince Edward Island Centennial Commission, 1973.

Bremner, Benjamin. *An Island Scrapbook, historical and traditional.* Charlottetown: Irwin, 1932.

Bremner, Benjamin. *Memories of Long Ago: being a series of sketches pertaining to Charlottetown in the past.* Charlottetown: Irwin, 1930.

Campbell, Duncan. *A History of Prince Edward Island.* Charlottetown: Bremner Brothers, 1875.

Collard, Edgar Andrew. *The McGill You Knew: an anthology of memories, 1920–1960.* Don Mills: Longman Canada, 1975.

Cotton, William L. *Chapters in Our Island Story.* Charlottetown: Irwin, 1927.

Croteau, John T. *Cradled in the Waves.* Toronto: Ryerson Press, 1951.

Dasgupta, Satadal, David Milne, and Verner Smitheram (Eds.). *The Garden Transformed, Prince Edward Island 1945–1980.* Charlottetown: Ragweed Press, 1982.

Dewar, George L. *Prescription for a Full Life.* Summerside: Williams and Crue, 1993.

Frost, Stanley Brice. *McGill University, For the Advancement of Learning,* Vols. I & II. Kingston: McGill-Queen's University Press, 1984.

Harris, Robin. *A History of Higher Education in Canada 1663–1960.* Toronto: University of Toronto Press, 1976.

Harvey, Daniel Cobb (Ed.). *Journeys to the Island of St. John or Prince Edward Island, 1775–1832.* Toronto: Macmillan Co. of Canada, 1955.

Jelks, Frank W. *The Parish of Charlotte and the Church of St. Paul's.* Charlottetown: Irwin Printing, 1991.

Knox, Henry Macdonald. *Two Hundred and Fifty Years of Scottish Education, 1696–1946.* Edinburgh: Oliver and Boyd, 1953.

Lang, Theo. *The Darling Daisy Affair.* New York: Atheneum, 1966.

Learned, William S., and Kenneth C. M. Sills. *Education in the Maritime Provinces of Canada.* New York: Carnegie Foundation, 1922.

MacDonald, G. Edward. *The History of St. Dunstan's University 1855–1956.* Charlottetown: Board of Governors of SDU and PEI Museum and Heritage Foundation, 1989.

MacDonald, G. Edward. *If You're Stronghearted.* Charlottetown: Prince Edward Island Museum and Heritage Foundation, 2000.

MacKinnon, D. A., and S. B. Warburton. *Past and Present of Prince Edward Island.* Charlottetown: Bowen and Co., 1906.

MacKinnon, Frank. *A Buffet of True Stories, Politics, Live Wires and Black Sheep.* Calgary: Detselig Enterprises Ltd., 1999.

MacKinnon, Frank. *Church, Politics and Education in Canada, The P.E.I. Experience.* Calgary: Detselig Enterprises, 1995.

MacKinnon, Frank. *The Government of Prince Edward Island.* Toronto: University of Toronto Press, 1951.

MacKinnon, Frank. *The Politics of Education: a study of the political administration of the public schools.* Toronto: University of Toronto Press, 1968.

MacLennan, Hugh (Ed.). *McGill: the story of a university.* London: Allen & Unwin, 1960.

Macphail, Sir Andrew. *The Master's Wife.* Charlottetown: Institute of Island Studies, 1994 (facsimile of 1939 edition).

McCabe, Kevin, and Alexandra Heilbron. *The Lucy Maud Montgomery Album*. Toronto: Fitzhenry and Whiteside, 1999.
McCourt, Peter. *A Biographical Sketch and Speeches of Edward Whelan, together with a compilation of his principal speeches*. Charlottetown: 1888.
McKenna, Mary Olga. *The History of Higher Education in the Province of Prince Edward Island*. St. John's, NF: Canadian Catholic Historical Association, Memorial University, 1971.
Middlemas, Keith. *The Life and Times of Edward VII*. London: Weidenfeld & Nicholson, 1972.
Pope, Joseph, and Maurice Pope. *Public Servant, The Memoirs of Sir Joseph Pope*. Toronto: Oxford University Press, 1960.
Prentice, Alison L., and Susan E. Houston. *Family, School and Society in 19th Century Canada*. Toronto: Oxford University Press, 1975.
Reid, John G. *Mount Allison University: a history, to 1963*, Vols. 1 & 2. Toronto: University of Toronto Press, 1984.
Roby, Kinley. *The King, The Press and the People*. London: Barrie and Jenkins, 1975
Rogers, Irene. *Charlottetown: the life in its buildings*. Charlottetown: Prince Edward Island Museum and Heritage Foundation, 1983.
Rubio, Mary, and Elizabeth Waterston (Eds.). *The Selected Journals of L. M. Montgomery, Vol. 1, 1889–1910*. Toronto: Oxford University Press, 1985.
Rubio, Mary, and Elizabeth Waterston (Eds.). *The Selected Journals of L. M. Montgomery, Vol. II, 1910–1921*. Toronto: Oxford University Press, 1987.
Scotland, James. *The History of Scottish Education*. London: University of London Press Ltd., 1969.
Sellick, Lester B. *My Island Home*. Windsor, NS: Lancelot Press, 1973.
Sellick, Lester B. *Some Island Men I Remember*. Hantsport, NS: Lancelot Press, 1980.
Snell, John Ferguson. *Macdonald College of McGill University*. Montreal: McGill University Press, 1968.
Tuck, Robert C. (Ed.). *The Island Family Harris: Letters of an Immigrant Family in British North America, 1856–1866*. Charlottetown: Ragweed Press, 1983.
Waite, P. B. *The Lives of Dalhousie University*, Vols. 1 & 2. Montreal: McGill-Queen's University Press, 1994/1998.
Waite, P. B. *Lord of Point Grey, Larry MacKenzie of UBC*. Vancouver: University of British Columbia Press, 1987.
Warburton, A.B. *A History of Prince Edward Island*. Saint John, NB, 1923.
Wilson, Donald, Robert M. Stamp, and Louis-Philippe Audet (Eds.). *Canadian Education, a history*. Scarborough: Prentice-Hall of Canada, 1970.
Zonta Club. *A Century of Women*. Charlottetown, 1967.

Theses, Memoirs, Lectures

Blanchard, John. "A Historical Development of the Educational System of Charlottetown" (1966–67).
Boates, Ed. "On the Boundary," valedictory address at Prince of Wales College convocation, May 16, 1969.
Brehaut, Willard. "Some Landmarks in Prince Edward Island's Educational History," paper presented to the Canadian Association of Professors of Education, Charlottetown, June 8, 1964.
Campbell, Alex. "The Birth of A Great Small University," University of Prince Edward Island Founders' Day Address, Sept. 4, 2003.
Cobb, Gordon. "The Formation of the University of Prince Edward Island: an example of elite accommodation in its last days on P.E.I." (BA thesis, UPEI, 1986).
Devereux, Joseph. "Looking Backward" (unpublished memoir).

Heber, Matthew R. "Education in Prince Edward Island" (MA thesis, 1938).
Hopkirk, Gail. "Prince Edward Island's First Normal School — A History, 1956–1969."
MacEwen, Horace. "Memories of Prince of Wales College" (unpublished memoir, 1978).
MacEwen, Horace. "Samuel Napier Robertson, Educator" (unpublished memoir).
MacKinnon, Frank. "Views from 150 Years," address on the occasion of the 150th anniversary of the beginning of higher education in Prince Edward Island, Charlottetown, Jan. 18, 1986.
McKenna, Mary Olga. "The Impact of Cultural Forces on Commitment to Education in the Province of Prince Edward Island" (doctoral thesis, Boston College, 1964).
McQuaid, C. R. "Early Island Schools and Schoolmasters," Charlottetown, 2000.
Moase, Lorne R. "The Development of the University of Prince Edward Island 1964–1972" (MEd thesis, University of New Brunswick, 1972).
Robertson, Ian Ross. "Religion, Politics and Education in Prince Edward Island, 1856–1877" (MA thesis, McGill University, 1968).
Sharkey, Charles Wilfred. "The History of Education in the Province of Prince Edward Island" (MEd thesis, Boston University, 1948).
Stetson, Kent. "Home from Away, Memory and Imagination in P.E.I. Culture," the inaugural Frank MacKinnon Lecture, Charlottetown, Oct. 27, 2002.
University of Prince Edward Island Extension Department. *Moments in Time and Other Memories: a compilation of stories by Centennial scholars,* Vol. 2, 1990

Reference Works
Appleton's Cyclopaedia of American Biography. James Grant Wilson and John Fiske (Eds.) Vol. 3. New York: D. Appleton and Company, 1894.
The Canada Council Third Annual Report to March 31, 1960.
The Canadian Parliamentary Guide (various years).
Church of Scotland Records.
A Cyclopedia of Canadian Biography. George MacLean Rose (Ed.). Toronto: Rose Publishing Co., 1888.
Dictionary of Canadian Biography On-line.
Executive Council Minutes (various dates).
Frederick's Prince Edward Island Directory and Book of Useful Information for 1889–90.
House of Assembly and Legislative Assembly *Journals* (1834–1965).
Hutchinson's Prince Edward Island Directory (1889).
Laws of P.E.I.
McAlpine's Prince Edward Island Directory (1880–1915).
Parliamentary Reporter abstract of Debates and Proceedings of the Legislative Council and House of Assembly of P.E.I.
Teare's Directory and Handbook of Prince Edward Island (1880–81).
Women in World History: a biographical encyclopedia, Vol. 16. Anne Commire and Deborah Klezmer (Eds.). Waterford, CT: Yorkin Publications, 1999.

Newspapers, Magazines, Diaries, Letters
Acadiensis
The Bathgate Gazette
The College Times
The Examiner (The Daily Examiner)
The Financial Post
The Guardian

Haszard's Gazette
The Island Argus
The Islander
The Island Magazine
The Journal-Pioneer
The Maritime Advocate and Busy East
The Monitor
The Patriot (The Daily Patriot)
The Prince Edward Island Magazine
Prince of Wales College annual reports 1965–68
Prince of Wales College calendars
The Prince of Wales College Observer
The Prince of Wales College Year Book
The Prince Edward Island Genealogical Society Newsletter
The Prince Edward Island Magazine
The P.E.I. Teachers' Federation Newsletter
The Protestant
The Protestant and Evangelical Witness
Ross's Weekly
The Royal Gazette
Book of Minutes of the Board of Trustees, Central Academy
Communications to Executive Council
Diaries of Henry Cundall
Letterbooks of Henry Cundall
Papers of Malcolm Beck, Alex Campbell, Andrew Macphail, Arthur Peters, William Peterson, Frank MacKinnon, Wanda Wyatt
Letterbooks of William Peterson

Interviews
Dianne Anderson, with Marian Bruce, July 25, 2003; June 4, 2004
Don and Cathy Anderson, with Marian Bruce, May 14, 2003; September 16, 2003
Doris Anderson, with Carolyn Roberts, August 6, 2002; with Marian Bruce, May 21, 2004
Wallace and Georgia Andrew, with Ryan O'Connor, August 7, 2002; with Marian Bruce, August 8, 2003
Malcolm Beck, Ryan O'Connor and Carolyn Roberts, July 18, 2002
Malcolm and Shirley Beck, with Ryan O'Connor, August 6, 2002
Francis Blanchard, with Marian Bruce, April 28, 2004
Rev. F. W. P. Bolger, with Ryan O'Connor, September 17, 2002
Austin Bowman, with Ryan O'Connor, August 13, 2002
Doug Boylan, with Marian Bruce, June 9, 2004
Elizabeth Brown, with Marian Bruce, September 23, 2003
Ian Brown, with Marian Bruce, June 3, 2004
Alex Campbell, with Marian Bruce, September 2, 2003
Dianne (Bennett) Campbell, with Carolyn Roberts, August 8, 2002
Roy Campbell, with Carolyn Roberts and Ryan O'Connor, August 1, 2002; with Marian Bruce, May 12, 2004
Horace Carver, with Marian Bruce, June 16, 2004
Catherine (Bethune) Coyle, with Carolyn Roberts, August 19, 2002

Keir Clark, with Marian Bruce, June 11, 2004
Katherine Dewar, with Marian Bruce, May 30, 2004
Ivan Dowling, with Ryan O'Connor and Carolyn Roberts, July 31, 2002
Lawson Drake, with Ryan O'Connor, August 9, 2002
Eileen (Burke) Ewing, with Carolyn Roberts, August 7, 2002
Robert Forsythe, with Marian Bruce, May 2, 2004
John Eldon Green, with Marian Bruce, August 14, 2003, August 21, 2003
Mary Beth Harris, with Carolyn Roberts, July 22, 2002
Catherine Hennessey, with Marian Bruce, May 20, 2003
Arnold and Marjorie Hiltz, with Marian Bruce, August 11, 2003
Anna (Bennett) James, with Carolyn Roberts, August 14, 2002
Rev. Bryer Jones, with Marian Bruce, August 21, 2003
Helen (Grant) Killorn, with Carolyn Roberts, August 22, 2002
Lloyd Lockerby, with Marian Bruce, July 25, 2003
Harry and Anne Love, with Ryan O'Connor and Carolyn Roberts, August 9, 2002
Eleanor Lowe, with Carolyn Roberts, July 17 and 24, 2002; with Marian Bruce, March 31, 2004
Peter MacKinnon, e-mail interview with Marian Bruce, November 5, 2004; February 7, 2005
Dorothy MacLure, with Marian Bruce, August 9, 2003
Zelda and Noel MacNevin, with Marian Bruce, May 21, 2003
Noel MacNevin, with Marian Bruce, April 27, 2004
Barbara Macnutt, with Marian Bruce, July 25, 2003; August 13, 2003
Ruby (MacMillan) Matheson, with Carolyn Roberts, August 5, 2002
John R. McGrath, with Marian Bruce, April 16, 2004
Glenn Palmer, with Ryan O'Connor, July 19, 2002
Murray Stevenson, with Ryan O'Connor and Carolyn Roberts, August 8, 2002
Clive and Fleur Stewart, with Carolyn Roberts and Ryan O'Connor, August 2, 2002
Lowell Sweet, with Carolyn Roberts, July 19, 2002
Gordon Tweedy, with Carolyn Roberts, August 14, 2002
Earl Wonnacott, with Carolyn Roberts and Ryan O'Connor, July 24, 2002
Milton Wood, with Ryan O'Connor and Carolyn Roberts, August 1, 2002
Frank Zakem, with Ryan O'Connor, August 26, 2002

Index

A

B

C

D

E

N

O

P

Q

R

S

T

U

V

W

ICH DIEN